Rethinking Nationalism

Also by Jonathan Hearn

Claiming Scotland: National Identity and Liberal Culture

Rethinking Nationalism

A Critical Introduction

Jonathan Hearn

First published 2006 by
PALGRAVE MACMILLAN
Houndmills, Basingstoke, Hampshire RG21 6XS and
175 Fifth Avenue, New York, N.Y. 10010
Companies and representatives throughout the world

PALGRAVE MACMILLAN is the global academic imprint of the Palgrave Macmillan division of St. Martin's Press, LLC and of Palgrave Macmillan Ltd. Macmillan® is a registered trademark in the United States, United Kingdom and other countries. Palgrave is a registered trademark in the European Union and other countries.

ISBN-13: 978–1–4039–1897–0 hardback
ISBN 10: 1–4039–1897–X hardback
ISBN-13: 978–1–4039–1898–7 paperback
ISBN 10: 1–4039–1898–8 paperback

This book is printed on paper suitable for recycling and made from fully managed and sustained forest sources.

A catalogue record for this book is available from the British Library.

A catalog record for this book is available from the Library of Congress.

10   9   8   7   6   5   4   3   2   1
15   14   13   12   11   10   09   08   07   06

Printed in China

Hear my prayer, O Lord,
And give ear to my cry;
Do not be silent at my tears;
For I am a stranger with You,
A sojourner, as all my fathers were.
Remove Your gaze from me,
that I may regain strength,
Before I go away and am no more.

Psalm 39: 12–13

To the memory of
Elinor Joy Scott Hearn

Contents

List of Figures

List of Boxes

Preface and Acknowledgements

This book aims to provide a critical introduction to the core literature in nationalism studies. It evolved out of my experiences teaching the subject of nationalism to undergraduates and postgraduates at the University of Edinburgh, and researching nationalism and national identity in Scotland. Like nationalism studies in general, it is interdisciplinary, drawing especially on the fields of sociology, politics, anthropology and history. Intellectually, having been trained in anthropology but having taught for several years in the areas of sociology and politics, I have become something of a 'man without a country'. Nonetheless, writing this book has brought home to me how that anthropological training has shaped my interdisciplinary perspective, including my interests in long-term social evolution, in social organization, and in how we conceptualize culture.

The book is about the phenomenon of nationalism but it explores it primarily through a selection of major influential texts on that subject, rather than through a direct consideration of cases. For that reason I regard it as a critical survey of concepts by means of which various thinkers have tried to understand nationalism. It is about nationalism, and the conceptual tools we use to grasp it. I do not advance a 'theory of nationalism', and share in the view of many specialists in the field that a single unified theory of nationalism is probably not possible. Instead my concern has been to grasp the general perspectives or approaches that have guided research, and to scrutinize the way key concepts have been formulated. My own point of view becomes apparent over the course of the book, but this is more a way of looking at nationalism, than a theory of nationalism. I hasten to add that while I think this kind of 'conceptual house cleaning' is necessary, and a good way to get an overview of a difficult subject, there can be no substitute for becoming familiar with, and conversant in, actual empirical case studies. To any student I would say that thinking critically about theories and concepts ultimately requires developing a feel for the complexity and particularity of real world instances of what is being theorized. There is no substitute for this, and it is the best way we have of checking aimless theoretical abstraction.

The contemporary literature on nationalism tends to get divided into

xii

two main perspectives (again, I am reluctant to call them theories), namely 'primordialism' and 'modernism'. The first half of the book overviews and engages with these approaches. Anthony Smith, a leading figure in nationalism studies, frequently maintains that the modernist approach, of which he is highly critical, is the dominant approach (1998). While this may be true among established scholars of nationalism, it has been my experience as one who teaches the subject that most people who come to it for the first time lean more towards a primordialist perspective. Moreover, popular discussions in the media often seem to uncritically invoke primordialist assumptions. Thus I have chosen to begin with primordialism in this book, because I think that is where most people begin at a common-sense level. My own perspective, however, while attempting to find merit in both approaches, leans decidedly towards modernism.

I have come to the opinion that the two most fundamental concepts one must grapple with, and that will have fundamental consequences for how one understands nationalism, are power and culture. For that reason the second half of the book explores the main ways those concepts have been handled in the literature, and argues for particular ways of conceiving them. The structure of the book is somewhat unusual, in that the internal chapters (2–9) come in pairs, the first one of each pair is expository, surveying major works under that heading while keeping critical engagements to a minimum, the second of the pair being critical and exploratory. Thus:

2 Primordialism	3 Rethinking Primordialism
4 Modernism	5 Rethinking Modernism
6 Power	7 Rethinking Power
8 Culture	9 Rethinking Culture

There is a certain affinity between the themes of primordialism and culture on the one hand, and those of modernism and power on the other. So in a sense the book returns to where it began, but in a way that problematizes the culture concept and its relationship to primordialism. The book's structure means that those newer to the subject, if more interested in a survey of the literature, can concentrate on the even-numbered chapters (which include case study 'boxes' to help flesh out the theories being discussed), while those more familiar with the subject may chose to concentrate on the more critical engagements in the odd-numbered chapters. This design is an attempt to 'practice what I preach'. I always tell students to respect the work of those they disagree with and try to understand it on its own terms as thoroughly as possible before engaging in critique. I've tried my best to take my own advice, reviewing literatures as sympathetically as I can, before raising my doubts and advancing my own perspective. One can never fully transcend one's own prejudices, but by organizing the book in this way I have tried to make the distinction between what others have said, and what I am saying, as clear as possible.

A single book can only cover so much ground without losing focus. There are three important areas of the literature on nationalism that I have thus chosen to largely leave aside. First, there is a more practical or applied literature that tries to imagine the best political, legal and constitutional means for dealing with national, ethnic and cultural diversity and conflicts, both within and between states. Second, there are normative debates in political theory and philosophy, about whether nationalism is a good thing or a bad thing, whether it has inherent affinities with either liberalism or ethnic chauvinism, whether it should be supported or opposed. And third, there are postmodern approaches that regard nationalisms primarily as socially constructed discourses and practices, and tend to view any treatment of them as relatively objective realities with suspicion. My primary purpose in this book is to offer a synthetic, descriptive understanding of nationalism, not to offer solutions to the problems it generates, to pass judgement on it, or to question its reality. Nonetheless I offer brief discussions of these 'roads not taken' in the Conclusion to provide a sense of other directions that the reader might want to explore.

Finally, there are many thanks to be made. I would like to thank all the students I have taught over the years in the MSc in Nationalism Studies at Edinburgh. The approach of this book and many of its ideas have been explored with them in lectures and seminars, and I have benefited from their engagements, both sympathetic and critical. My colleagues at the School of Social and Political Studies have provided a stimulating and supportive intellectual environment. I have gained much from my conversations with James Kennedy and David McCrone, who also generously read and commented on a full draft of the book. The book was also improved by helpful comments from Palgrave Macmillan's anonymous reviewer. My publisher Steven Kennedy gave me good advice as well, and was very patient and supportive as the demands of new empirical research, and the more pressing project of starting a family, slowed down the journey from book proposal to manuscript. In addition to her critical eye, Gale Macleod gave me understanding and emotional support throughout, lifting me when I became dispirited. Iskra, who was born about the time the book was conceived, and Lovel, who was born as the manuscript was being completed, have brought me great happiness. All three have helped me keep things in perspective, by filling my days with love.

JONATHAN HEARN

Acknowledgement: Parts of the text on pages 196–7 draw substantially on a book review by the author of Rogers M. Smith's *Stories of Peoplehood* published in *Contemporary Political Theory* (Hearn 2005) by permission of Palgrave Macmillan.

1

Introduction: Knowing Nationalism

Before delving into more specific perspectives and approaches, we need to appreciate the fundamental difficulties involved in defining nationalism and formulating core concepts to guide our investigations of it. Sensitizing us to these difficulties is the main objective of this introduction.

Perplexing Variety

How do we know when we are looking at an instance of nationalism? Consider the examples from the recent past in Box 1.1.

Which, if any, of these diverse episodes best exemplifies nationalism? Some readers may only regard some of these examples as clear instances of nationalism, and each one can, of course, be viewed through other conceptual lenses – constitutional reform, regime collapse, ethnic politics, international *realpolitik*. They are not offered as any sort of easy demonstration of what nationalism is, but to sensitize us to the diversity and complexity of the processes we routinely attach to this term, and the likelihood of misunderstanding and miscommunication on this topic. Their causes and contexts are highly varied – shifting distributions of governance in an evolving Europe, a weakened state following the collapse of the USSR, inter-ethnic conflict on a small island with a restricted economy and a global super-power asserting its international strength in a domestic atmosphere of insecurity. No doubt in each case there are elites and factions vying to mobilize popular support around particular agendas, and complex combinations of calculated interests, collective sentiments and evocative symbols shaping the course of events. And specifying how these play out in each case is fundamental to explaining them. But these are the stuff of politics and society in general, and not peculiar to nationalism. So what is it that makes us look at examples like these and so often think: 'nationalism'?

Box 1.1 Exemplifying Nationalism

Example 1: On 11 September, 1997, the people of Scotland voted in a referendum, by a strong majority, to establish a Scottish parliament with legislative authority over much of Scotland's domestic affairs. The new parliament was officially opened on 1 July 1999. This was the outcome of decades of building political pressure for greater self-government in Scotland, and Britain-wide pressures for constitutional reform. Some supporters are content with this new arrangement, others would like to see the parliament's range of powers increase, and still others would like to see Scotland become an independent nation-state, while retaining membership in the European Union.

Example 2: In February 1998 Slobodan Milosevic, President of the Federal Republic of Yugoslavia, sent Serbian troops into parts of Kosovo controlled by the Kosovo Liberation Army, triggering brutal guerrilla warfare, urban riots and abortive peace negotiations. On 24 March NATO launched a campaign of air bombardment that lasted for 78 days, finally achieving an agreement to the withdrawal of Serb troops on 9 June. These events arose out of Milosevic's rescinding of the provincial autonomy of Kosovo in 1989, the general disintegration of the Yugoslavian state after 1991 and the Bosnian War of 1992–5, with its 'ethnic cleansing' in the Serbian parts of Bosnia. At the time of writing all that remains of Yugoslavia is the loose federation of Serbia and Montenegro.

Example 3: In May 2000 Fijian businessman George Speight led a small private army in a coup, seizing control of the Fijian parliament. He

→

When we focus on the more abstract language of theories and generalization it is easy to lose sight of the messy reality we seek to understand. To help offset this tendency, throughout this book in the even-numbered expository chapters I have offered case study boxes to illustrate some of the issues under discussion. It is in the nature of concrete examples, however, that they can exemplify many different themes at once, and at the same time they highlight general issues in idiosyncratic ways. Some cases are included because they are paradigmatic for the literature (e.g. Czech nationalism in nineteenth-century Bohemia), others because they are likely to be less familiar and perhaps counterintuitive (e.g. spirit mediums mediating territorial attachments in the insurgency that transformed Rhodesia into Zimbabwe in the 1970s). Thus some examples are meant to help strengthen the reader's familiarity with cases that have strongly influenced the literature, while others are meant to tease the mind a bit in relation to the discussions they are located in. But most fundamentally

> → sought to remove the Indian-descended Prime Minister Mahendra Chaudry, and called for a new constitution guaranteeing the political supremacy of indigenous Fijians. After holding the Prime Minister and his cabinet hostage for 56 days, Speight and his army surrendered, ushering in a period of martial law. This was the third coup d'état since 1987 led by indigenous Fijians (around 50 per cent of the population) in response to perceived political domination by Indo-Fijians (around 44 per cent of the population). Descended from indentured labourers brought to Fiji under British colonial rule in the late nineteenth and early twentieth centuries, the Indo-Fijians today dominate the economic sector, while the military is controlled by the indigenous Fijians.
>
> *Example 4*: Between 20 March and 15 April 2003, after failed attempts to get full UN backing and strong resistance from France and Russia, a 'coalition of the willing', led by the US with its main partner the UK, waged a war against Iraq, toppling the regime of Saddam Hussein. The war was justified on various grounds: that Saddam Hussein had weapons of mass destruction and was prepared to put them into the hands of terrorists, posing an imminent threat to the US and the UK; that Hussein had flaunted UN resolutions calling him to disarm for over a decade and had to be brought to heel; and that he was a brutal tyrant and deposing him was a humanitarian act, liberating the Iraqi people. More broadly, the war arose out of the Al Qaeda terrorist attacks on the US on 11 September 2001, which triggered a US policy of heightened national security and an international 'war on terrorism', in the first instance on Al Qaeda and their Taliban allies in Afghanistan.

they should keep reminding us of the perplexing variety that lies beneath the conceptual abstractions. I have also tried to achieve a reasonable amount of global and historical scope overall in the examples chosen.

Competing Definitions

If we survey a few examples of how the nation and nationality have been defined by major commentators, the results are just as diverse. One established approach to these questions is to begin with the assumption that 'nationalism' is what 'nations' do. In a famous essay of 1882 the French rationalist scholar Ernest Renan defined the nation broadly as a combination of social solidarity built up out of historical contingencies, with a voluntary collective will in the present to continue to build on that solidarity:

A nation is a soul, a spiritual principle. Two things, which strictly speaking are just one, constitute this spiritual principle. One is in the past, the other in the present. One is the common possession of a rich legacy of memories; the other is actual consent, the desire to live together, the will to continue to value the heritage that has been received in common. (Renan 1996: 57–8)

In the 1950s, strongly influenced by the developing field of cybernetics, the political scientist Karl Deutsch emphasized the frequency and density of social communication, a theme that continues to be central to many conceptions of nationalism (e.g. Anderson 1991):

What is proposed here, in short, is a functional definition of nationality. Membership in a people essentially consists in wide complementarity of social communication. It consists in the ability to communicate more effectively, and over a wider range of subjects, with members of one large group, than with outsiders. This overall result can be achieved by a variety of functionally equivalent arrangements. (Deutsch 1953: 97)

Yet another key theme, prevalent in many popular (as well as scholarly) definitions, has been to stress notions of ancestry, kinship and descent. The nation is an imagined extension of bonds of blood relationship:

Our answer, then, to that often asked question, 'What is a nation?' is that it is a group of people who feel that they are ancestrally related. It is the largest group that can command a person's loyalty because of felt kinship ties. . . . The sense of unique descent, of course, need not, and *in nearly all* cases *will not*, accord with factual history. (Connor 1994: 202, emphasis in original)

And again, in a line of thought running from Emile Durkheim (1965 [1915]), through Carlton Hayes (1960), up to Benedict Anderson (1991: 5–6), the parallels between nationalism and religion have often been noted, many seeing the national community as a modern replacement for religious community, supplying a criteria for ultimate good and a focus for social solidarity. As Josep Llobera puts it:

The nation, as a culturally defined community, is the highest symbolic value of modernity; it has been endowed with a quasi-sacred character equalled only by religion. In fact, this quasi-sacred character derives from religion. In practice, the nation has become either the modern, secular substitute of religion or its most powerful ally. In modern times the communal sentiments generated by the nation are highly regarded and sought after as the basis for group loyalty. As a symbolic value, the nation is the stake of complex ideological struggles in which different groups participate. That the modern state is often the beneficiary should hardly be surprising given its paramount power. (Llobera 1994: ix–x)

And recently, in the face of highly negative conceptions of nations and nationalism as malign forces inevitably leading to chauvinism, social conflict and violence (e.g. Hobsbawm 1996), some have tried to articulate more philosophical justifications for why nations may be necessary and even beneficial:

Consider what is involved in a set of people forming a team. When we describe a group of people in this way, we imply that they work or play in close proximity to one another. But we also imply more than this: we imply that they see themselves as co-operating to achieve some end, that they regard one another as having obligations to the team. These two parts of the definition can pull apart. For instance, we might say 'The England cricket team isn't really a team at all; they're just a bunch of individuals . . . We can imagine two participants arguing about such a claim, one seeing individualism where the other sees co-operation, and we could see that it would not be easy to decide who is right . . . Nations are like teams in this respect.' (Miller 1995:17–18)

So which is it? Is the nation a historically formed community, an artefact of communicative interaction, an imagined macro-family, a pseudo-religion, a team? While not absolutely incompatible, these various definitions point us in different directions, and each seems to work better in some cases than others. We will attempt a 'working definition' of nationalism towards the end of this introduction. For now what we need to appreciate is that our definitions do not so much delimit the subject matter as direct our attention towards specific aspects of a complex phenomena that has proved very difficult to encapsulate in a few words.

Underlying Assumptions

Most of us bring fundamental assumptions about what kind of thing nationalism is to our studies of nationalism, assumptions that shape from the outset our attempts at more formal definitions. We need to be aware of our own prejudices in this regard, because they have a powerful affect on how we read – what we find appealing and unappealing, convincing and unconvincing. The usual starting points are:

Nationalism is a feeling: At bottom, nationalism is made of passions, emotions and sentiments. It arises out of the subjective experiences of those who consider themselves nationalists, and patterns of sympathy among those with similar feelings. For this reason it is ultimately irrational or at least non-rational (Mill 1996; Connor 1994; Grosby 1995).

Nationalism is an identity: It is a way of categorizing oneself and others, which fulfils a fundamental human need for such labelling. While the social divisions and attendant labels of nationalism may be viewed as socially and historically contingent, the need to anchor the self in relation to others is a necessity (McCrone 1998; Penrose 1995; Reicher and Hopkins 2001).

Nationalism is an ideology: It is a particular system of morally charged beliefs about the world, which sees the world as naturally made up of discrete nations, each with a natural right to self-determination. This ideology can seize the minds of key thinkers and spread to entire populations, creating a worldview that directs collective behaviour (see Kedourie 1993 [1960]; Greenfeld 1992; Smith 1991: 74).

Nationalism is a social movement: Feelings, identities and ideas can be amorphous and elusive, their social effects difficult to demonstrate. Better to look for actual behaviour, social action in the name of the nation, people organizing themselves on a substantial scale to achieve nationalist goals. Only by tying it to observable behaviour can we give the concept reliable meaning (see Breuilly 1993; Hroch 2000; Hechter 2000).

Nationalism is a historical process: While usually encompassing the previous premises, which are all undoubtedly historical processes, by this we mean something broader – the tendency to view nationalism as a world historical trend, which has localized beginnings, most would agree in Europe, but which spreads to encompass the globe. In the guises of ideology, social movement and historical process, nationalism is closely identified with modernization in general. The key point with this last, however, is that nationalism is seen somewhat coolly, as a process that can be described with some detachment, and that objectively exists apart from the sentiments and convictions of actual nationalists (see Kohn 1967; Gellner 1983; Mann 1992).

My own position is that nationalism can be all of these things at once – feeling, identity, idea, movement and process – though certain cases, and approaches to research, will tend to direct our attention to some aspects more than others. And in practice most students of nationalism observe this catholicity of understanding, despite tending to anchor themselves in one of these broad conceptions. What I want to suggest here at the outset is that we should not let our biases towards one of these conceptions impede our ability to grapple with the ideas of those who see it differently.

Primordialism versus Modernism

Since the 1970s students of nationalism have increasingly been viewed as falling into two great camps: primordialists versus modernists (Özkirimli 2000; Smith 1996a, 1996b; Gellner 1996a). Surveying these approaches and assessing their strengths and weaknesses is the main purpose of the first half of this book. Briefly, primordialists tend to view nationalism as a variant of ethnicity, often emphasizing its emotional dimension, and arguing that many modern nations have evolved continuously out of premodern ethnic formations. Modernists, on the other hand, tend to see nations as concomitants of the formation of modern states and economies, often emphasizing their ideological dimension and seeing them as evidence of the plastic and socially constructed nature of ethnicity.

While this dichotomy encodes some very real and fundamental differences in the conception and understanding of nationalism, it has also become a somewhat sterile framework for making sense of nationalism. What once fruitfully stimulated debate and forced people to articulate their arguments has increasingly become a pair of entrenched, ritually opposed positions, which many would now like to move beyond (e.g. Nairn 1997). Among other things, I will be arguing in the chapters that follow that although primordialist approaches pay salutary attention to the role of feelings in nationalism, the social nature of feelings is frequently under-theorized, and too easily attributed to the power of symbols. On the other hand, modernist approaches, while rightly drawing attention to the historical specificity of nationalism, have a misleading tendency to represent modernity as a relatively stable state, failing to appreciate the accelerating dynamism of modernity, which continues to generate new nationalisms.

Ethnicity and the State

The concept of ethnicity tends to become unhelpfully blurred with those of culture and nationalism. I would define ethnicity as the process generating relatively bounded, self-identified groups, defined in relation to similar groups, usually through notions of common descent and practices of endogamy, and often occupying a distinctive economic or ecological niche (see Eriksen 1993: ch. 1). The crucial ideas here are, first, that there is more to an ethnic group than common social traits such as language variety, religion, skin colour, customs and so on. Indeed an ethnic group might be quite diverse in terms of such traits, or share such traits with other distinct ethnic groups. What matters is that the group regards itself as a unique population, with a name for itself, some sense of collective history and ways of symbolically marking membership in the group. Second, ethnic groups by definition come in contrastive sets, the notion of 'us' is defined in contrast to other such groups, to 'them' (Barth 1969).

Thomas Eriksen usefully lists some of the typical headings under which we encounter ethnic groups: (1) urban ethnic minorities, where processes of immigration in search of work have brought people of different origins together in the same urban space; (2) ethnic groups in 'plural societies', usually colonially created states in which pre-existing ethnic diversity and labour immigration combine to create an ethnically segmented citizenry; (3) indigenous peoples, whose identities have been embedded and maintained within nation-states (sometimes called 'first nations'); and (4) proto-nations, groups usually arising out of 2 or 3 above, and politically organized to actively pursue nation-statehood (1993: 13–14). Such groups are shaped by inter-ethnic competition and cooperation, which in turn is conditioned by the number of groups interacting in any given setting, and their relative sizes and strength. Typically ethnic identity is sharpened by competition between groups for advantages within a specific urban and/or state context, or by having their distinctiveness institutionalized by state structures, and/or by resistance to the state and dominant ethnic groups. The crucial point to make here at the outset is that the pursuit of equal representation and rights by ethnic groups within a given political system is ethnic politics, not nationalism.

Only when such groups make claims to jurisdiction, to some degree of self-government in a given territory, have we entered the realm of nationalism. Ethnic groups that are strongly embedded in urban contexts and relatively detached from homelands of origin, have little ability to engage in nationalism in that urban context, although they may be able to influence nationalisms in their distant homelands (Anderson 1998: ch. 3).

Related to but distinct from the opposition between primordialism and modernism, is a general tension in nationalism studies between those who assimilate the concept of the nation to that of ethnicity (Smith 1986) and those who assimilate it to that of the state (Breuilly 1993). Either nations and nationalism are a particular kind of ethnicity, or they are ideologies that necessarily accompany the state (especially the modern state). If we encountered a debate among meteorologists, one side arguing that thunderstorms are caused by masses of cold air, the other by masses of warm air, we would surmise that both sides had fundamentally misconstrued the process in question, failing to understand that thunderstorms are caused by the encounters between masses of colder and warmer air. Broadly speaking, I argue that nations and nationalism are more usefully thought of as arising precisely out of the interactions of ethnicity-making and state-making processes, as, in an important sense, 'neither here nor there'.

A word on terminology is in order here. The point has often been made that if by 'nation-state' we mean the congruence of a single ethnicity with a single state, then these are rare creatures indeed (see Connor 1978). However, there is a convention of using this term more loosely to label powerful modern states that claim to bind the allegiance of their citizens through a shared identity, often styled as national, notwithstanding underlying ethnic or national diversity in their populations. When I use the term in this book, it is in this latter, putative sense that it is intended. Nation-states are those that subscribe to this dominant idea, which should not be taken as an adequate description of their social composition.

Power and Culture

My own perspective, developed in the second half of the book, is that the study of nationalism necessarily relies heavily on concepts of power and culture, and thus how we conceive of these will fundamentally affect our understandings of nationalism. Few would deny this although, as we will see, some place more emphasis on the one and some on the other. There is a tendency, however, for those who emphasize power to define

nationalism primarily in terms of the pursuit of state power, and the ideological power of the state to generate social identities and political allegiance. While agreeing with the importance of this dimension, I think we
need to conceive of power as something that permeates social relations
and forms of social organization, not just as something locked up in the
state and that emanates from it. Thus understanding nationalism is often
a matter of grasping how the power inherent in less manifestly political
forms of social organization – ethnic groups and associations, religious
communities and institutions, speech communities, urbanism, gender
relations – articulate with the powers of the state and provide the necessary infrastructures for challenging and pursuing state power. In saying
this I am not trying to be novel, but rather to move to the fore an aspect of
nationalism that is too often taken for granted. To do this I will try to
bring some general theories about the nature of social power to bear on
nationalism studies.

Culture, on the other hand, has a tendency to be disassociated from, or
even opposed to power. Here I make two arguments. First, to the degree
that we define culture in ideational terms, as a system of ideas, attitudes
and values embodied in symbols and myths, we need to appreciate the
difficulty of distinguishing between culture and ideology, in other words
ideas bound up with the making and unmaking of power. In fact, the
distinction is probably a hazardous one, and we should always look for
the political charge in the mental representations that suffuse nationalism. Second, and here I will draw particularly on the history of how
culture has been conceptualized in the discipline of anthropology, I argue
that there is another, often forgotten sense of the term culture, that should
be restored. In this second sense, culture is not a set of ideational *contents*
– symbols, myths, values and so on – but rather a pattern of *relations*
among all kinds of social phenomena, ideational, but also emotional,
institutional, organizational, material, which makes them appear to 'hang
together' (Deutsch 1953: 88).

It is the influence of centres of power, created through myriad forms
of social organization, which patterns relations among social phenomena
such that they appear to hang together through their common orientations
to power. Thus culture, especially in this second sense, far from being
opposed to power, is a conceptual guide to the perception and analysis of
power and its workings. The point of view I have just sketched and will
elaborate later on, with its interdependent conceptions of power and
culture, is obviously a general one, which I would advocate for all social
enquiry, not just the investigation of nationalism. But because nationalism is such a complex and pervasive aspect of our times, and we regularly

invoke notions of power and culture in wrestling with it, I think it is valuable to try to work through what we mean by power, culture and nationalism, together. Whether or not readers find this perspective appealing, it
should provide a way of directing attention to fundamental issues, and of
interrogating some of the conceptual assumptions of nationalism studies.

A Working Definition

I have suggested that defining nationalism is a particularly problematic
task. Nonetheless, I'm obliged in a book like this to offer some sort of
working definition, a general guide to what I have in mind when I talk
about nationalism. Let me offer a relatively short definition, to be
followed by some elaboration and qualification:

> Nationalism is the making of combined claims, on behalf of a popula-
> tion, to *identity*, to *jurisdiction* and to *territory*.

This definition, while not reducing nationalism to a political ideology,
nonetheless stresses that at its core it involves the assertion of social
claims, and that these claims are normally articulated and advanced by
smaller social groups in the name of a larger population, which may or
may not follow. Three particular kinds of claims are specified. The first,
to *identity*, is not just to a common name or label shared with the rest of
the national group, but to substantive content that characterizes the
group. This claim may include such 'cultural' factors as religious
beliefs or language, or notions of shared biological substance, or of
inherited historical experiences, but it can also invoke more abstract
qualities such as core values (e.g. egalitarianism, liberty, democracy).
The kinds of content that make up the claimed identity can be quite
variable. The second claim, to *jurisdiction*, asserts entitlement to power
and the authority to make and enforce laws, although this may be
claimed only to a degree, within a larger political system. Frequently
this aspect of nationalism's claims is specified with the terms 'self-
government' or 'sovereignty'. I choose the less common term jurisdiction because it tends to direct our attention to the goal of translating
aspects of identity into laws, and the fact that laws, to be real, must be
in force 'somewhere'. This takes us to the third claim, to *territory*,
which normally concerns lands that at least some of the national group
occupies, but can also concern lands from which the group has been
wholly displaced. Usually when we think about nationalism, the issue

of territory is problematic, because the territory claimed is embedded within a larger territory that is otherwise claimed, and/or divided between the jurisdictions of separate states. The crux however is that there needs to be a real place where jurisdiction can secure identity. Thus in some forms of nationalisms, such as the official nationalisms of well-established states, the issue of territorial claims is not problematic, and only implicit, and thus nationalism reveals itself primarily through the other two claims. To be nationalism, these three kinds of claims have to come together as a package, and be viewed as interdependent by those who make these claims.

In discussions of nationalism, it becomes almost unavoidable that one moves back and forth between fairly narrow senses of the term such as the one above, and a much broader sense of nationalism as an epochal social process shaping modern world history. It is usually clear from the context which sense is meant, and I use the term in both senses in this book. The definition above is meant to help us decide what to designate as nationalism when we look around the world today. But it is somewhat historically under-specified. Something like these three combined claims can be found around the globe throughout much of human history (a point I would expect the committed primordialist to seize upon!). To specify nationalism in the fully modern sense, we need to say something about how these claims are *legitimated* and how they are *communicated*. Modern nationalism seeks broad popular support, casting political leaders as the agents of a collective will of the people. Large, complex political systems have always had to take some account of the sentiments and opinions of those at the base of the social hierarchy, but the processes of expressing consent to leaders was generally enchained, such that any support at the bottom for power at the top was heavily mediated through intervening layers of authority and consent. Modern politics is dominated by the idea that power at the top gets its legitimacy directly from the base, whether through democratic elections, or attendance at mass public rallies. Such processes of mobilizing popular support and gaining consent are greatly facilitated by means of mass communication. The expansion of literacy and the printed word, beginning about 500 years ago, and more recently the development of electronic media have extended, intensified and accelerated communications between the base and the top of the social hierarchy. Without such technologies it is difficult for the full-fledged claim-making process of nationalism to get off the ground.

I have chosen to define nationalism in the first instance, rather than nations. I would avoid the hyperbolic position that nationalism always comes first, making nations where none existed (Gellner 1983) – the relationship between the two is more dialectical than this suggests. But it is collective social action, rather than its effects, that should be our starting point. Finally, the social world is too complex and messy to ever be adequately contained by such working definitions. These can at best guide our enquiries. If some cases appear marginal, falling neither clearly inside nor outside our definition, then recognizing that may itself be useful for understanding such cases.

Historical Orientation

There is a fairly conventional historical narrative about the rise and spread of nationalism that informs most academic discussions, and what follows is a schematic account of that narrative, more chronology than history. It is not offered as gospel truth, but simply as a synopsis of how the story routinely gets told, highlighting some of the major historical reference points, to help readers contextualize some of the discussions in this book. Most writers on the subject are either taking for granted, or arguing for or against, a story of unfolding forms of nationalism that goes something like this.

Forerunners and Preconditions

Glimmers of precocious nationalism have sometimes been discerned in the societies of the circum-Mediterranean world in the first millennium BC, particularly in the religiously integrated but politically marginalized Israelites, in the semi-democratic city-states of Greece and in the early Roman republic. However, in keeping with the modernist view, most have regarded these as at best distant relatives, seeing nations and nationalism as such as outcomes of long-term social transformations in Europe beginning around the fourteenth century.

Two processes are usually thought of as laying some of the groundwork for modern nationalism. First, the Renaissance (c. the fourteenth to sixteenth centuries) saw the rediscovery and revival of the classical art, literature and learning of the ancient Greco-Roman world. A new style of humanist thought, concerned with the study of human affairs rather than theological debate, developed in the Italian city-states and spread throughout Europe. A crucial aspect of this period was the recovery of classical republican and democratic ideas, and their reapplication in the early modern context. Second, the Reformation (sixteenth century), stimulated in part by the critical style of humanist thought, had several important effects. It led to the establishment of break-away 'national' churches in the newly Protestant countries, thus obliging the Catholic Church in the countries of the counter-reformation to take on a more national form. It promoted the expansion of literacy through the translation of the Bible into vernacular languages. It also stimulated the idea of a horizontal community of individuals with direct relationships to God, in contrast to an institutional hierarchy mediating that relationship, thus laying ideological groundwork for the idea of a mass society of equals. And new attention by Protestants to the Old Testament revived the notion of 'chosen peoples' in Western political thought. Thus the Renaissance and the Reformation together profoundly altered intellectual and political horizons in Europe.

The Reformation led to intense religious factionalism and fighting between Protestants and Catholics throughout Europe. The political effects of the Reformation took important institutionalized form in the Treaty of Westphalia (1648). This treaty ended the Thirty Years' War (1618–48) between Catholic and Protestant forces in Europe. It established France, the United Netherlands (newly independent from Spain) and, for a time, Sweden, as major European powers. But more crucially for our story, it broke the overarching power of the Holy Roman Emperor, allowing the rulers of German states to determine the religion in their lands. In the study of international relations it is often regarded as one of the foundations of the modern system of nation-states in Europe, with its conventions of international diplomacy, and as marking a shift from wars based on reasons of religion, to wars based on reasons of state.

Two intellectual movements in Europe are also usually highlighted in historical discussions of nationalism: the Enlightenment and Romanticism. In some respects a further development of the Renaissance, the Enlightenment was centred on the eighteenth century, although it had important precursors in the previous century. In general key figures such as Francis Bacon, René Descartes, John Locke, Issac Newton, Voltaire and Immanuel Kant argued for the powers of human reason and science, and against superstition and the veneration of tradition for its own sake. Spurred on by advances in the physical sciences and global exploration, the Enlightenment thinkers typically argued that by approaching the world rationally and critically, humans could achieve progress and social improvement. Romanticism was centred around the late eighteenth and early nineteenth centuries. Whereas the Enlightenment tended to combine philosophy and science, Romanticism tended to combine philosophy and art. Influenced by such figures as Jean

Jacques Rousseau, Johann Gottfried Herder and Johann Wolfgang von Goethe, it celebrated the authenticity of strong emotions, the beauty of nature and individual imagination and artistic genius. This frequently took the form of an interest in reviving languages, cultures and folk arts, which were seen as embodying the spirit and genius of a people, especially when these were seen as threatened by the more dominant languages and cultures of Europe. Romanticism is often viewed as a reaction to the cold rationalism of the Enlightenment, and as a response of Germanic society to the domination of France. There is truth to this, but they might also be viewed as symbiotic and roughly contemporaneous reactions to modernity. Both placed new value on the individual, and were critical of an archaic aristocratic social order, although the Enlightenment tended to emphasize mastering the future through reason, while Romanticism focused more on the reform of the soul through art.

The Heyday of Nationalism

The main arc of the story of nationalism is often seen as running from the French Revolution to the end of the Second World War (1789–1945). For many, *the* pivotal event in the rise of nationalism is the French Revolution (1789–1802), with its determination to overturn the old monarchical politics of the *ancien régime* with principles of 'liberty, equality and fraternity'. Arguments for republicanism, constitutionalism, democracy, equality, natural rights and the sovereignty of 'the people' reached a kind of climax in this event. After the violent chaos of the final years of the Revolution French people welcomed the stability of Napoleon's imperial rule (1804–14). Napoleon rendered the ideas of equality among citizens and the sanctity of property rights as laws in the famous *Code Napoléon*, which was then instituted in the various countries conquered by the French imperial forces, thus helping to disseminate this new worldview throughout Europe. It is worth tempering this Francocentric view, however, by remembering that France was only the centrepiece in a wave of republican rebellions and revolutions in both Europe and the European colonies in that period. Others include: Corsica (1755, 1793), Geneva (1768), South-East Russia (1773), the United States (1776), Dutch Netherlands (1784), Austrian Netherlands/Belgium (1787), France (1789), Liège (1789), Hungary (1790), Poland (1791), Haiti (1791), Sardinia (1793), Ireland (1798), Serbia (1804), Spain (1808), Tyrol (1809), Spanish America (1810).

The 'Age of Revolutions', with its ideas of liberalism, democracy and republicanism, is widely seen as spawning an initial wave of modern nation-building in Western Europe and the Americas, especially in Britain, France, Spain and the US. In Western Europe, long-standing dynastic integration of territories provided a foundation for this transformation. In the Americas, European settlers (that had subjugated and displaced indigenous populations) were able to innovate, developing new constitutions and political systems based on the new ideology. In both cases, the wealth generated by imperial global trade, industrialization and capitalism facilitated this new consolidation of power around the nation-state.

Following the lead of these rising powers, a second wave of nation-building in Europe is normally identified in the unification of the fragmented principalities of Germany (1815–71) and Italy (1848–61, 'the *Risorgimento*'), through the expansion of the small states of Prussia and Piedmont-Sardinia, respectively. This process was aided by a relatively high degree of linguistic and cultural continuity within these politically unifying areas, and was partly stimulated by a new wave of liberal revolutions (1848–9) that were quickly crushed by reactionary conservative powers. Nonetheless, by the 1870s the modern nation-states of Germany and Italy had taken shape. The model begun on the Atlantic coasts of Europe and America appeared to be radiating eastward through Europe.

Further East in Europe, the fates of three empires were crucial to the unfolding of a third wave of nationalism in the Balkans and Eastern Europe more generally. Control of the Balkans was fought over from the west by the Austro-Hungarian Empire (1867–1918), from the east by the Ottoman Empire (c. 1400–1923) and from the north by the Russian Empire (1682–1917). Unlike the German and Italian regions, this area was more of an ethnic, linguistic and religious patchwork, shaped by centuries of wars, population movements and imperial designs. Within the Austro-Hungarian and Ottoman empires, from the 1860s to the 1920s, various ethnic groups that occupied subordinate positions in the social hierarchy – for example, Magyars, Czechs, Croatians, Serbs, Romanians, Greeks – struggled for greater political autonomy or national independence. By the eve of the First World War (1914–18) the great powers of Europe, each with its own imperial interests within Europe and/or abroad, were aligned in two great blocs. In the war these became the Central Powers (Germany, Austria-Hungary, the Ottomans and Bulgaria), and the Allied Powers (United Kingdom, France, Russia and Serbia, later joined by Italy, Portugal, Romania and Greece, and crucially the United States in 1917). In 1917 the Bolsheviks seized power in Russia and sued for peace (either ending Russia's imperial history or beginning a new kind of empire, depending on how one defines 'empire'). After the war, the Austro-Hungarian Empire was dismantled, and the Balkan region was 'reconstructed' in a series of treaties (1919) with the defeated countries of the Central Powers in an awkward attempt to make states and nations match more closely. By 1923 the Ottoman Empire, reduced in territory and weakened by the war, was transformed into Turkey by modernizing nationalists. To this day, the Balkans remain a 'hot spot' of ethnic and nationalist conflicts.

The humiliations of defeat in the First World War and the severe economic and social strains of global depression (1929–39) inspired many to seek a remedy in the new, extremist and expansionist nationalism of fascism, especially in Germany and Italy. Fascism took hold first under Mussolini's dictatorship in Italy (1922–45), where it focused on the cult of his leadership and ambitions of regional hegemony. In Germany under Hitler (1933–45), fascism's cult of leadership was wedded to the racial essentialism of Aryanism and anti-Semitism, and an elaborated mythology of national history and destiny. Meanwhile, Japan was heavily burdened by the depression, and sought national revival in rapid industrialization and military-imperial expansion, particularly against China. These three countries became allies in the Second World War (1939–45) through the 'axis' agreement, waging war on multiple fronts. However, they were unable to match the combined industrial and military might of the allied powers – the United Kingdom, Russia and the United States – and were ultimately defeated in 1945. This period has left a complex legacy of guilt, ambivalence and resentment in regard to national identity in Germany and Japan today.

A Continuing Story

The years between the world wars are often seen as marking the apotheosis of nationalism, in the extreme form of fascism, followed by a new form of bi-polar geopolitics, determined by ultimate allegiances to capitalism and Communism rather than nations. But others have seen the Cold War as a process that put European nationalism in suspended animation, only to be released again with the collapse of the Soviet Union (1989). At the same time, the post-Second World War growth of international organizations such as the United Nations, NATO and the World Trade Organization has suggested to some that a post-national age was beginning to take shape from this time. However, a broader view suggests that nationalism never really went away and is far from over.

The years following the Second World War saw waves of nationalist struggles for independence against European colonial powers in Africa, the Middle East, the Asian subcontinent and South-East Asia (c. 1945–77). This created a series of often very ethnically diverse states, whose territories had been defined somewhat arbitrarily by colonial geopolitics, with little regard for the actual distribution of ethnic groups. Perhaps in part to overcome these divisions, these movements were often inspired by marxist ideologies, receiving military and financial backing from the USSR. Similar insurgencies and revolutions were happening in Latin America, but because these states had already won independence from Spain and Portugal under the rubric of an earlier liberal nationalism, these movements often were viewed as more purely a matter of Cold War geopolitics. However, often this same global context obscured the nationalist dimension of all these struggles in the minds of Western political observers and theorists.

Such anti-colonial nationalisms are sometimes viewed as the final wave of the global form of the nation-state, radiating throughout the world as colonized peoples adopted and adapted to the modern political form created by the colonizers of the West. This reading of events has its detractors, however, and does not work so well for those new nationalisms, sometimes called 'neonationalisms', that have gained strength in the older, established liberal nation-states of the modernized West in recent decades (c. 1960–present). Primary examples include Scotland and Wales in the United Kingdom, Catalonia and the Basque Country in Spain, Quebec in Canada, Brittany in France and the Flemish in Belgium. These nationalisms have often been seen as the result of rising expectations in the affluent West being regionally stimulated and/or frustrated by uneven economic fortunes, and thus as merely 'regionalism', and not qualifying as 'true' nationalisms. They are also commonly regarded as defensive responses to increasing global political, economic and cultural integration. Nonetheless, they frequently draw on long-standing cultural, linguistic and religious divisions, often combining 'ethnic' notions of national identity with liberal and civic political ideologies, and can be difficult to define in terms of a left–right political spectrum.

The most recent 'wave' of national independence movements has been associated with the collapse of the USSR and the end of the Cold War (1989–present), including Estonia, Latvia, Lithuania (i.e. the Baltic States), Belarus, Ukraine, Kazakhstan, Azerbaijan, Georgia, Armenia and Chechnya. To the west, Czechoslovakia has split into two republics, eastern and western Germany have reunified and the Balkans have been in a state of violent transition with the collapse of former Yugoslavia. Many regarded the USSR as, in effect, the last of the Eurasian empires, its collapse allowing the messy but unfinished process of political and economic modernization to resume in its former domain.

Summing Up

In this schematic account, just when you think it's over, another wave comes along. This should make us sceptical about eager predictions of the end of nationalism. That is not to say that the world is not changing, or that nationalism will be with us always – but it does appear to be something we are still 'in the middle of'. This story is conspicuously Eurocentric. It is difficult not to see Europe (perhaps in tandem with its American colonies) as the epicentre of this process. Nonetheless certain parts of the world – China, Latin America, Australia – tend to get marginalized in this account, even though we know nationalism is a part of their histories as well. And important current processes can be difficult to integrate into this story. The movements for political autonomy by 'first nations', ethnic groups based on indigenous populations embedded within modern Western states (e.g. the Nunavut in Canada), seem to partake of aspects of both anti-colonial nationalism and neonationalism. The rise of Islamism in recent decades clearly articulates with many nationalist projects, but has a distinctive transnational religious and ideological agenda. So, this outline history of nationalism is in no sense plain truth, but rather a summary of the academic discourse about nationalism, an imperfect map to guide us, and perhaps be amended along the way.

Further Reading

For key articles and chapters exploring the conceptual problems involved in defining nationalism, see especially Brubaker (1998), Connor (1978), Hall (1993), Hechter (2000: ch. 1) and Nairn (1997: ch. 1). Several edited readers provide good collections of essays by major figures in the field, giving an initial sense of the scope of nationalism studies. Among the best of these are: Guibernau and Hutchinson (2001), Balakrishnan (1996), Hutchinson and Smith (1994) and Eley and Suny (1996). There are a growing number of major reference volumes for libraries that offer entries on many sub-topics within nationalism studies by specialists in the field. These can be particularly helpful for initiating research. See: Leoussi (2001), Leoussi and Grosby (2003), Motyl (2001) and Smith and Hutchinson (2000).

2

Primordialism

This chapter offers a thematic introduction to what have often been termed 'primordialist' approaches to the study of nationalism. By exploring treatments of race, kinship, territory, language, history and ethnicity we will familiarize ourselves with the work and ideas of some key figures in nationalism studies.

What is Primordialism?

The term 'primordialism' as it is commonly used in nationalism studies (e.g. Özkirimli 2000: 64–84) designates not so much a specific theory as a related family of concerns and approaches. The thinkers we want to discuss are various and distinctive from one another in their views, but nonetheless can be bundled together according to certain similarities. As we did in the Introduction (Chapter 1), let us begin with a working definition. By 'primordialism' we will mean those academic approaches to nationalism that emphasize one or some combination of the following:

- Dominant themes of common descent, territorial belonging and shared language in discourses of national identity.
- Historical depth – the idea that nations generally evolve rather organically out of a pre-existing substrate of ethnicity.
- Underlying emotional bonds and feelings of attachment, and their evocation through nationalist language and symbols.

These three dimensions already suggest the main lines of variation we will find among those labelled 'primordialists'. It is also evident from this definition that primordialism offers a conception of ethnicity in the first instance, and nationalism in the second, by extension. Primordialists tend to make ethnicity central, in a causal sense, to their understandings of nationalism, and thus nationalism is understood as a late development of much older processes of ethnicity. All theories of nationalism incorporate concepts of ethnicity, but for many it is one force among several, such as state-building and economic modernization, that varies in importance from case to case.

Before going further, it is useful to make a distinction between primordialist theories and what we might call 'true primordialism'. The latter is the position often found in dedicated nationalists who are true believers in their own cause, and take the essential identity with their co-nationals (whether attributed to blood, spirit, culture, or whatever) as somehow self-evident. The 'primordialism of the theorists' addressed here does not take ethnic essentialism at face value, but rather takes the process of essentializing identities through symbols very seriously, seeing it as an important part of what causes national identity (cf. Penrose 1995). The pejorative use of the term primordialism in theoretical debates sometimes elides this distinction.

Descent

Perhaps the most central theme of primordialism is that of descent. Notions of concrete biological ties, of blood, kinship and ancestry often play a key role in the imagining of national bonds. Before exploring primordialist approaches to descent, let us examine the often confusing relationship between racism and nationalism. George Mosse (1995) has compellingly argued that we undermine our ability to make important analytical distinctions when we treat these as different names for the same thing. Racism is a certain kind of ideology based on beliefs about biology and external, bodily signs of difference; nationalism is a much more flexible ideology taking many forms. While nationalism has often been found in combination with racism, most memorably in the context of German fascism, it also combines with other ideologies such as liberalism, conservatism and socialism. In some cases of nationalism the accent on racial and ethnic distinction is quite strong, in others where concepts of territoriality and civic duty are dominant, racial or ethnic criteria can be weak or absent. Finally, nationalism can provide other criteria besides race for inclusion in or exclusion from the nation, such as legal citizenship or language competency (cf. Brubaker 1992).

If the folk theories of biology that inform racial beliefs are often vague and intuitive, the designated signs of difference are usually vivid and concrete, or imagined to be so. In his account of the rise of racism in Europe, Mosse emphasizes the aesthetic dimension of racism, 'Racism like nationalism had its symbols, but for the most part these were not abstract – like flags or national anthems – but concrete, centred upon the human form' (1995: 165, see also 1985a). He argues that in the late eighteenth and nineteenth centuries in Europe, a new 'natural scientific' view of the world focused attention on the body and the physical world for answers to social questions. Tastes cultivated in the Enlightenment fed into a 'cult of beauty' based on classical Greek sculpture, which elevated the ideal of male youth and virility. At the same time, with industrialization and burgeoning urban growth, a new concern with hygiene was mapped onto social relations between middle and poorer classes, both urban and rural. The rise of gymnastics and programmes to expose young people, especially boys, to exercise in the countryside, reflected these heightened concerns. Increased contact with physically and culturally different populations through the process of colonial expansion also stimulated the production of these ideas. The body mattered on another level as well – as a metaphor for society as a whole. Threats to the social body could be symbolized as a biological threat to the purity and wholesomeness of real physical bodies (cf. Douglas 1982: 65–81). Thus the increasing use of race and physical characteristics to distinguish between nationals and 'dangerous others' combined these various ideas of the body and hygiene.

The rise of 'scientific racism' was related closely to this process (Stanton 1960; Stepan 1982). The new social aesthetic of the body was accompanied by 'scientific' (as opposed to biblical) attempts to explain human variation and hierarchy. Darwin's theory of natural selection presented in *The Origin of Species* in 1859 provided a new framework for thinking about race. It became possible to argue that many types or races could arise out of a single stock, becoming distinct over time. Races were commonly ranked in terms of degrees of advancement; stages of technological development were mapped onto racial types and given biological explanations. Developing anthropological sciences supplied new, supposedly scientific ways of measuring racial and hereditary differences. These so-called sciences, far from challenging, sought to confirm popular stereotypes and assumptions. Techniques such as phrenology, the measuring of bumps on the skull, and physiognomy, which examined facial and bodily proportions, rested on a metaphorical notion that the inner being (soul, psyche, mind) could be measured and evaluated by the outward form. Moreover, they served to reinforce two different kinds of social distinction: between 'racial' groups, and between 'deviants' (e.g. criminals, homosexuals) and 'normals' (i.e. respectable middle classes) within the same 'race'.

Mosse affirms that the integral nationalisms of the late nineteenth and early twentieth centuries provided the context in which this classic

European racism flourished, most notoriously in the rise of the Third Reich in Germany with the racial demonization of the Jews and the conception of a pure Aryan race (Mosse 1985a; Poliakov 1974). But it is important to understand this as a historical conjunction of relatively distinct ideological processes. Racial discourses such as these, though hardly eliminated, have been marginalized in the post-1945 period for a variety of reasons. First, the victory of the allied powers, and particularly the US, was linked to a moral argument condemning the racial ideology of the Nazi regime and the terrible price paid by the European Jews. The legitimacy of new world powers on both sides of the Atlantic was now tied to anti-racist arguments. This, along with better genetic science, placed constraints on scientific racism and its potential to become wedded to state ideology in its former heartland. In recent years, the use of genetics in academic discourse has more commonly been used to legit-imize the social stratifying effects of market economies (cf. Herrnstein and Murray 1994), rather than to demonize alien races. More generally, fluid and relatively open market economies require flexibility and mobil-ity in the workforce and citizenry. While racial boundaries can serve to divide and control workforces to the advantage of economic firms, too much or too rigid a set of institutionalized boundaries places a brake on economic development. Racism of course still exists in the liberal democracies of the 'West', but there are practical obstacles to it becom-ing fused with nationalism as it did in the inter-war years. Nonetheless, it is worth noting that Mosse's themes of the aestheticization of the body as a response to the pressures of modern life, and its associations with power, health and social prestige, lives on in the guise of advertising, the images of popular entertainers in music, television and film, and more general concerns about diet, health and fitness. Uncoupled from rigid notions of race, the ideal of the beautiful body as a mark of success permeates the world's most affluent populations. Moreover, while the legitimacy of racial discourses has weakened, the notion of ethnicities, cultures and even 'civilizations' (cf. Huntington 1998) as highly distinct and bounded entities has gained ground with popular discussions of multiculturalism, thus providing a new, non-biological way of reifying social groups and boundaries.

Contemporary theorists of nationalism's primordialism, while reject-ing scientific racism and accepting Mosse's distinction between national-ism and racism, will see a confirmation of their general position in the power of racist ideas and their putative claims to shared substance and common descent. One rather controversial theory seems to occupy a grey area between attributing nationalism to genetic causes, and the more

---

Box 2.1 The Idea of Race in Modern China

The confluence of racism and nationalism in the modern era is primarily associated with Europe and the decades leading up to the Second World War. In his essay 'Group definition and the idea of "race" in modern China (1793–1949)' (1990) Frank Díkötter outlines another variant of this widespread process. From ancient times the Middle Kingdom was conceived of as the centre of civilization, with outlying groups categorized as 'barbarians' who could potentially learn Chinese ways and become culturally assimilated. As contact with Westerners increased from the late eighteenth century onwards, this model of the social universe began to be disrupted. This created anxieties about domination by Western 'whites', and the need to incorporate other 'races' into a larger worldview. Basic racial categorizations emphasizing the paleness and hairiness of 'whites', and backwardness of darker-skinned populations developed over the nineteenth century, stimulated especially by 'scholar-officials involved in foreign affairs' (p. 422).

Defeat in the Sino-Japanese War (1894) led to new patriotic and intellectual ferment often expressed as heightened concern about preservation of the race. In a syncretism of traditional Chinese categorizations of barbarians according to colours, and borrowed Western 'science' of racial categories, reforming intellectuals such as Yan Fu (1853–1921) and Liang Qichao (1873–1929) developed hierarchical racial systems in which 'whites' and 'yellows' (Chinese) struggled for superiority at the top, while 'reds', 'blacks' and 'browns' were seen as the weaker, inferior races. At the same time, traditional Confucian scholars were critical of such racial

→

---

common position of saying it is *the idea* of common descent that matters. Pierre L. van den Berghe (1995) offers what he sees as a sociobiological explanation of racism, ethnicity and nationalism. Sociobiologists look for genetic causes to social behaviour (Wilson 1975). A general rule of Darwinian evolution is that those organisms that successfully reproduce the most will leave more of their traits in succeeding generations. A key concept in sociobiology is that of 'inclusive fitness', the idea that genetically based behaviours that increase the reproductive success of close kin will be selected for. In the animal world there are many curious cases of seemingly 'altruistic' behaviour where organisms will sacrifice themselves to protect the lives of their siblings and offspring. At first glance this would seem to decrease or eliminate their genetic contribution to the next generation. But in fact, as they share much genetic material in common with their close kin, such behaviours can maximize the presence of their genes in the population

→

thinking and its tendency to displace an older Sino-centric view of social order.

By the first decade of the twentieth century a new generation of radical students studying in Japan were importing new ideas about the essential unity of race and nation, tending to narrow down the Chinese race to the main ethnic group, the Han. The revolutionary generation elevated the figure of the Yellow Emperor to first ancestor of the Han, 'initiator of the Chinese race' (p. 426), linking this national symbol to traditional values of filial piety, ancestor worship and clan loyalty. In this context the nationalist intellectual Zhang Binglin (1869–1936) argued that racial strength was a result of an ability to 'group' (i.e. unify, coordinate) – only the 'white' race had shown itself superior to the 'yellows' in this regard. The iconoclastic New Culture Movement (1915–49) borrowed from the West even more enthusiastically, advocating the adoption of Western forms of democracy, culture and science, including pseudo-sciences of race, disseminating these ideas more widely. The concept of evolution led to greater concern for racial purity and origins. Eugenic programmes to improve the racial stock were advocated, and the discovery of Peking Man (now classified as *Homo erectus*) at Zhoukoudian bolstered arguments that China was the original seat of humankind.

After the Revolution in 1949 racial discourse was expressly forbidden and replaced by one of international class struggle. Nonetheless, the central axis of opposition is still China and the West, in a sense reconstituting, in marxist terms, the old idea of a civilized centre and barbarian periphery, and notions of race are still present as an ideological undercurrent, just as they are elsewhere in the globe.

over time. Thus, by sacrificing themselves, organisms, in effect, can help guarantee that the very genes that prescribe such self-sacrificing behaviour are passed on to the next generation.

Van den Berghe argues that a genetically determined preference for the needs and well being of one's own kin, what he calls 'nepotism' in preference to 'altruism', is the basis of racial, ethnic and national ties. He concedes that there are no biologically bounded races in our species, but argues instead that our socially constructed notions of race have a basis in evolutionary biology. He claims that as social organisms we are 'biologically programmed' to behave favourably 'to others in proportion to their real or perceived degree of common ancestry' (1995: 360). While our genetic commonality with immediate kin is usually obvious, what we share with broader racially or ethnically defined social groups is not. For van den Berghe, this is precisely why notions of race and ethnicity seize upon highly visible markers such as skin colour or traditional dress, to compensate for the lack of obvious information about relatedness. Thus, race and ethnicity over-generalize relatedness beyond immediate kin, while also establishing the limits to beneficial nepotistic behaviour at the boundary of the racial or ethnic group. Where physically distinct populations have been brought together by migration, slavery, conquest, etc., bodily signs of race will do the job. When physically similar but relatively endogamous populations live side by side, cultural markers such as language, dress, body adornment and alteration, will serve this purpose. The fact that the limits of biological relatedness established by ethnic and racial boundaries are rather arbitrary is of no consequence according to van den Berghe, because as long as most individuals tend to have more genetic material in common with other members of their race/ethnic group, nepotism will tend to enhance inclusive fitness, and be selected for.

This kind of argument that seeks a 'real' material basis for race and ethnicity is usually associated with conservative and politically rightward currents of thought. It is worth pointing out that van den Berghe is a left-leaning academic with a critical attitude towards economic stratification and coercive state power. His recourse to biological science to try to explain the phenomena of race and ethnicity neither implies that he sees nepotism as the only principle organizing human social relations, nor that he would want to privilege it. Be that as it may, van den Berghe's theory is itself a curious cross-breed. A truly sociobiological theory must make connections between genetically determined behaviours and the increase or at least preservation of those genes/behaviours in successive generations. But this theory does not really address the actual reproductive success of ethnic and racially defined populations, it simply assumes without demonstrating that nepotism works to the group's benefit. Moreover, the gist of the argument is that while cultural definitions of the social group are consciously believed in and acted upon, the desire to look after one's own is, at base, instinctual and automatic. But if an instinct requires conscious will and intention for its realization, is it really still an instinct? The argument rests on an enticing metaphor – nepotistic behaviour within the racial/ethnic/national group is likened to altruistic self-sacrifice within the family. But the causal argument is not clear. On the one hand, biological principles of inclusive fitness seem to generate complex sets of cultural behaviours, but on the other these same sets of behaviours seem to parasitically attach themselves to the much more limited processes of inclusive fitness among close kin.

Unlike van den Berghe, most theorists of nationalist sentiment see no need to trace it back to actual biological causes. They are content simply to observe that themes of consanguinity and ancestry are present in most nationalist discourses, and to treat these as particularly powerful ideas shaping belief in the reality of the nation (e.g. Bauman 1992; Erikson 1993: 12; Smith 1991: 161–2). Two of the strongest statements of this position come from Donald L. Horowitz (1985) and Walker Connor (1994).

Horowitz's primary concern is with the logic and dynamics of ethnic conflict, particularly in Africa, Asia and the Caribbean. He has been concerned to show why ethnicity, more so than class, has had a dominant role in shaping politics in these regions.

To view ethnicity as a form of greatly extended kinship is to recognise, as ethnic groups do, the role of putative descent. There are fictive elements here, but the idea, if not always the fact, of common ancestry makes it possible for ethnic groups to think in terms of family resemblances – traits held in common, on a supposedly genetic basis, or cultural features acquired in early childhood – and to bring into play for a much wider circle those concepts of mutual obligation and antipathy to outsiders that are applicable to family relations. (1985: 57)

According to Horowitz, ethnicity, as a 'fictive' extension of kinship, gets its strength both from the fact that it provides a metaphorical language of unity for the group, and from the fact that actual networks of kinship relations provide an important infrastructure for ethnic groups, even if the social range of the ethnic group extends beyond clear-cut kin connections (1985: 57–64).

Horowitz is circumspect in drawing connections between ethnicity and nationalism. He observes that the principles of liberal democracy in modern territorial states assume 'congeries of free-floating individuals' unconstrained by ascriptions of kinship. For this reason liberalism has trouble 'constructing bonds of community' (1985: 87). There is a fundamental tension between the ideals, institutions and mechanisms of liberal democracies and principles of ethnicity. This is revealed in the way democratic party politics is undermined when votes are mobilized on the basis of ethnicity and majority ethnic groups within a country are thus able to hold a *de facto* monopoly on power (1985: 83–5). It also comes out most distinctly in the 'logic of secessions and irredentas' (1985: 229–88), where ethnicity is often the basis for challenges to the integrity of the territorial state that seek to break away and/or unify with co-ethnics across existing state boundaries. Thus Horowitz's aim is not to equate ethnicity and nationalism, his approach leaves room for national identities based on civic rather than ethnic principles. But he highlights the substantial bearing ethnicity has on nationalist politics, which is rarely purely civic, especially outside the heartlands of modern liberal democracy.

As we saw in the Introduction (Chapter 1), one of the most emphatic statements of the link between kinship and nationalism comes from Walker Connor (1994: 196–209):

> Our answer, then, to that often asked question, 'What is a nation?' is that it is a group of people who feel that they are ancestrally related. It is the largest group that can command a person's loyalty because of felt kinship ties; it is, from this perspective, the fully extended family. (1985: 202)

To those who would object that national and ethnic groups are not, in fact, closely related kin he avers that it is not *the fact*, but *the perception* that matters. If people think this way then it has consequences, and nation-builders are aware of these perceptions and repeatedly exploit them. Connor supports his argument by citing numerous uses of kinship-laden language in a variety of nationalist discourses, from Hitler's fascism, to Mao's communism, to the appeals of the colonial revolutionaries to their 'British brethren' in the US Declaration of Independence. A particularly vivid example comes from Adolph Stocker, a nineteenth-century German author:

> German blood flows in every German body, and the soul is in the blood. When one meets a German brother, and not merely a brother from common humanity, there is a certain reaction that does not take place if the brother is not German. (quoted in Connor 1994: 204)

For Connor, countering such language with reasoned objections based on the realities of biology, or supplying more rational explanations for why people identify in national terms, would be futile. This language of kinship works precisely because 'the national bond is subconscious and emotional rather than conscious and rational in its inspiration' (1994: 204). This is why music and poetry have so often been central to nationalist discourses, because they reach deeper into the psyche than rational modes of understanding: 'The core of the nation has been reached and triggered through the use of familial metaphors which can magically transform the mundanely tangible into emotion-laden phantasma . . .' (1994: 205).

Despite their common emphasis on kinship, we can see clear differences in the perspectives of Horowitz and Connor. Horowitz sees kinship as forming both the ideology and social organization of ethnicity, and ethnicity as caught up in, but not entirely defining nationalist politics. He treats ethnic politics as a relatively rational though problematic response to certain political conditions. Connor, on the other hand, focuses more strictly on the ideological dimension of kinship language, and sees the prevalence of such language as evidence of a basic continuity between ethnicity and nationalism. He locates nationalism, or as he prefers to call it, 'ethnonationalism' (1994), in the emotions and the subconscious. This move would seem to call for some kind of psychological or social psychological theory, but Connor offers none. Instead, the tendency of his approach is to place nationalism beyond our explanatory reach, arguing that because ethnonational beliefs are non-rational, they cannot be rationally accounted for. One problem here is that it is not enough to point to the use of kinship language. We need to know exactly when and under what conditions such language has psychological and ideological force. When monks refer to each other as 'brother' and 'father' they understand this as metaphorical and are not confused about their biological relationships. In the quote above, Stocker uses the term 'brother' to refer *both* to his fellow Germans, and to 'common humanity', so obviously something more than the kin term is needed to invoke that special relationship to fellow nationals.

Having said this, there is no doubt that relations of blood, ancestry and kinship are routinely invoked in nationalist discourses, both in ethnically and racially charged contexts, and in more sedate civic discourses of national solidarity. In fact, as just suggested with the example of the monks, the metaphor of kinship permeates social life and is operative in many non-national contexts. That such language is so pervasive and always to hand is hardly surprising. People everywhere live embedded in kin relations, no matter how attenuated by modern life. More profoundly, for much of human history kinship, always partly fictive, did provide the major ligaments of social organization, mobilizing social labour, and regulating the distribution of wealth and power (cf. Wolf 1982: 88–100). Even the dynastic states and far-flung empires such as that of the Habsburgs, which survived into the modern period, evolved out of earlier principles of kingship, involving complex symbolic and political extensions of earlier forms of kin-based social organization. Indeed, Horowitz's primary concern is with parts of the world where kinship still serves more of these regulative purposes than it does in the 'modern' industrial and post-industrial countries. At the very least, this raises the question of

---

Box 2.2 Guerrillas and Spirit Mediums in Zimbabwe

In his book *Guns and Rain* (1985) anthropologist David Lan offers an impressive symbolic analysis that hinges on themes of land and kinship. He studied the Shona people living in the Dande region of northern Zimbabwe, bordering on Mozambique, during the period between 1966 and 1980 when the guerrillas of the Zimbabwe African National Liberation Army (ZANLA) were making incursions into what was then Rhodesia, from bases in Mozambique, through the Dande region.

In seeking support for their struggle among the Shona of Dande, the guerrillas, often from other ethnic groups, had to be assimilated to traditional conceptions of legitimacy and authority. According to Lan, in the pre-colonial period chiefly authority over the land and the people was tied to the ability to bring much needed rainfall. Candidates for the office of chief normally came from a pool of descendents of a royal lineage (there are several royal lineages associated with particular territories among the Shona). The process of selecting the chief was partly guided by a spirit medium who, possessed by the spirit of a dead royal ancestor (*Mhondoro*), would pass judgement on the qualification of the candidate for office.

During the colonial period this traditional political system broke down as the colonial state claimed the authority to select and appoint chiefs, and the spirit mediums, while still serving the religious needs of their communities, became detached from the political process. This marginalization made them prone to become sources of criticism of the colonial political system, sometimes engaging in elaborate practices of purity and taboo, in which contact with Western objects and persons was seen as polluting and thus avoided.

As the anti-colonial war developed some of these spirit mediums became central in legitimating the activities of the guerrillas and garnering local support for them. Although they were 'outsiders', under the guidance of *Mhondoro* spirits, the mediums identified the guerrillas as liberators of the land from colonial oppression, and thus as the legitimate successors of the chiefs of old, unlike the co-opted chiefs of the present. In effect the traditional system of political legitimation was reconstituted with the guerrillas supplanting chiefs, the bringers of guns supplanting the bringers of rain. In Lan's analysis we can see a complex fusion of 'traditional' ethnic politics and 'modern' nationalist movement in which ideas of territory and kinship are crucial.

---

whether the extreme elaborations of racial and kinship language in the modern nationalisms of Europe c. 1870–1945 should be taken as a sign of the continuing importance of kinship for social life, or of anxieties about its increasing subordination to more impersonal bureaucratic forms of social organization.

Territory

In terms of sentimental attachments, the theme of kinship is often closely linked to that of territory. We will hear more about types and causes of territorial power struggles in later chapters, here we are only concerned with the primordial dimension. In keeping with his characterization of nationalism as an emotional bond of presumed kin ties, Walker Connor (2001) also speaks of a 'homeland psychology', citing the prevalence of such terms as 'fatherland', 'motherland' and '*blut und boden*' ('blood and soil') in nationalist discourses. For him the word 'homeland' is particularly telling:

> In the case of homeland, territory becomes intermeshed with notions of ancestry and family. This emotional attachment to the homeland derives from perceptions of it as the cultural hearth and, very often, as the geographic cradle of the ethno-national group. (2001: 53)

Connor emphasizes the power the image of homeland has to mobilize people in national and ethnic conflict, whether to defend existing state borders, to liberate an ethnic heartland, or to purge a country of those perceived to be 'alien'. Thus he argues that national liberation movements that employ guerrilla tactics within their own ethnic homeland are particularly difficult to eradicate because of the support they receive from local people, but by the same token, nationalist movements that aim to expand beyond an ethnic homeland will run into difficulties (2001: 60–2). Again, he understands the phenomenon in question as basically non-rational, an almost instinctive emotional affirmation: 'The notion of primal ownership – that only the members of my people have a "true right" to be here – is characterized by a mind-set that perceives privileged status for the homeland people as a self-evident right' (2001: 64).

In a rather more complex argument, with weberian overtones, Steven Grosby (1995, see also 1994 and 2001a) has tried to explain the compelling force of territorial ties. He argues that land, country and nation are figures in a complex pattern of inherited meanings that are invested with a 'charismatic' quality, in other words a certain authority or truth that is embodied in their immediate presence. In this light he offers:

> By the term primordial, I do not mean a racial or genetic predisposi-
> tion; rather it refers to the significance of vitality which man attributes
> to and is constitutive of both nativity and structures of nativity,
> whether that structure be the relation of lineage, for example, the
> family, or the relation of area, for example, the locality in which one is
> born and in which one is sustained. (1995: 144)

In short, Grosby argues that we are all born to someone, somewhere, and the group we are born into, and the place we are 'from', become fundamental categories of thought for understanding our place in the world and our general well being. Our own lives make sense in the context of larger genealogies associated with particular places (1994: 169). Nationalism partakes of this more basic social patterning. Rejecting classic sociological arguments that propose a secular shift away from social organizing principles of 'kinship' to those of 'territory' with the transition from premodern to modern society (e.g. Morgan 1985 [1877]), Grosby believes that kinship and territory are originally linked and endur- ingly tied to one another (1995: 157). He also believes that current social theory seriously overestimates the role of secular, rational, voluntaristic modes of thought and interaction, neglecting the way human behaviour is over-determined by systems of cultural meaning in which ties to kin and place are fundamental.

Language

Running through the themes of kinship and territory discussed above is a notion of essential connectedness – shared substances of blood or genes, rooted in lands passed down through generations. A third key element in this nexus of essential bonds is language. The most resound- ing statement of this idea over the centuries has been that formulated by the German philosopher of history Johann Gottfried Herder (1744–1803) in the late eighteenth century (cf. Barnard 1969; Kedourie 1993 [1960]: 48–57; Llobera 1994: 164–70; Penrose and May 1991). Reacting to the hyper-rationalism and cosmopolitanism of the Enlightenment, and the tendency of educated classes in (what would become) Germany to emulate French styles and mores, Herder made the organic processes of language central to his conception of society, and his celebration of German culture:

> Has a nationality anything dearer than the speech of its fathers? In its speech resides its whole thought domain, its tradition, history, religion and basis of life, all its heart and soul. To deprive a people of its speech is to deprive it of its one eternal good . . . With language is created the heart of a people. (Herder, 1783, quoted in Fishman 1972: 1)

Herder's rhapsodies to the essential virtues of German language and culture have often been seen as romantic irrationalism, and as forerunners of the racial essentialism, xenophobia and chauvinism of Hitler (cf. Dumont 1986). But the quote above is about the virtue of national languages in general, without preference for Germany in particular. In fact, Herder's views are more akin to current ideas of multiculturalism, and defences of the inherent value of cultural traditions often espoused by anthropologists. In human social variation, arising out of adaptations to differing climates and environments, he saw a pattern of God-given diversity that ought to be cultivated. For him, language was a means through which distinctive peoples came to know God, their natural world and themselves, and the ideal social arrangement was one in which language, nation and government were congruent, developing together. Thus he repudiated the multinational empires of the Habsburgs and the Ottomans as unnatural, and advocated the self-government of language groups as the necessary path to an authentic life.

The socio-linguist Joshua Fishman (1972) has picked up on this theme of 'authenticity' in his attempts to understand why language has so often been central to the nationalisms of new states breaking away from European empires. Fishman accepts the point often made by others, that modern nation-building requires the codification and dissemination through education of a common vernacular, for the practical purpose of social integration (Gellner 1983). But for him the power of language is much more than this:

> Modern mass nationalism goes beyond the objective, instrumental identification of community with language (i.e., with communication) to the identification of authenticity with a particular language which is experientially unique and, therefore, functional in a way that other languages cannot match, namely, in safeguarding the sentimental and behavioral links between the speech community of today and its (real or imaginary) counterparts yesterday and in antiquity. (Fishman 1972: 43–4)

Box 2.3 Language and Nationalism in Quebec

Recent decades have seen a rise in nationalist sentiments among the people of the province of Quebec in Canada. In *Nationalism and the Politics of Culture in Quebec* (1988) Richard Handler focuses on the period between 1976 and 1984 when the *independantiste* Parti Québécois was in control of the provincial government, highlighting the importance of language in Quebec nationalism. From the mid-nineteenth to the mid-twentieth century Quebec francophone culture was shaped by a conservative clerical nationalism that centred on the Catholic Church and espoused rural and familial values. In these terms Quebec francophone elites sought to preserve a distinct national identity and set of institutions (church and education), not separation. But by the 1960s this elite vision of society was out of step with most francophone experience. Urbanization, secularization, Americanization, growing labour organization and the spread of new liberal values among younger francophone intellectuals had set the stage for a rearticulation of Quebecois identity and political demands. In 1960 the Liberal government of Jean Lesage initiated a programme of catch-up modernization which came to be known, along with the broader social changes that led to it, as the 'Quiet Revolution'(pp. 83–4; see also Keating 2001: 78–80).

   Significantly, while religion and rural class structures had weakened as bases for francophone identity, language remained central, and perhaps became more problematic. In the urban environment, especially in Montreal, French increasingly interacted with English, and existed in a multilingual environment due to increasing immigration from outside Canada (Italian, Portugese, Greek, Vietnamese). Handler describes the various discourses about the French language he encountered among Quebec nationalists. By the time of his research an older nationalist argument, that the French language was the guardian of the Catholic faith (*La langue, gardienne de la foi*), and was peculiarly suited to Catholic ideas, mores, traditions, and culture, was losing salience. But people frequently argued, after the manner of Herder, that the language carried a 'distinctive style of thought and way of looking at the world' (Handler 1988: 160). Some went so far as to claim the 'superior clarity and rationality of French language and thought' (Handler 1988: 160). Others simply made a categorical equation between language and identity, as one person put it: 'your language, that's you' (Handler 1988: 161).

→

He stresses the way language implies for many nationalists an almost mystical link with the past, and stands as a testament to the nation's authenticity. On the one hand, this 'authenticity' is experienced directly by language users in a speech community. Even if a nation lacks strong traditions of written history and political autonomy, the language itself

→

In a larger frame, Handler outlines a 'linguistic dilemma' (1988: 164) defined by the poles of purity and pollution. On the one hand there is a long history of anxieties about the integrity of the French language, with purists denouncing Anglicization and mixtures called '*franglais*'. One major object of scorn has been the language variant called '*joual*', associated especially with the francophone urban working class of Montreal. *Joual* involves pronunciations different from standard French, significant borrowings from English, as well as its own distinctive words, not found in French or English. However, during the Quiet Revolution there was a movement among some intellectuals to revalorize *joual*, seeing it as a part of a distinctive indigenous culture, rather than a degraded form of French. Another dimension of the language debates in Quebec is bilingualism. Handler was told that exposing a francophone child too early to English would 'produce children who, having mastered neither French nor English, would be maladjusted and unable to think clearly' (1988: 168). This complex of anxieties about language and national identity is well illustrated by a quote offered by Handler from a speech about the quality of French in Quebec:

> Our language patrimony (*patrimoine langagier*) is a mass of words and expressions that we all share – all of us five or six million franco-phones. We have in common a patrimony that comes to x billion words. This is our treasure, like a natural resource. When six million people lose three, four, five words, our patrimony is reduced by that much: we lose ten, twenty, thirty million words. (1988: 167)

This context of popular concerns about language and national identity helps explain the evolution of language and education policy in Quebec, leading to the Charter of the French Language (Bill 101) in 1977. This bill sought to make French the only official language of Quebec, the language of choice in public administration, the private sector, in commerce and publicity. It also sought to make French the compulsory language of education in Quebec except for the indigenous anglophone minority. In response to objections from the anglophone and allophone (neither French nor English as a first language) communities, some of these requirements have subsequently been relaxed and moderated. But particularly in the field of education, the effects of the bill have been marked (see Keating 2001: 103–10).

conveys a kind of cultural history, encoded in its words, grammar and rhetorical styles, that has been passed down over generations. Language is experienced as an evolving but relatively stable 'substance' that is shared and exchanged by those who speak it, and that provides a funda-mental means of intimacy. Even when specific languages are understood as a cultural rather than a genetic endowment, there is still an important sense in which, at least metaphorically, they have a life of their own, and speakers partake of that life communally. On the other hand, a people's linguistic heritage will also include written and/or oral 'products of verbal versitility' (Fishman 1972: 50) – poems, epics, folk tales, songs, jokes, proverbs and such. Whether or not these contain explicit national-ist themes, and they often do, being conversant in them is a key badge of cultural membership, and participating in them a way of affirming community.

Herder, Fishman and a host of nationalists ('true primordialists') have been sensitive to these more sentimental and intuitive dimensions of language and its role in national identity, a role that has often been over-looked in favour of language's instrumental function in national unifica-tion. Fishman's writing has been stimulated by the practical problems of 'language planning' faced by new states after decolonization – how to select and standardize a 'national language' out of a continuum of dialects; whether to borrow loan words from the colonizer's language or coin new ones to name objects of technology imported from 'outside'. Fishman draws our attention to how these practical problems ultimately bear upon deeper feelings of linguistic authenticity that language plan-ners are obliged to take into account.

History

There is a difference between 'historical' and 'historiographic' ques-tions. By the former we normally mean enquiries that assume some kind of objective temporal framework within which human events unfold, offering hypotheses about how and why things unfold as they do. By the latter we generally mean investigations into history as representation, into how and why such accounts are constructed, what interests direct them, what narrative models shape them and so on. We ask these ques-tions both of professional historians, and of historical notions that inhabit popular imaginations. These two dimensions of history can never be entirely separated, we can always ask historiographic questions about supposedly 'objective' histories, but the practice of doing history, espe-cially in regard to nationalism, tends to diverge along these two lines. Sometimes we simply assume there is a general story to be told, and at others we ask questions about the story itself. Historiographic questions have been prevalent in the study of nationalism (Calhoun 1997: 51–65; McCrone 1998: 44–63), of concern to both 'primordialists' and 'modernists' and those in between. We will return to such questions under the heading of 'culture' in Chapter 8. Here I want to focus on 'primordial' approaches to the *history* of nations and nationalism, focusing particularly on the influential work of Anthony Smith (see also Hastings 1997; Hutchinson 2000).

In a debate published in the journal *Nations and Nationalism*, Smith and Ernest Gellner outlined their differences on this question (Gellner 1996a; Smith 1996a; 1996b). Gellner, the arch-modernist, argued that nations don't have 'navels', or if they do, they are unnecessary. By this he meant that whatever a modern nation's connections to its past (as our navels connect us to our mothers) these are relatively inconsequential for understanding them. Nations are primarily functional adaptations to the pressures and requirements of societal modernization, the need for a relatively uniform mass culture sharing a common language, so that a national sphere of industrial productivity and prosperity can be achieved and consolidated (Gellner 1996a: 366–70). Smith by contrast, has tirelessly argued that nations usually develop out of pre-existing ethnic formations, and can best be understood as such developments, concretely linked to an ethnic past (Smith 1986, 1989, 1996b: 371–88). Because of this stance, he has often been labelled a 'primordialist' by Gellner and others (Gellner 1996a: 366; Breuilly 1996: 150–1), but he rejects this label (Smith 1996b: 385), distancing himself from primordialism, while constantly positioning himself as a critic of the idea that nations lack premodern antecedents (Smith 1986: 1–18). Smith prefers to call his approach and those similar to it 'ethno-symbolism' (see Smith 1998: 170–98). As this approach ultimately rests on a particular conception of culture, we will treat it more fully in Chapter 8.

Nonetheless, conceding that the label is contested, we can still examine Smith's argument as one that emphasizes the historical depth of nations and nationalism. Smith sees modern nations as modifications, under the right circumstances, of pre-existing ethnic communities, which he calls '*ethnies*', borrowing the term from French. Throughout his work he has tried to capture this relationship of continuity with conceptually overlapping but distinct ideal-typical definitions of *ethnies* and nations. For Smith an *ethnie* is 'a named unit of population with common ancestry myths and shared historical memories, elements of shared culture, a link with a historic territory, and some measure of solidarity, at least among the elites' (2001a: 19). In contrast, a modern nation is 'a named human population sharing a historic territory, common myths and historical memories, a mass, public culture, a common economy and common legal rights and duties for all members' (2001a: 19).

The parallels between these definitions are obvious; and with them Smith invites the reader to make a genealogical inference from one form to the other. This is a very different conceptual approach to the one I offered with my working definition in the Introduction (Chapter 1). There I chose to define the process of nationalism (rather than an entity such as an *ethnie* or a nation) as: the making of combined claims, on behalf of a population, to the jurisdiction over a common identity within a distinct territory. I further qualified this definition, suggesting that nationalism in the full sense of the word is what happens when this general type of political mobilization happens under conditions of mass communication and the influence of the idea of rule by popular consent. I point this out to remind the reader that definitions encode assumptions about the nature of the object under study. Where, for me, the object is a general type of socio-political mobilization under specified historical conditions, for Smith the objects are types of social organization defined as sharing similar cultural or ideological features.

A crucial analytic distinction for Smith is that between two ideal types of *ethnie*, the lateral and the vertical:

[The lateral] type of *ethnie* was usually composed of aristocrats and higher clergy, though it might from time to time include bureaucrats, high military officials and the richer merchants. It is termed lateral because it was at once socially confined to the upper strata while being geographically spread out to form often close links with the upper echelons of neighbouring lateral *ethnies*. As a result, its borders were typically 'ragged', but it lacked social depth, and its often marked sense of common ethnicity was bound up with its *esprit de corps* as a high status stratum and ruling class . . . In contrast, the 'vertical' type of *ethnie* was more compact and popular. Its ethnic culture tended to be diffused to other social strata and classes. Social divisions were not underpinned by cultural differences: rather, a distinctive historical culture helped to unite different classes around a common heritage and traditions, especially when the latter were under threat from outside. As a result the ethnic bond was often more intensive and exclusive, and barriers to admission were higher. (1991: 53)

In Smith's view, the transition from *ethnie* to nation typically follows one of two paths, depending on which kind of *ethnie* provides its basis. In aristocratic/lateral cases, such as France, a core *ethnie* with aristocratic position spreads its elite culture to outlying groups through bureaucratic incorporation into more formalized state structures. In demotic/vertical cases, such as the Czechs c. 1780–1848, the intelligentsias of politically marginalized *ethnies* develop and popularize programmes of ethnic rediscovery in response to the incursions of nation formation of the first type (Smith 1989: 349–56).

As Smith points out, debates about the antiquity of nations, mostly carried out among historians, hinge on when particular cases can be seen as fitting more closely to his model of the nation as opposed to the ethnie (2001: 14–18). He notes that those prepared to push back the beginning point for nations tend to fall into two groups, those who see nations or at least relevant antecedents in the European medieval period (e.g. Hastings 1997; Reynolds 1984; Llobera 1994) and those who see proto-nations in the circum-Mediterranean ancient world, especially among the Jews, the Armenians and the Hellenes (e.g. Armstrong 1982; Grosby 1997; Kohn 1967: 27–60). Smith's general tactic is to argue that although nations as such are modern, some premodern *ethnies* are markedly closer to the nation-type than others (1994; cf. Routledge 2003). Thus ancient Egypt is viewed as more of an 'ethnic state' with overarching religious practices and a relatively unified ruling class, but economically localistic and with profound social barriers between nobles and commoners; whereas ancient Israel in the Second Temple period seems to have had a fairly integrated system of law and religious practices uniting the social hierarchy, and intensified by collective hardship, periods of religious reform and strenuous claims to territory. Clearly there is an echo in this comparison of Smith's lateral and vertical *ethnies*. Similarly, Smith contrasts the histories of Russia and France, two medieval dynastic states with strong legitimating ideologies about defending their own variants of the Christian faith. By 1500 Russia had achieved a degree of elite unity partly through identification with the cause of the Orthodox Church but the incorporation of territorially outlying *ethnies* and reimposition of serfdom made this, again, more of a socially divided ethnic state. France on the other hand, was more territorially compact and hemmed in by other European powers, identification with the state intensified by repeated Anglo-French wars.

As Smith notes, one of the main bases for disagreement about the search for premodern nations is the question of 'social penetration' – it is very difficult to know how far down the social scale the fragments of nationalist-sounding discourses preserved in the historical record actually penetrated (1986: 70–3). Most modernist approaches are reluctant to recognize 'nations' much before the late eighteenth century, with the political revolutions spreading out from France, and the industrial revolutions spreading out from England as the key markers of the beginning of the nationalist era. Such approaches tend to stress the 'mass' nature of national identity, and a relatively secular conception of the nation on the model of the French Revolution. But if we allow that elite and middle-class ideas of nationhood constitute a form of nation, even before these ideas and identities have been effectively disseminated to a wider society, and that nationhood can be articulated within a religious idiom, then the conceptual continuum (rather than a sharp break) between *ethnie* and nation begins to look more fluid and ambiguous, and the chronology of nations less fixed (Smith 2001a: 20–2; cf. Grosby 1997: 2; Hutchinson 1994: 23–4)

In Smith's conceptions of ethnicity and nationhood, compared to some of those we have discussed above, there is a distinct shift away from actual or imagined biological and kinship ties, to a more general notion of shared heritage:

> *ethnies* are constituted, not by lines of physical descent, but by the sense of continuity, shared memory and collective destiny, i.e. by lines of cultural affinity embodied in distinctive myths, memories, symbols and values retained by a given cultural unit of population. (1991: 29)

Nonetheless, in trying to account for the enduring power of national identities the familial imagery is back in force:

> [The nation] can offer a glorious future similar to its heroic past. In this way it can galvanize people into following a common destiny to be realized by succeeding generations. But these are the generations of 'our' children; they are 'ours' biologically as well as spiritually, which is more than any class or Party can promise. So the promise of life immortal in our posterity seems genetically vindicated. (1991: 161)

> [One] function of national identity is the prominence it gives to realizing the ideal of fraternity. The ideal itself suggests the close relationship between the family, the ethnic community and the nation, at least on the ideological plane. *Ethnie* and nation are seen simply as families writ large, a sum of many interrelated families, brothers and sisters all. (1991: 162)

In characteristic fashion, after the passage just quoted Smith goes on to stress again that this identity is sustained through countless symbolic processes, large and small: 'parades, remembrance ceremonies, anniversary celebrations, monuments to the fallen, oaths, coinage, flags, eulogies

Box 2.4   Israel – an Ancient Nation?

The Jews and Greeks of antiquity have long been regarded as precocious forerunners of modern nationhood (e.g. Kohn 1967). Whether and when ancient Israel took a shape that could reasonably be classified as 'a nation' has been a core concern of Steven Grosby's research (1991, 1999). Our main source for the early history of the Israelites is the Old Testament, which appears to have begun taking shape with the book of Deuteronomy in the late seventh century BC, in a period of religious reform and political consolidation. Thus it is very difficult to separate history from myth in the sacred story of Abraham and his descendents down to Moses, and the exile into Egypt. Grosby observes that there is fragmentary archaeological and historical evidence for the existence of a people of Israel as far back as the late thirteenth century BC, but these people appear to have consisted of loose confederations of clans and tribes that were often at war with each other, and observed diverse religious practices, which included the god Yahweh, but variously combined this with the worship of the fertility/nature god Baal and Asherah, a goddess consort of Yahweh. A degree of political unification was achieved with the alliance of the 'House of Saul' reigning over Israel in the north and the 'House of David' reigning over Judah to the south, brought more firmly together under the kingdom of David and his son Solomon (1006–926 BC) but then divided again by a war that Grosby suggests was only a 'civil war' from the subsequent perspective of the authors of Deuteronomy who were concerned to portray a religiously and politically unified people stretching back into the past (1991: 257–8).

The crucial period for the consolidation of a more nation-like identity for the people of Israel appears to have been the century between the fall of the northern kingdom of Israel to the Assyrians in 721 BC and the fall of Judah in the south to the Babylonians in 597 BC. In this imperilled environment, especially under the reign of Josiah (637–607 BC), a period of intensive religious reform and identity consolidation was driven forward. The Book of Law (Deuteronomy) was 'discovered', and the new unity of 'all Israel' was promulgated, requiring that only Yahweh be worshipped in the land of Israel, that his laws be obeyed, that Jerusalem was the religious centre of the people, and that the tradition of Passover marking the people's covenant with Yahweh be 'revived' (or perhaps created), a covenant which entailed Yahweh giving the lands 'from Dan to Beersheba' to the chosen people. Grosby argues that it is this fusion of the monolatrous worship of a single deity, whose laws have jurisdiction over a defined people and territory, with a clear symbolic centre in Jerusalem, that mark this out as an early example of nation formation.

of heroes and memorials of historic events' (1991: 162). He is determined
not to be understood as saying that there is some universal deep psychology that automatically creates the bonds of ethnicity and/or nationhood,
and herein lies his desire to distance himself from the label of 'primordialism'. Rather, the national disposition is sustained by a chain of
communication. But as the subject matter itself is always an enduring
identity, symbols of land and descent are eminently serviceable for this
purpose, appearing again and again.

Conclusion

I hope this overview of primordialist themes has served to show the
diversity within this category. Let us return to the dimensions of primordialism we laid out at the beginning, paying attention to the fact that the
thinkers we have been discussing incorporate them to varying degrees in
their approaches.

Among those we have discussed, only van den Berghe sees a need to
trace links between actual biological processes and nationalist beliefs and
behaviours. All would acknowledge the centrality of notions of kinship
and territory for nationhood, although Horowitz and Connor place particular emphasis on the former, and Connor and Grosby have paid more
attention to the latter. Fishman has been something of a lone voice in his
stress on the power of linguistic 'authenticity' in nationalism. As we have
said, the prominence of these themes is widely recognized across the field
of nationalism studies, but these approaches tend to move them centre
stage and give them greater explanatory weight.

In various ways all these writers are concerned with the historical depth
of nationalism in premodern social forms, but Smith and Grosby have
been particularly preoccupied with identifying early, premodern forms of
nationhood. By contrast, Connor, despite his conception of 'ethnonationalism' as imagined kinship, argues that nationalism *per se* is a distinctively
modern, mass phenomenon. When confined to elite groups as it generally
was before the late nineteenth century it is not truly nationalism (1990).
Thus he quipped on the platform at the annual conference of the
Association for the Study of Ethnicity and Nationalism in March 2001 that
his colleagues don't know how to place him – is he a 'primordial
modernist' or a 'modern primordialist'? This puzzle should alert us to the
fact that we cannot rely on simple equations in which ethnicity is aligned
with a premodern past, and nationality is aligned with a modern present.
Whether modern nationalism is ultimately a variation on ethnicity (as

Connor argues), and whether we can find ethnic formations approximating modern nations in the premodern era (as Smith argues), are two separate questions.

What does tend to run throughout these approaches is a concern for nationalism as a process involving powerful feelings that have to be taken into account, and not simply treated as epiphenomenal, as secondary by-products of elite manipulations of larger populations, or adjustments to the social structures of modern life. Whether in terms of van den Berghe's 'instincts', Fishman's 'authenticity', Connor's 'psychological bond', Grosby's 'structures of vitality', or Smith's 'lines of cultural affinity', ethnicity and nationhood are seen as pervasive worldviews grounded as much in feelings, intuitions and sentiments as in reasoning, conscious motives and explicit ideologies. But here again there are differences. Locating the springs of nationalism in human biology, as van den Berghe does, or deep in the subconscious, as Connor does, tends to push the causes of nationalism beyond the bounds of rational inspection. Nationalism becomes part of our basic human nature, and explicit ideologies of the nation, however conditioned by modernity, become reflections of that nature. Grosby and Smith, on the other hand, treat ethnicity and nationalism more as an emergent historical processes of '*la longue durée*'. Moreover, for them aspects of affect and attachment are constantly linked to more accessible processes of cognition, symbolization, representation and knowing. The latter are not reflections of, or driven by, the former – they are two sides of the same process.

In closing this chapter we should simply appreciate that primordialism, however loosely defined here, does direct our attention to important matters in nationalism studies. First, it encourages us to think about the continuities between contemporary nationalisms and earlier, similar cultural and political processes, whether or not we chose to categorize these as forms of nationalism. And second, it directs our attention to recurrent core themes in nationalist discourses, and calls upon us to ponder the relationship between the explicit ideological articulation of these themes and the powerful emotions and attachments they can mobilize. We will explore these issues further in the next chapter.

Further Reading

Grosby (2001a) offers a good general theoretical statement of the primordialist position. This is also one of the clearer statements of his own position, which can be difficult to grasp. Connor (1993) is a key statement of the position that nationalism is ultimately a non-rational matter of psychology and emotions. Prime examples of various sub-types of primordialist arguments include: from the sociobiological perspective, van den Berghe (1978); regarding language, Fishman (1972); and regarding the historical roots of nations in ethnicity: Hastings (1997), Hutchinson (2000) and, of course, Smith (1989).

3
Rethinking Primordialism

This chapter will take a more critical look at the themes of primordialism surveyed in Chapter 2. I will start by examining some well-established lines of criticism of primordialism, providing a general overview of debates about the primordialist approach. I will then go on to develop my own somewhat different critique. My main arguments will be: (1) that primordialist approaches have tended to neglect the importance of social scale and organization in understanding the nature of emotional bonds; (2) that questions of social scale and structure must have bearing on the efficacy of nationalist symbols and discourses about kinship, territory and so on; and (3) that the importance of social scale, and thus 'primordial emotional bonds', needs to be understood in the context of the evolution of ever larger and more complex forms of social organization. In other words, the issues of 'emotional bonds' and 'historical depth' are concretely interrelated, but in ways not often appreciated by primordialist theories. My aim is not to utterly refute the primordialist approach, but to raise questions and suggest what lines of argument need to be developed if primordialist approaches (broadly defined) are to be rendered more compelling.

Three Critiques of Primordialism

The Modernist Critique

As we saw in Chapter 2, Anthony Smith and Ernest Gellner have debated the importance of historical depth for modern nations. From the modernist perspective, John Breuilly (1996) has also been a particularly forceful critic of Smith's 'primordialism' (bearing in mind Smith's resistance to this term). While he does not dispute the premises that ethnicity can be found long before nations and nationalism, and that '*ethnies*' can provide some of the materials out of which modern nations are forged, for him these points are of little significance in explaining modern nationalism. To begin with he worries that attempts to discern the roots of modern nations in pre-existing *ethnies* tends to 'buy into' the prejudices of nationalist themselves, that is, 'true primordialists' (see also: Hobsbawm 1996), and to confuse contingent preconditions with real causes (Breuilly 1993: 405–6). He argues that the complexes of myths and symbols that Smith makes central to his conceptions of both *ethnies* and nations are poor predictors of nationalism – modern nations have taken shape regardless of how well developed these ideological preconditions are. Moreover, much of the original context of 'ethnic statements' made by cultural elites in the distant past has been lost, making it very difficult to judge the broader social meaning, salience and popular reception of high cultural assertions of ethnic identity. He also notes that the primary difference between Smith's definitions of '*ethnie*' and 'nation' (see Chapter 2) lies in the addition of pervasive legal, political and economic institutions in the definition of nations. For Breuilly it is precisely these institutions that define modern national identity (cf. Zubaida 1989). While he accepts that institutions of religion and dynasties were carriers of 'myth-symbol complexes' in premodern times, he regards these as highly ambivalent in regard to national identity, in that they involved universalistic and trans-ethnic creeds and political projects. In the case of religion, churches became bound up with national identities precisely when larger confessional and dynastic-imperial institutions in which they had once been embedded were unravelling (1996: 150–4).

Debates about the antiquity of nations hinge on how one defines terms such as 'nations' and 'nationalism' and what questions one is asking about them. In other words these debates are often more about the terms of analysis than the substance of history. Breuilly rightly characterizes the difference between himself and Smith as lying in the fact that where Smith is struck by continuities, he finds discontinuities more salient (1996: 151). Smith proceeds by defining both *ethnies* and nations primarily in terms of social solidarity generated through culture and symbols, with allowances for the differences between modern and premodern institutions and their roles in regulating society. More generally, Smith's focus on the ideological or cultural dimension naturally leads him to concentrate on its manifestation in the form of discourse, myths, symbols and such. This in turn results in a prominent role for elites, as the primary generators of such discourses, in his analyses. Smith himself has noted this tendency, describing his own intellectual trajectory in this regard as involving an early focus on the role of intellectuals and elites followed by an increasing concern with the impact of cultural discourses on wider populations (1998: 190). This general approach implies certain underlying research questions, about how social solidarity and political legitimacy are ideologically created and sustained. These are very general questions and there is no reason to assume that there is nothing to be learned from comparing these processes across very different cases, of both ancient and modern polities. But by the same token, making these comparisons does not oblige us to accent the underlying similarities between Smith's *ethnies* and modern nations – the fundamental differences between these two ideal types may be what makes the comparison most interesting and illuminating.

By contrast, Breuilly's approach defines the nation as an ideological solution to political problems generated by modernization. As societies became less a cluster of interdigitating corporate bodies (e.g. burghs, craft guilds and religious orders) and more a fluid labouring population, and as governing functions became more concentrated in the state, notions of 'culture' and 'nation' served as a kind of ideological glue to bind the new kind of society and state together (2001: 37). Significantly for this debate, Breuilly's interest in the first instance is in 'nationalism' not as a shared ideology, but as actual instances of political mobilization in the pursuit of statehood. Thus his focus is more on the social, economic and political processes that make modern mass societies, and how and why these masses become mobilized. He eschews the idea of a general theory of nationalism, seeing the phenomenon as too variable for this, preferring instead to conceptualize typical patterns of nationalist mobilization, understanding nationalism as one of many forms of the pursuit of power (1993: 420–1). Because modern mass society and the modern state are constitutive parts of Breuilly's definition of nationalism, his comparisons are logically contained within a modern historical frame. Smith and Breuilly define nations and nationalism differently, because they are ultimately asking different questions, the former about the nature of culture and ideology, the latter about the conditions of mass mobilization.

The Instrumentalist Critique

Paul Brass (1991) shares many of Breuilly's objections to the primordialist approach, but with a particular emphasis. He draws a fundamental contrast between 'primordialism' and 'instrumentalism'. He understands primordialism as holding that 'ethnic attachments belong to the nonrational part of the human personality' and that 'ethnic groups properly so-called are groups based on distinctive cultures or origin myths or patterns of exchange with other groups that have core features that persist through time' (1991: 72). He counters this with his own instrumentalist position:

the study of ethnicity and nationality is in large part the study of polit-
ically-induced cultural change. More precisely it is the study of the
process by which elites and counter-elites within ethnic groups select
aspects of the group's culture, attach new value and meaning to them,
and use them as symbols to mobilise the group, to defend its interests,
and to compete with other groups. (1991: 75)

Thus Brass's approach requires that there is a strong 'rational' dimension to ethnic identity formation, and that cultures are quite malleable. He
allows that elites and counter-elites are constrained by the cultural materials with which they must work, but nonetheless sees them as having
considerable latitude to strategically and instrumentally chose which
cultural symbols to manipulate for political gain, and how (although they
may blunder in these efforts).

This position developed partly through a series of exchanges with
Francis Robinson (1994) regarding the development of Muslim identity
in South Asia, and more particularly Uttar Pradesh in northern India.
Robinson stresses 'the formative influence of the ideal of the Islamic
community on Muslim political behaviour' (1994: 215), arguing that the
tradition of Islamic thought contains powerful moral injunctions for
political leaders to seek the power to establish separate communities
living according to Islamic religion and law, and that the pursuit of this
goal is widely evident in Islamic political behaviour across the globe.
Whether in the form of Muslim minorities seeking political separation, or
of political parties in Islamic states advancing a particular vision of the
true *umma*, the call to form the ideal Islamic community is a powerful
shaping force. Brass, on the other hand, has argued that Muslim identity
in India was only weakly defined before the late nineteenth century.
Despite a set of common religious beliefs, variations in religious practice,
language and historical origins militated against an integrated Muslim
community (1991: 87). From the late nineteenth century on, however,
diversification among Muslim elites led to competition over political
leadership and over definitions of ethnic identity through differing selec-
tions of symbols. In summary: the traditional religious leaders of the
ulema sought to preserve and reinforce religious and legal autonomy,
emphasizing the *shari'a*; Muslim aristocrats, landlords and government
servants sought to secure their privileged positions in a changing political
system, emphasizing their regional history of political dominance; and
after the First World War a rising group of middle-class professionals and
politicians increasingly sought national self-determination, emphasizing
a full-blown national identity including distinctive religion, philosophy,

literature and language. In effect the competition between these elites 'ratchets up' the definition of a distinctive Muslim community in India.

Both Brass and Robinson are willing to acknowledge the other's position to a degree. The difference is one of emphasis, the former seeing culture as relatively flexible and manipulable, the latter seeing it as having a kind of inertia that constrains and powerfully shapes choices. Once again these differences are more a matter of asking different questions, of what one is trying to explain, than they are of historical facts. Brass is interested in why things change, why political movements develop where they had not existed previously. Robinson is concerned to explain a perceived widespread similarity in Muslim demands for political autonomy.

In Brass's instrumentalism the role of elites, by definition, becomes particularly prominent. As we have seen with Anthony Smith, primordialists sometimes emphasize the role of elites, but many tend to treat them as a component in a larger *sui generis* process, and not as a primary cause of ethnic and national formation. It is worth noting here that whether or not national identity is 'socially constructed' is not a key axis of difference. There is general agreement amongst researchers that it is, even though some critics of primordialism accuse primordialists of failing to recognize this fact (see below). But as Virginia Tilley has suggested, primordialists tend to see social construction as a more socially diffuse process, rather than always led by intellectuals and elites (1997: 512).

The Anti-Essentialist Critique

Perhaps the most emphatic attack on the primordialist approach has come from Jack Eller and Reed Coughlan (1993) who see it as 'unscientific', 'unsociological' and 'vacuous'. The central thrust of their objections is that primordialism essentializes ethnic identity, failing to appreciate the socially constructed nature of ethnicity. Their critique targets the formulations of the weberians Edward Shils (1957) and Clifford Geertz (1973) who are usually treated as the originators of the concept of primordialism. Eller and Coughlan structure their critique around Geertz's discussion of primordialism, so I introduce Geertz here, turning to Shils at the beginning of the next section, for reasons that will become apparent.

Like Shils, Geertz was concerned with modernization and nation-building in the 'new states' emerging out of post-Second World War decolonization, a process he called 'the integrative revolution'. In a passage worth citing at length he explains:

the new states are abnormally susceptible to serious disaffection based on primordial attachments. By a primordial attachment is meant one that stems from the 'givens' – *or, more precisely, as culture is inevitably involved in such matters, the assumed 'givens'* – of social existence: immediate contiguity and kin connection mainly, but beyond them the givenness that stems from being born into a particular religious community, speaking a particular language, or even a dialect of a language, and following particular social practices. These congruities of blood, speech, custom, and so on, *are seen to have* an ineffable, and at times overpowering, coerciveness in and of themselves. One is bound to one's kinsmen, one's neighbor, one's fellow believer, ipso facto; as a result not merely of personal affection, practical necessity, common interest, or incurred obligation, but at least in great part by virtue of some unaccountable absolute *import attributed to* the very tie itself. The general strength of such primordial bonds, and the types of them that are important, differ from person to person, from society to society, and from time to time. But for virtually every person, in every society, at almost all times, some attachments *seem* to flow more from a sense of natural – some would say spiritual – affinity than from social interaction. (Geertz 1973: 259–60; emphasis added)

Eller and Coughlan (1993:186–92) take this passage to be asserting that ethnic identities are *a priori* facts beyond analysis (i.e. 'givens'), that they are uniformly irresistible and 'overpowering' for members of the ethnic group, and that ethnic identity is 'essentially a question of emotion or affect' as opposed to 'interests' for instance. There is no doubt that the term primordialism is often used loosely and without elaboration in ways that suggest all these assumptions. However, several authors (Özkirimli 2000: 73; Smith 1998: 155–6; Tilley 1997: 501) have recently pointed out that this is a serious misreading of Geertz, in that the stuff between the first pair of dashes makes it clear that by 'givens' he means what is *believed* to be natural and beyond question. As this passage and the other words and phrases italicized in the quote above indicate, Geertz is concerned here with relatively unquestioned systems of belief, and not with some unanalysable first principle. The assertion of the variability of primordial bonds in the next to last sentence clearly implies that they are sociologically analysable. And as we saw repeatedly in the previous chapter, primordialist approaches usually stress that it is what people believe about their social relations, not actual ties of blood, etc., that is at the heart of the matter.

More generally, Geertz's original argument set up 'primordialism' as one half of a dialectical equation, complemented by a demand for 'civil politics'. He was not trying to define ethnicity, nations or nationalism in terms of primordial ties, whether 'real' or simply 'believed', but rather in terms of a deep tension between principles of traditional social organization and modernization. By the end of the essay he speculates that in some countries, under the right conditions, a proper, stable balance between primordial and civic attachments can be established, once these new states have weathered the transition to the modern world. His treatment is very much in the Gellnerian mode of nationalism as an ideology of transition to modernity (Gellner 1983).

A crucial issue in this debate is the relationship between affect and cognition. Steven Grosby (1994) has rebutted Eller and Coughlan by claiming that they fail to understand that 'emotions are aroused by the cognition of an object' (166). Far from a vague emotionality, for him primordialists attempt to account for ethnic ties in terms of 'a pattern of orientation of human society' (1994: 167) and objectified systems of meaning. Primordial symbols may be widespread and long-standing, and they may sustain and mobilize sentiments, but they also constitute cognitive maps of reality and how the social world works.

Virginia Tilley (1997) has made an admirable attempt to rehabilitate Geertz's conception of 'primordialism' by stressing its culturally constructed nature (*pace* Eller and Coughlan). She counters objections to allowing amorphous notions of affect to do explanatory work by arguing that such patterns of affect as understood by Geertz and other anthropologists are inevitably grounded in systems of meaning embodied in symbols and routinized practices. To this end she describes certain rules of courtesy and etiquette in sharing drink and showing hospitality among Palestinian Arabs and the lowland Quichua of Ecuador in order to show how feelings of pride, honour, offence and so on are sustained by micropractices that articulate with universes of explicit symbols concerning good behaviour. As she puts it:

> Although such meanings shape our social universe, they are elusive to conscious consideration; many of us, experiencing a visceral reaction to some social moment, would be hard pressed to articulate exactly what principles were violated by the offensive action or abrasive individual . . . Yet those principles must form a pre-existing basis for the emotional reaction or it would not have arisen. (1997: 505)

Tilley's call for a more careful attention to the subtle details of social universes of meaning is welcome, because all too often these are rather blithely assumed or ignored while vivid key symbols of consanguinity, descent and place are treated as self-evidently effective and powerful. Nonetheless, Tilley perhaps over-compensates in emphasizing the cognitivist frame of systems of meaning, stopping short of a fuller consideration of the more elusive realm of sentiments and emotional bonds. Surely it is our sense that with nationalism, powerful emotions are frequently being mobilized, not simply convincing or habitual ideas (although these count too), that makes the primordialist account seem compelling, and the instrumentalist and modernist accounts seem some-how incomplete. But, as we have seen, what primordialists tend to do is to highlight (and less often analyse) systems of symbols, and then assert the emotive power of the same. No doubt symbols are evocative and do have an ability trip a spark across the gap from the cognitive to the emotional sides of our beings, but there is much more to human affect than this. We will examine problems of symbolic analysis more closely in relation to conceptions of culture in Chapter 9. For the rest of this chapter I will concentrate more on questions of social structure and social scale. What all these accounts fail to pay attention to is how actual affective ties between socially related persons come into play in the process of nationalism. Our emotional natures are governed not simply by ideologies and symbols, but fundamentally by the degree of intimacy and familiarity we share with other human beings – it is these ties that must be put into motion. And yet primordialists generally content them-selves with describing anonymous processes in which abstract persons are assumed to respond to emotive language full of symbols of kinship and soil. They demonstrate the mobilization of minds by symbols, but not the mobilization of hearts. We will pursue this problem more closely in the next section.

Shils Revisited

Having reviewed and raised some objections to how primordialists have handled primordialism, let me see if I can now build a more positive account of what is at stake here. To begin with, if we take a closer look we will find that Edward Shils' much cited article 'Primordial, Personal, Sacred and Civil Ties' (1957) was actually concerned with matters strik-ingly different from those primordialists have tended to pursue.

The essay is, in fact, a piece of intellectual autobiography meant to show that the relationship between research and theory in socio-logical enquiry is often oblique and circuitous, and that aspirations to the theoretical rigour of the hard sciences are misplaced. Within this personal account Shils lays out a critique of the classic sociological notion of a shift from *Gemeinschaft* to *Gesellschaft*, from a universe of intimate and solidaristic social relations to one of anonymous functional integration. He argues that a variety of foci of close personal ties continue to operate effectively within large modern societies, and that what needs to be understood is the interrelations between these levels, rather than assuming some process of replacement. But strikingly, although it is often cited as the *locus classicus* of the idea of 'primordial ties', that concept plays a relatively minor role in this essay (but see Shils 1995). Instead, Shils spends much more time focusing on the concept of 'primary groups' as adapted from the American sociologist Charles Cooley. While these might be based on kinship or co-residence in a territory, they might just as well be based on some other principle of association. Shils gives further credit to the German sociologist Hermann Schmalenbach, saying:

> He saw that it was possible for a state of intense and comprehensive solidarity to exist without those who shared it possessing either a common territory or origin and residence, a common place of work or ties of blood and sexual connection. When these primordial concepts were isolated from the original concept of *Gemeinschaft*, the residue was the *Bund*, for which such terms as confraternity, brotherhood, league, band, gang are all poor translations but each of which brings to the fore the element of intense mutual attachment independent of primordial ties. (1957: 133–4)

Indeed, Shils' own research in which he developed the significance of the concept of primary groups focused on the primary fighting units within military organizations (e.g. platoons), while drawing out comparisons to other types of primary groups based on industrial activity and religion. Later in his career, in the 1950s, when he began to be involved in research on family and kinship in the East End of London, he did become convinced that the bonds of kinship involve 'a certain ineffable significance . . . attributed to the tie of blood' (1957: 142) that is not reducible to the effect of social interaction. But this is a relatively minor qualification on the larger argument about the variable and shifting fit between primary groups and society as a whole.

Shils was also wrestling with the question: how do large ideological systems succeed or fail in insinuating themselves into the fabric of primary groups? Or, to put it another way, how do such primary groups succeed or fail in resisting such insinuations? Thus he was also concerned with Weber's concept of charisma and the idea of personal leadership and value commitments within these primary groups. In his studies of German and Soviet soldiers of the Second World War he had found that soldiers were by no means uniform in this regard, some of the higher ranking officers having strong commitments to the state ideologies they served, while others were more motivated by obligations to the soldiers that served under them. In the Soviet case he found that the soldiers in general were motivated by a complex of sources: 'the morale of the small unit . . . the cult of manliness . . . diffuse patriotism . . . and . . . fear and awe of authority' (1957: 141). In short,

> The military studies revealed that participation in the central value system was very unequal in intensity and continuity, and that a large social organization could maintain a high degree of effectiveness (integration) with only a modicum of attachment to its value system. (1957: 141)

Cooley's whole point about primary groups had been that they could provide the basis for the creation and reproduction of solidaristic values that could then feed into and sustain a potentially anomic and impersonal modern society. But Shils had come to an almost opposite conclusion, that the values of primary groups and those of the larger society were as likely to be disjunct in nature:

> Man is much more concerned with what is near at hand, with what is present and concrete than with what is remote and abstract. He is more responsive on the whole to persons, to the status of those who surround him and the justice he sees in his own situation than he is with the symbols of remote persons, with the total status system in the society and with the global system of justice. Immediately present authorities engage his mind more than remote ones. (1957: 130)

Writing in a tradition of suspicion towards powerful state ideologies, Shils seems to take comfort from this conclusion that ideological zeal and enthusiasm are as likely to be diffused as sustained by the subtleties and intricacies of primary bonds. Thus the 'sacred' can become bogged down in the 'primordial' and 'personal', leaving space for more moderate 'civil' ties to prevail.

Thinking about Feeling

There are powerful echoes here of the ideas of the thinkers of the Scottish Enlightenment, particularly David Hume and Adam Smith, who were deeply concerned with affective dimension of human social life. Both argued that there is a self-evident propensity in human nature to partake, in moderated form, in the feelings of others, through our capacity for sympathy. We both instinctively echo the feelings of those around us and evaluate the propriety of each other's actions according to the degree to which we are able to identify with the feelings of the various persons involved in any interaction. It is this emotional capacity which forms the initial foundation of our moral life, not any complex cogitation on ethical principles.

Discussing the social basis of our moral sentiments Smith makes an observation that prefigures Shil's discussion of primary groups:

> Among well-disposed people, the necessity or conveniency of mutual accommodation, very frequently produces a friendship not unlike that which takes place among those who are born to live in the same family. Colleagues in office, partners in trade, call one another brothers; and frequently feel towards one another as if they really were so. Their good agreement is an advantage to all; and, if they are tolerably reasonable people, they are naturally disposed to agree. We expect that they should do so; and their disagreement is a sort of small scandal. The Romans expressed this sort of attachment by the word *necessitudo*, which, from the etymology seems to denote that it was imposed by the necessity of the situation. (1984 [1790]: 223–4)

This points to a problem however. Smith builds up an image of concentric spheres of affective and moral ties, beginning with the family, moving out to circles of friendship, association and frequent interaction in public life, out to the level of national society and, finally, towards humankind as a whole. But as one moves out through these spheres, the vivacity of our emotional bonds naturally grows weaker. To be effective, our moral sentiments require some sort of supplementary process. In another celebrated passage, Smith asks us to imagine a representative European confronted with the knowledge that the entire population of China had been swallowed up in an earthquake. While sensible of the tragedy, this person would only be moderately discomforted, and yet if confronted with the loss of his or her own little finger, the anguish would be extreme:

If he would lose his little finger to-morrow, he would not sleep to-night; but, provided he never saw them, he will snore with the most profound security over the ruin of a hundred million of his brethren, and the destruction of that immense multitude seems plainly an object less interesting to him, than this paltry misfortune of his own. (1984 [1790]: 136–7)

Smith goes on to argue that this sad state of affairs in human nature is somewhat compensated for by the fact that, out of the habits of sympathy and wanting to be well regarded by others, we develop a conscience (what he often called 'the impartial spectator') which calls us to evaluate our own actions from a more disinterested perspective. In the most virtuous persons this can lead to magnanimous interest in human affairs, and even profound self-sacrifice in the larger interests of humanity. If Smith's compensating factor for our affective limitations is found in a certain potential in the human character, David Hume points more to the role of social institutions. Like Smith he believed that moral sentiments arose naturally out of the emotional bonds of family and other close relations. But as society grew in scale it became necessary to develop the 'artificial virtues' of systems of government and justice, derived from the 'natural virtues' that normally sustained stable intimate relations. Precisely because our moral sentiments based on our passions have a limited range, our powers of reason come into play, correcting this shortcoming by imitating and expanding through social institutions the natural benevolence and fairness found in the family (see Hume 1978 [1740]: 477–84; Baier 1988).

Whether or not these refinements of human character and social institutions are adequate to the ethical challenges they confront, probably more daunting now than 250 years ago, is not our question here. The point is that Hume and Smith thought these formulations, or something like them, were necessary because they had shown that our natural affectivity was the basis of our moral sentiments, and that these affections are naturally limited in scope. On this point, I think they were and are absolutely right. They may not have the right answer, indeed, there may not be one, but they have *the right problem*. Any one of us who stops to ponder it will quickly have to concede that the number of people in the world for whom we would more or less automatically be sympathetically moved if we learned they were experiencing either great good fortune or misfortune, is alarmingly small – perhaps a dozen to 40 or 50 at the most. Across that number the intensity of our natural sympathy will fade, dropping off sharply beyond its extremes. Many variables come into play affecting the intensity of our feelings: physical proximity, frequency of contact, duration of relations, intensity of shared experiences. To return to our main theme, surely any 'primordial' theory of nationalism must explore, in some detail, how nationalisms activate these rather constrained spheres of emotional ties. Just as Smith's hypothetical European gentleman understands the plight of his fellow human beings in China, but only dimly feels it, it is perfectly possible to be confronted by all kinds of nationalist rhetoric, parading images of kith and kin, but to not be particularly moved. Beneath the ideas and symbols of primordiality lies a concrete social reality of actual social relations, involving countless small, but interdigitating social spheres of powerful affective ties, grounded in propinquity. We need to ask questions about how, in particular social settings, these spheres are created and sustained, and through what kinds of institutions and modes of communication.

A basic interest in the role of emotions in social life runs from these Scottish Enlightenment thinkers through modern sociology, in the work of major figures such as Durkheim, Weber and Simmel (Shilling 2002), but it has often been marginalized by rationality and cognition as more dominant themes in social analysis. In the last few decades, however, there has been a growing interest in the sociology of emotions (Barbalet 2002a; Kemper 1978; Layder 2004). Recent theorists have emphasized the complexity of emotions, understanding these as the composite outcomes of social situations and relationships, and bodily feelings generated through physiological processes (Barbalet 2002b: 3–4). Although emotions clearly can be triggered by forms of language and cognition, by powerful symbols and rituals, they are not simply reflections of these. Emotional processes involve subtle interactions of actual social relations, the embodiment of feelings, and linguistic forms, which cannot be reduced to any regular causal relations between these (Kövecses 2000; Burkitt 2002). Moreover, there is a further level of difficulty in conceptualizing how individual emotional experiences are aggregated into collective experiences. Theodore Kemper (1978) suggests that when people share similar structural circumstances they are likely to have similar emotional responses. Wary of any notion of 'group emotions' Jack Barbalet suggests an alternative notion of 'emotional climates':

> An emotional climate does not require that every person subject to it experiences the same emotion. As emotional climates are group phenomenon and as different people occupy different positions within groups, perform different roles and have different capacities, it is indeed likely that individuals will differ from each other in their

emotional experiences. Yet in their relationships they will each contribute to the feeling of the group *qua* group, to its emotional formation or climate. (2002b: 5)

By either formulation, one must go some way towards specifying the social relations that anchor emotional processes. For these reasons, the rather automatic and unspecified connections between ideas of kinship and affective bonds of large social groups, which some theorists of nationalism want to infer, are too crude.

There is a striking convergence among theorists of emotion on the idea that matters of power, control and security lie at the heart of emotional processes. Kemper's (1978) model sees most basic emotions, such as anger, fear, sadness, joy, guilt and shame, as reactions to changes in one's social relations of power and status, or to success or failure in behaving according to one's perceived positions of power and/or status. Thus to the degree that one social group collectively experiences certain power and status relations to another social group, characteristic feelings are likely to be generally present among each group, reflecting their relations of inferiority/superiority. Derek Layder argues that our emotional well being, sense of identity and personal agency are indissolubly linked:

The idea that power and emotion are everywhere found together gets to the heart of the issue. Power is not the special preserve of the 'movers and shakers' of the world, nor can it be regarded as something closeted away and 'revealed' only on special occasions. It saturates our very being and existence as actors whoever and wherever we are in the social world. (2004: 17)

Layder thus conceptualizes emotions as concomitants of our ability to achieve an adequate degree of control over ourselves and our identities, over our interpersonal relations and over our wider social environment, in expanding layers outward from the self. Though Layder is less concerned with emotions at the collective level, it seems fair to assume with Kemper that when these existential problems of personal control take similar forms, encounter similar crises, for many members of a social group, then a certain convergence of emotions within the group is likely. Again, I am trying to suggest that these specific combinations of personal and collective power situations provide necessary clues to when and how affective bonds are formed. These may get expressed through primordial discourses, but these discourses should not be confused with the existential situations and relations of power that render them salient.

This leads us back to the questions that troubled Shils, about how larger ideologies and discourses seize upon emotions. David Kertzer has emphasized the ways elaborately choreographed political rituals trigger emotions through the theatrical manipulation of physical stimuli (light, colour, movement, setting, etc.), and the ability of symbols and rituals to merge cognitive and emotional experiences in one process (1988: 11, 99). And Mabel Berezin further notes the way politicians opportunistically capitalize on events in which the emotional charge is, in a sense, 'ready-made', as when

> British Prime Minister Tony Blair attempted to feed off the emotional energy generated by the thousands who flocked to London when Princess Diana died. He was quick to label her the 'People's Princess' – no doubt hoping to infuse his Labour Party with Diana's charisma. (2002: 40)

I am not denying the importance of these ways of fusing politics and emotions, but they seem to me to provide only half the story, the other half lies in the specific social structures of primary groups. Concrete affective ties can cut various ways. Jeff Goodwin's (1997) study of the Communist-led Huk rebellion in the Philippines (1946–54) examines how the solidarity among the male cadre of this high-risk social movement was weakened both by bonds to families back in peasant villages and by affective and sexual ties that developed between male militants and young women brought into the rebel camps to provide support. Reinterpreting David Laitin's (1995) attempt to explain why there have been high levels of nationalist violence in the Basque Country of Spain, but not in Catalonia, Berezin suggests that the 'more rural form of social organization characterized by high levels of youth association' in the Basque Country provided strong bonds of loyalty and friendship that nationalist activists could mobilize for 'outbursts of nationalist violence' (2002: 46–7). These two examples minimally suggest that the dynamics of affective ties within primary groups are highly variable, and that their suitability to ideological mobilization will be very particular.

Nonetheless we can attempt some cautious generalizations. Different kinds of primary groups are probably more or less responsive to different rhetorics and symbols. It seems reasonable to hypothesize that discourses emphasizing consanguinity will have more 'bite' where kin ties play a strong role in social organization, that 'mother tongues' will be especially evocative where certain speech communities are set apart from the rest of society through residence, occupations and such. By the same token, we might expect that primary groups formed around professions and bureaucratic careers may be more susceptible to rhetorics that associate those groups with abstract and 'patriotic' values such as 'freedom', 'social improvement' and 'civilization'. Nonetheless, metaphors of kinship and place may be particularly apt for representing affective bonds within all kinds of primary groups. Our core experience of primary group-ness derives from the experience of familial relations, and thus kinship language will universally provide a key metaphor for expressing exceptional intimacy, as Adam Smith suggests when he refers to co-workers calling each other 'brother'. Likewise, primary groups will almost always be brought together through some form of space (clan lands, the office, the synagogue, perhaps even the 'virtual spaces' of internet chat rooms), and thus territorial metaphors of 'our place' are likely to be drawn upon. This general utility of these kinds of symbols may have bearing on their frequent presence in nationalist discourses, but we should distinguish between the purchase that rhetorics of kin and place have because they seem to concretely relate to personal experience, and their use as convenient metaphors for social bonds with other bases.

On the other hand, it probably matters whether or not core, local level social units of work and production and political decision-making are strongly articulated by actual kinship relations. And indeed, this tends to be more the case in the peasant sectors of less industrialized societies, which are often considered to have a susceptibility to violent, ethnically based nationalist mobilization (Nairn 1998). In situations where many members of society have suffered violence and the loss of loved ones within their natural spheres of sympathy, the ability to sustain a constant level of resentment and grievance in ethnic-nationalist terms is likely to be high. But this is not just because the symbols of kinship are powerful and compelling in and of themselves, but instead because many people have lost, or know someone close to them who has lost friends and kinfolk at the hands of ethnic enemies. Once these kinds of injuries become a widespread and entrenched part of the emotional fabric of daily life, there is a distinctively emotional process in motion, and complex reasoning about shared blood and ethnic essences may manipulate this process to a degree, but it is in some sense secondary.

Finally, primary groups and their affective ties are probably crucial for all kinds of social cohesion and mobilization, not just in regard to ethnicity and nationalism. For instance, mass mobilizations around identities of class and gender will depend not just on ideologies and political programmes, but on the cultivation of identities and motives within very specific social settings – mining communities, unions, factories, campaigning groups, student cohorts in universities, intentional communities and so on. If I am right, and the mobilization of emotional bonds can only be properly understood within a context of primary groups, and primordial approaches to nationalism rely on the idea of such emotional bonds, then 'primordialism' becomes one variant of a much more general social process.

When was Primordialism?

Smith's limited spheres of moral sentiment, and Shils' primary groups, like everything human, have a history. Because I have argued that these should be prominent in any notion of primordial bonds, and because primordialism usually assumes that such bonds have considerable historical depth, let me try to trace out that history. Our limited capacity for affective ties has obvious roots in our natural history. As Robert Wenke has observed:

> If we truly want to follow the Socratic dictum to know ourselves, at least in the sense of ourselves as a biological species, we must examine the past two million years and try to understand what forces and factors produced us. As farmers and city-dwellers we are only a few thousand years old, so everything of importance that we are biologically is the result of the long thousands of millennia, the millions of years that we spent under the tutelage of natural selection, as we evolved into our modern form. We are, simply put, largely what 'worked' throughout our great antiquity. (1990: 136–7)

Neither Wenke nor I would want to reduce what we are to our biological inheritance. In fact that is precisely the point – the last few thousand years has been a story of cultural, not biological adaptation, the latter becoming much less significant. But our focused capacity for emotional bonding and sympathy is not a recent cultural development, but rather an aspect of our general primate inheritance, filtered through that long march of human evolution over the past two million years or so.

We can outline what we might call our original 'primordial situation'. Up until about 10,000 years ago, all humans lived primarily in relatively small foraging (i.e. hunting and gathering) bands, centred on a few 'families', with probably somewhere between 20 and 80 members. Such social groups sustained themselves by extracting naturally available food resources from the environment, and thus had to maintain low and widely dispersed population numbers according to the carrying capacity of their environment. We need to be careful not to be misled by the rather idealized image of foraging peoples promulgated by popularized anthropology (see Wilmsen 1989). The situation just described is an ideal-typical model, derived from the ethnographic study of recent foraging groups, ethnohistorical records and archaeological reconstructions of prehistoric life-ways. Nonetheless, for most of humanity, most of the time, survival and general well being depended primarily on the mutual support and coordinated activities of the smaller band unit. It is within this context that food-getting, shelter-making, child-rearing and predator avoidance would have been achieved on a daily basis. These were the original primary groups. In such societies the survival of the individual and the group depends upon individual behaviour being oriented towards the well being of the whole, and our capacity for sympathy, for being sensitive to emotional cues and identifying with the feelings of others, enables this kind of small social unit to function cohesively. Limited in its social extent, but profound in communicative subtlety, human sympathy was a mainstay of our foraging band way of life for hundreds of thousands of years.

Over the last 10,000 years, this norm of human existence has become buried under an accumulation of new strategies for social life. Nomadic foraging bands become settled tribes engaged in agriculture and pastoralism, which in turn grow larger and develop more hierarchical political structures, which in turn grow into ancient agrarian states, which finally, in the last millennium, have issued forth the modern industrial society that now dominates the globe. There is no reason to think that this progression is inevitable, and considerable archaeological evidence of societies that never headed down this path, or that took a few steps 'up' the evolutionary ladder (or down, depending on one's perspective), only to abandon the project and return to 'earlier' forms of social organization. But it does seem that in some cases, once things had developed far enough along this path it becomes difficult to turn back and, instead, the new principles of social organization spread laterally, pulling outlying populations into the new orbit of power, dragging societies 'up the ladder'. In other words, the general image one should have of this historical process is not one of all humanity moving either in lockstep, or in staggered individual sequences up the ladder of social evolution. Rather, by fits and starts, probably for very historically particular ecological and demographic reasons, some societies began to travel down this path and, as they did so, becoming larger, more centralized and powerful, they tended either to absorb or displace their neighbours, or to trigger in them similar transformations.

Having said this, the sketch of 'post-primordial' human history goes something like this. About 10,000 years ago, for the first time in the Near East, but again later independently in the Asian subcontinent, China, the New World and Africa, people began to settle in stable farming villages, combining simple forms of agriculture and pastoralism. This is often referred to as the 'neolithic revolution' (after Childe 1951). With time agriculture became more extensive and intensive, and by about 5,000 years ago the first archaic agrarian states took shape in Mesopotamia, with early forms of writing linked to bureaucratic record-keeping developing in tandem, and significant advances in metallurgy soon to follow. By about 300 years ago, after millennia of reliance on human and animal labour power, modestly supplemented by fire, water and wind, the developing capacity to harness new forms of energy trapped in fossil fuels provided the basis for the phenomenal explosion of modern industrial society.

Against this rather materialist account we can place a corresponding sequence of changes in dominant principles of social organization. From the foraging bands right through to the early agrarian states, systems of kinship provided a key infrastructure for most people, defining their primary universe of social identity and moral obligations. Rights in land, ritual offices, exchanges of goods and services, obligations for military support all tended to be regulated and mobilized by ties of obligation defined in terms of degrees of kin relatedness. Kinship systems, however, tended to become much more elaborated with the shift from small mobile foraging bands to larger settled farming communities. As societies became still larger and more complex, tending towards the early state form, kinship systems increasingly provided the framework for social stratification, with certain lineages within the system making claims to privileged, royal and divine status (cf. Kirchhoff 1968). Such 'chiefly' societies may often have provided a political basis for the formation of early states around royal lineages. With this internal stratification of the kinship principle and its embedding within the archaic state came a parallel shift from the dominance of principles of reciprocal exchange between individuals and kin groups, to one of the centralization of resources in the hands of the elite lineage and/or the state, allowing these new centres of power to redistribute wealth between the members of society, as well as to use surplus resources to underwrite their own power, in the form of courts, bureaucracies, armies, priesthoods and artisans. These new, more centralized forms of social organization seem to have provided a spur to trade and commerce, partly because of elite consumption driven by status competition between rival elites. Market behaviour was incubated and regulated within these tribute-extracting agrarian states for four millennia, only to become the fully dominant principle of the social distribution of wealth and power, that is, capitalism, with the incredible boost to markets of industrial production (Polanyi 1957: ch. 4; Wolf 1981).

This entire sequence can be summed up as one of demographic increase, and steady urbanization, but as we know, with this last, 'modern' phase, and especially the last century, a story of long and steady growth becomes one of skyrocketing change. Now we find an odd fact, which is behind this detour through human history. The great debate between 'modernists' and 'primordialists' is generally made to hinge on the rise of modernity (somewhere between 1500–1789), synoptically viewed as a transition from *Gemeinschaft* to *Gesellschaft*, from status to contract, from stasis to change. The 'primordialist' typically argues that the new nation-states and nationalist movements achieve an identity and legitimacy by invoking a premodern heritage of kinship-based, territorially bounded communal life, reshaping it to fit modern conditions. But as we have seen, the conditions for our core primordial ties as outlined above, were unhinged in the first instance not by the industrial revolution, but by the neolithic revolution. Expanded forms of social organization have confronted the task of mobilizing our narrow fields of emotional bonds not for the last 300–500 years, but for the last 10,000 years.

The overall effect of primordialist arguments is to imply that nationalism is a reflection of a transhistorical human nature – emotional attachments to kin and place are eternal verities, that may operate within new, more modern contexts, and are no doubt socially constructed, but are themselves social constants. One of the points of the synopsis of human history offered above is that, in fact, these elements have become important for human beings in a historically layered way. During our long sojourn in foraging bands, kinship and territorial ties were necessarily much looser, because of ecological demands for flexibility. With sedentarization and the passing on across generations of rights in land and other properties and offices, the territorial and kinship dimensions become elaborated. But the relationship between the original 'primordial situation' in which our affective capacities were first cultivated and attuned to relatively small social groups, and the phase in which kinship became the complex ideological infrastructure of society, is sequential. These two elements of primordialism are not parts of a primeval bundle, but actually reflect functionally different principles of social organization. From our modern vantage point they may appear as one, but, in fact, they derived from distinct periods of human social evolution.

What I hope to have conveyed here is that the story of our social evolution is not so much one of progressing through stages, marching from one social form to the next, but rather one of the overlaying of older forms with newer ones, such that principles that were once dominant in governing human behaviour are not so much replaced as encysted within new and more complex forms, in which what were once minor principles (centralized redistribution, market exchanges) become dominant ones. In conceptualizing the shift from premodern societies made up of numerous bounded corporate groups, to modern societies with much more mobile and fluid populations, we often arrive at an exaggerated notion of modern society as simply a mass of autonomous individuals. Primary groups endure, with their special attachments, embedded within new structures, shaping the dynamics of larger social processes. What changes is that kinship plays a less prominent role in these groups, and their structural bases become more numerous and differentiated. Moreover, modern society evolves new kinds of primary groups suited to its needs. It is worth recalling that Shils paid special attention to primary groups within military structures. This reminds us that not only do modern nation-states draw support from the primary groups that their civil societies generate, but for that most central of national institutions, the modern military, they perfected the art of fabricating primary groups of soldiers ready to die for the national cause. That is the purpose of boot camp – to bend our emotional inheritance from our pre-neolithic past in band societies to one of the key needs of the modern state.

Conclusion

I have tried to argue that any approach, such as that of primordialism, that emphasizes the importance of emotional bonds is obliged to give serious attention to the nature and history of primary groups. In short, social scale and structure matters for primordialism. Some may want to respond to this by saying 'yes, but when all is said and done we know that symbols of kinship and strong emotional feelings are regularly involved in nationalism – isn't that enough?' I do not think so. We must not avoid dealing with a very basic aspect of how social cohesion and mobilization work, simply because it renders the question much more complicated. It also renders the question more interesting, suggesting lines of enquiry for understanding why ethnic and nationalist politics play out in different ways in different settings. In sum, to understand better the importance of human sentiments in the formation of nationalism, what is needed is detailed case and comparative studies that look at the actual interface of primordial discourses of kinship, territory and language, and primary groups in specific social structures, and the workings of national discourses in those contexts, whether playing upon primordialist themes or not. Only in this way can we really understand the interactions of reason and passion in nationalism.

Further Reading

It is worth returning to the key early statements of Shils (1957) and Geertz (1973) when critically engaging this subject. Several key debates have defined critical responses to primordialism more generally. See the exchanges between Brass (1979) and Robinson (1979); between Eller and Coughlan (1993) and Grosby (1994); and between Smith (1996a) and Gellner (1996a) in the 'Warwick Debate'. The latter has been reproduced in Mortimer (1999), which also includes an exchange between Robin Cohen and Terrance Ranger on the subject. Most recently Conversi's (2002) edited volume exploring the work of Walker Connor contains chapters by Joshua Fishman, Donald Horowitz and Anthony Smith addressing primordialism.

4
Modernism

Modernists generally argue that nations and nationalism arose some-where between the sixteenth and the late eighteenth centuries, in Europe in the first instance, largely caused by social structural transformations in that period. In this chapter we survey the main themes of modernist approaches: economy, state and mass culture, acquainting ourselves with leading figures in the modernist approach.

What is Modernism?

The term 'modernist' tends to encompass an array of approaches that are more coherently unified than those of the 'primordialists'. Three main themes, which interpenetrate, can be identified:

- The demands of industrial and capitalist economies in generating rela-tively unified national identities. A major sub-theme in this regard is the idea of the 'uneven development' of the modern economy as a stimulus to nationalism.
- The modern state as a bureaucratic and legal institution generating new conceptions of citizenship. A particularly important sub-theme here is the concept of 'civil society'.
- The spread of literacy, linguistic homogenization and standardized education as the cornerstones of a mass culture and unified national identity.

Modernists generally emphasize all of these themes in combination. The main variations concern how different theorists place the accent on these themes in their conceptions of modernization and its role in creat-ing nationalism. Reflecting his central position in the literature, we shall use Ernest Gellner as a guiding thread in our survey of these various emphases.

Economy: Industrialism, Capitalism and Uneven Development

Beginning with his influential 1964 book *Thought and Change*, Ernest Gellner developed a powerful argument about the role of industrialization in the formation of nationalism. Gellner proposed that there was a 'new social contract' abroad in the world, negotiated according the following terms:

> In our time, a social order is valid, has rightful claims on the loyalty of the members of the society, under two conditions:
> (a) It is bringing about, or successfully maintaining, an industrial affluent society.
> (b) Those in authority are co-cultural with the rest of the society. (1964: 33)

This is perhaps the starkest statement of Gellner's theory of nationalism. On the one hand he sought to argue, against marxism, that the dominant value of the modern era was not to overcome class-divided industrial society, but to become a member of such a society. As long as major divisions in social power were not underscored by cultural differences, and there were opportunities for increasing one's wealth, industrial life would enjoy legitimacy. On the other hand he was also arguing rather specifically against Elie Kedourie, who had recently portrayed nationalism as an ill-advised doctrine of self-determination, with roots in the Enlightenment (1993 [1960]). Where Kedourie saw a philosophical line of thought gone awry, Gellner saw a system of values strongly conditioned by economic forces. Thus it has often been commented that Gellner was an anti-marxist materialist (Szporluk 1998: 25–7).

Gellner's approach reflected the functionalist anthropology and Oxbridge philosophy in which he had trained. He saw human history as outlining a fundamental shift from agrarian to industrial forms of social organization. According to Gellner, before the modern era the horizons of most people's lives were relatively confined to localized communities of kinship, co-residence, production and consumption and states and their political, religious and military elites sat on top of a few or many such communities, without interfering much in their daily life. This highly segmented political structure meant that a great deal of cultural diversity could be tolerated. While a degree of ideological integration was required within local communities and among leading elites, the entire system required little in the way of unified culture (1983: ch. 2).

With the rise of industrial society, there is a new demand for the social and geographic mobility of workers, and flexibility in their capabilities, as the industries and employments thrown up by the new form of society rise and fall at a much faster pace. As Gellner puts it: 'Nationalism is rooted in a *certain kind* of division of labour, one which is complex and persistently, cumulatively changing' (1983: 24, emphasis in original). In this context the rigid, localized social structures of traditional societies become brakes on the system, and need to be weakened or dismantled. In their place develops a new and more fluid society, in which the population is much more 'modular', able to switch functions as the economy demands (Gellner 1995). Gellner argues that as social structures of kinship, caste, differential property rights and such become less able to functionally integrate society, a new form of mass culture develops to do the job. Mass education spreads literacy and a common language to the general populace, helping to facilitate their mobility and interchangeability. In the ancient agrarian states clerics were an elite group specific to the state bureaucracy, in modern society everyone is a clerk (Gellner 1964: 160). Gellner characterizes this as the generalization of a 'high culture', once reserved to premodern elites, to the broader population. He recognizes that this takes the form of a non-elite popular culture, but the central issue for him is the spread of literacy, which had once been the preserve of a narrow band of elites involved in the high arts of state and religion.

For Gellner, nations and nationalisms are the products of this long-term structural transformation. In time the functional requirements of industrial society became fully articulated as a theory of political legitimacy, held by modern nation-states and those aspiring to that condition, one

> which requires that ethnic boundaries should not cut across political ones, and, in particular, that ethnic boundaries within a given state – a contingency already formally excluded by the principle in its general formulation – should not separate the power-holders from the rest. (Gellner 1983: 1)

Gellner almost always spoke in terms of 'industrial' rather than 'capitalist' society. Anthony Giddens has pointed to the significance of this choice of terms in social theory in general, observing that the former is associated with a notion of modern society as functionally integrated, and of history as converging on that model, whereas the latter is associated with a model of underlying social conflict between the economic classes generated by modern industrial capitalism (1987a: ch. 2). In contrast to Gellner, the marxist historian Eric Hobsbawm works with the governing concept of capitalism rather than industrialism. Thus, while the same general historical process lies behind the rise of nationalism for both of them, where Gellner sees the formation of a social identity that is functional for life under modern conditions, Hobsbawm sees an identity that is an ideological illusion, generated by the interests of those benefiting from the capitalist state, and the fears and uncertainties of those confronting the dissolution of more traditional ways of life in the face of capitalist 'progress'.

In his book *Nations and Nationalism Since 1780* (1992), Hobsbawm offers a sweeping evolution of nationalism through several phases, ending with intimations of its impending demise. Early on Hobsbawm isolates a paradox: that nationalism came into its own in the nineteenth century at the same time that liberal political economic theories of Adam Smith and others were conceptualizing individuals, firms and markets as the fundamental components of economic growth, not nations or states (1992: 24–5). But while free trade was espoused in principle, in practice the economy of the national state was the focus of concern among economists and politicians. Significantly, a more nation-state centred developmentalist economics arose in those countries that felt the need to keep pace with burgeoning British economy, places such as the USA and especially Germany, with its 'historical school' of economics led by Friedrich List (Hobsbawm 1992: 29–30). Hobsbawm argues that List and his followers articulated a point implicitly accepted by most liberal economists – that nation-states need to reach a certain threshold in size to be economically viable, a point amply demonstrated by Britain and France. More generally Hobsbawm argues that the entire thrust of nineteenth-century liberal nationalism was towards expansion and unification, as in Germany and Italy, not secession. Nation-states were seen as a stage in the evolution of an ever more integrated global liberal society, one which would necessarily entail many local languages, dialects and cultures falling by the wayside, a prospect countenanced with minimal sentimentality. The more closed, ethnically defensive versions of nationalism were a reaction to this expansionist liberal nationalism, developing after about 1870.

Hobsbawm avoids any crude economic determinism, recognizing a degree of autonomy in economic, political and cultural processes. He conceives of national identities as complex formations built both from the bottom up, out of raw materials of language, descent and religion, and from above, by states seeking to homogenize their subject populations to facilitate governance. In regard to 'top down' processes, he has articulated the influential concept of 'the invention of tradition' (which we will examine more closely in Chapter 8), to describe the new national states' role in synthesizing and fabricating a national culture to encourage national loyalties. But true to his marxist orientation, the key agents in this process are the state and its functionaries, on the one hand, and various middle-class strata, those made most acutely conscious of either the opportunities or the liabilities of the forming nation-states that confronted them. As he says, discussing cases of nationalism where language was a central issue:

> The classes which stood or fell by the official use of the written vernacular were the socially modest but educated middle strata, which included those who acquired lower middle-class status precisely by virtue of occupying non-manual jobs that required schooling. The socialists of the period who rarely used the word 'nationalism' without the prefix 'petty-bourgeois', knew what they were talking about. The battle lines of linguistic nationalism were manned by provincial journalists, schoolteachers and aspiring subaltern officials. (1992: 117; see also pp. 92, 109, 130)

Recently Liah Greenfeld has weighed in on this subject with her book *The Spirit of Capitalism: Nationalism and Economic Growth* (2001). Greenfeld's first book on nationalism (1992) was highly distinctive in its weberian emphasis on status groups and the social consciousnesses and identities through which they understand themselves. Her argument, in short, was that 'nation' was in the first instance the banner of a new forming and rising elite in sixteenth-century England, a mantle that became generalized to a wider population in the seventeenth century. As elites in other countries observed the successes of the new social construct, they followed suit, forming concepts of nationhood specific to their historical situations. Thus, where Gellner and Hobsbawm tend to see material economic processes driving ideological ones, Greenfeld sees a novel ideological construct leading to political and economic transformations. In *The Spirit of Capitalism* she seeks to correct her relative neglect of economics in the first book. She agrees that economics is indeed central to nationalism, but in opposition to structural economic approaches, she argues that it is the novel idea of the nation that stimulated the modern quest for endless economic growth. Economics becomes the key medium of status competition between nations. Thus where most argue that modernity made nations, Greenfeld counters that nations made modernity, and supplied the orientation of values and motivation necessary for the phenomenal rise of capitalism (2001: 1–26).

In various ways all three of these authors include a prominent place for the idea of 'uneven development' in their theories, but this is made most explicit in Gellner's writings. His version is drolly sketched in his allegory of 'Empire of Megalomania' and its embedded territory of 'Ruritania' (1983: 58–62). The Ruritanians were largely peasants speaking a patchwork of dialects and observing a religion different from the language and religion of the Megalomanians, who constituted the dominant class of the major urban centres of the empire named after them. In the nineteenth century, under the pressures of rapid population growth in the countryside, industrialization in the cities and substantial rural to urban migration, the Ruritanians are made rudely aware of how different they are, and how difficult it will be for them in the changed order of things. Gellner sums up:

> What all this amounts to is this: during the early period of industrialization, entrants into the new order who are drawn from cultural and linguistic groups that are distant from those of the more advanced centre, suffer considerable disadvantages which are even greater than those of other economically weak proletarians who have the advantage of sharing the culture of the political and economic rulers. But the cultural/linguistic distance and capacity to differentiate themselves from others, which is such a handicap for individuals, can be and often is a positive advantage for entire collectivities, or potential collectivities, of these victims of the newly emergent world. It enables them to conceive and express their resentments and discontents in intelligible terms. (1983: 62)

In other words, it provides the basis for nationalist mobilization, and possibly national independence. With this allegory Gellner clearly had in mind the multiplicity of ethnic groups embedded within the collapsing Habsburg Empire, but he also saw it as a general pattern reflected in later waves of nationalism associated with decolonization. There is an important sense in which Gellner's notions of modernization and nationalism were articulated in the context of debates about Third World development and anti-colonial nationalisms in the 1950s and 1960s, and then projected back onto the European past (Hall 1993: 5). Writing within a marxian framework shaped by this same context, and trying to account for the rise of neonationalisms in Britain, Tom Nairn (1981 [1977]) seized upon Gellner's model, translating it into the language of cores, peripheries and imperialism (Wallerstein 1974):

Real, uneven development has invariably generated an imperialism of the centre over the periphery; one after another, these peripheric areas have been forced into a profoundly ambivalent reaction against this dominance, seeking at once to resist it and to somehow take over its vital forces for their own use. This could only be done by a kind of highly 'idealist' political and ideological mobilization, by a painful forced march based on their own resources: that is, employing their 'nationality' as a basis. The metropolitan fantasy of even development had predicted a swelling, single forward march that would induct backward lands into its course; in reality these lands found themselves compelled to attempt radical, competitive short-cuts in order to avoid being trampled over or left behind. (Nairn 1981 [1977]: 341)

As we have seen, Hobsbawm also recognizes this dynamic, particularly in the later ethnic and reactive nationalisms of Europe c. 1870–1945. The various middling classes that he identifies as key agents in nationalism are usually confronting some version of uneven development. And operating on a more purely ideological and psychological plane, Greenfeld focuses on a similar dynamic. But her attention is particularly on national elites that lead broader populations in a search for dignity, reacting against supposedly superior external nationalities:

Every society importing the foreign idea of the nation inevitably focused on the source of the importation – an object of imitation by definition – and reacted to it. Because the model was superior to the imitator in the latter's own perception (its being a model implied that), and the contact more often than not served to emphasize the latter's inferiority, the reaction commonly assumed the form of *ressentiment*. A term coined by Nietzche and later defined and developed by Max Scheler, *ressentiment* refers to a psychological state resulting from suppressed feelings of envy and hatred (existential envy) and the impossibility of satisfying these feelings. (1992: 15)

The point to remember here is that for Greenfeld this collective psychological dynamic is the motivating factor behind the modern economy. It is not just that relative economic deprivation creates envy and a demand for nationhood, but that this nationally encoded envy is a spur to economic competition in the first place. A final point to be made is that there is a classic problem of pristine and secondary formations here (see Fried 1967: ch. 6). It would seem that fundamentally different forces formed the first, pristine nations, from those that formed the later 'reactive' nations, so in

---

Box 4.1 The Czechs of Bohemia

The emergence of a modern Czech national identity in Bohemia in the eighteenth and nineteenth centuries is one of the iconic instances of nationalism that has influenced much theorizing. In the twelfth century, with the encouragement of Czech kings, the medieval kingdom of Bohemia, where Czech was the dominant language, saw an influx of German settlers, concentrated in towns and specializing in handicrafts and mining. Under the religious leadership of Jan Hus (1369–1415) Bohemia was one of the first Catholic countries to experience a large-scale Protestant Reformation, which was successfully defended against largely German-speaking crusading armies in the Hussite Wars of 1419–37. For about two centuries following there developed a Bohemian kingdom including both Protestants and Catholics, and speakers of Czech and German. But the Thirty Years' War (1618–48), triggered by a revolt of the Bohemian nobility, led to defeat by the Habsburgs, who re-imposed Catholicism and supplanted the indigenous nobility with families from other parts of Europe. By the end of the seventeenth century, German had become the language of the aristocracy and the merchants and officials in the towns, and Czech had become the language of the peasants.

By the mid-eighteenth century the enlightened absolutist rulers of the Habsburg Empire began to introduce modernizing reforms, first under Maria Theresa, and then under Joseph II. These included: religious toler-ance and the reducing of the Catholic Church's powers; the abolition of serfdom; new legal notions of the equality of citizens; the spread of elementary education; and state support of Enlightenment ideas of science and secularism. These changes provoked reactionary opposition from segments of the nobility and Church, but also provide a stimulus to a

→

---

what sense are they all the same thing? We will pursue this puzzle further in the next chapter.

Politics: the Modern State

Although Gellner couched his theory broadly in terms of transition from agrarian to modern states, and often characterized nationalism as a 'polit-ical principle' (1983: 1), he had relatively little to say about the state *per se*, leading Brendan O'Leary to conclude that his 'almost Olympian apoliticism' (1998: 78) comprised the main weakness in Gellner's impressive theoretical apparatus. Ultimately for Gellner, states took the form and pursued the ends industrial society required. Others, however,

→
developing Czech national identity. The new religious and intellectual environment created space for the recovery of Czech Protestant writings, and for secular studies of the geography and history of the country, thus fostering the idea of a distinct nation of land and people with their own history. But political reforms were differentially experienced, as emancipated German and Czech peasants moved into towns dominated by the German language, and promising Czech students confronted universities where German was the language of education. On top of this, the influence of the radical ideas of the French Revolution combined with reports and experiences of the revolutionary and later Napoleonic Wars sharpened a sense of national identity among educated Bohemians.

Across the nineteenth century a Czech bourgeoisie developed, with its own schools, newspapers, publishing houses, theatres and even a large Czech-owned bank. Demands for equal recognition of the Czech language with German, and for the constitutional devolution of powers to the predominantly Czech regions of Bohemia, Moravia and Silesia, developed in parallel. Miroslav Hroch (2004) describes various strains of 'patriotism' at work during this period, but the most crucial difference was between older elite strains oriented to aristocratic stewardship of the land and the economy on the one hand, and towards the enduring institutions of the kingdom and Catholic Church on the other, and a rising new strain of the Czech intelligentsia oriented towards 'improving the cultural standard and education of the most neglected part of the population – the Czech-speaking part' (p. 102). It was this view, combined with the frustrations to social mobility caused by the dominance of German-language institutions, that led to a modern Czech national identity in Bohemia and Moravia, frequently pitted against a German identity more often oriented towards Vienna and Austria (see Hroch 2004; Klima 1993; Seton-Watson 1977: 149–57).

have been more concerned with the state as a key agent in the formation of both nationalism and modernity.

Applying the ideas of Max Weber, Reinhard Bendix (1964, 1978) focused particularly on the transformation of political authority, from the patrimonial rule of kings to the bureaucratic rule of states. 'Patrimonialism' refers to rule by the head of a household (usually male as the root of the word suggests) by merit of personal authority and tradition, and more specifically to political systems in which a royal household rules over society through a hierarchy of noble households. According to Bendix:

In the medieval conception the 'building block' of the social order is the family of hereditary privilege, whose stability over time is the foundation of right and of authority, while the rank-order of society and its transmission through inheritance regulates the relations among such families and between them and the supreme ruler . . . The modern nation-state presupposes that this link between governmental authority and inherited privilege in the hands of families of notables is broken. Access to important political and administrative posts in the governments of nation-states can be facilitated by wealth and high social position through their effect on social contacts and educational opportunities. But facility of access is not the same as the prerogative which aristocratic families in medieval politics claim by virtue of their 'antiquity of blood'. (1964: 106)

The political decisions and actions of the monarch, however constrained by the need to keep subordinate nobles 'on-side', have considerable latitude for arbitrariness and favouritism. In contrast, the modern state, in principle, regulates and administers society through a bureaucratically defined system of offices and responsibilities, staffed by trained, full-time professionals who obtain their offices on merit, and who are themselves as subject to legal authority as those they help govern. Along with this social structural shift in the nature of authority is a corresponding shift in the principles of legitimation. Whereas monarchs ultimately traced their authority to a combination of divine sanction and the precedent of tradition, constantly having to court the support of religious authorities and maintain a coterie of loyal retainers, the modern state is legitimated by being the instrument of 'the people', who created it, elect representatives to it and are loyal to it. In theory the modern state is a case of the people actively governing themselves according to agreed terms, rather than merely being governed by their monarch and nobles. It is this turning to the people for legitimacy that makes modern states nation-states. Bendix was well aware that these are ideal types, derived from Western European examples, from which reality often diverged. Nonetheless he saw this historical model as illustrating a general rule – that to be stable, power requires modes of authority and legitimacy, and that this shift from 'kings to people' (1978) was at the heart of the rise of modernity (cf. Carr 1945).

John Breuilly (1993) has made the state central to his conception of modernization. He has much to say about the historically specific power dynamics that determine the various forms that nationalist movements take, and we will consider these more closely in Chapter 6. Here we are concerned with the nature of the modern state, and why it cultivated national identities. Echoing most classical theories of modernization,

Breuilly points to a shift from a 'corporate' to a 'functional' division of labour (1996: 163), that is, from one in which the economic, political and cultural needs and interest of most individuals were mainly met through single corporate organizations that heavily shaped their lives (e.g. craft guilds, religious orders, peasant communes), to one in which these purposes were increasingly met by separate, function-specific organizations (e.g. trade unions, political parties, schools and universities), and all under the umbrella of a large, bureaucratic, functionally differentiated state. This process of functional specialization was combined, particularly in the early liberal nation-states of the nineteenth century, with a growing separation of public and private spheres:

> The modern state originally developed in liberal form – that is, it involved a concentration of 'public' powers into specialized state institutions (parliaments, bureaucracies), while leaving many 'private' powers under the control of non-political institutions (free markets, private firms, families, et cetera). That involved a double transformation of government; institutions such as the monarchy lost 'private' powers (for example, the principal source of revenue from royal lands and the granting or possession of monopolies); other institutions such as churches, guilds and lordships lost their 'public' powers to government. In this way a clear and distinct idea of the state as 'public' and 'civil society' as 'private' was elaborated and seemed to have some hold upon reality. (Breuilly 1996: 164)

Thus, for Breuilly, new notions of national identity were developed, from both above and below, to provide a kind of ideological glue to reconnect the privatized populations with their more extensive and uniformly sovereign states:

> The breakdown of corporate ties meant that within both state and civil society there was a new emphasis on people as individuals rather than members of groups. The main problem for those seeking to establish as well as those trying to understand political order in such situations came to be how to make the state-society connection; how to maintain some harmony between the public interests of citizens and the private interests of selfish individuals (or families). Nationalist ideas could be related to both of the major forms taken by attempts to solve this problem: one imposing citizenship ideals upon society; the other imposing interests (individual or class) within civil society upon the state. (1996: 165)

In a similar fashion, Anthony Giddens has portrayed nationalism as a worldview that necessarily accompanies the extended powers of the modern state, with its new and more effective levels of sovereignty:

> Nationalism is the cultural sensibility of sovereignty, the concomitant of the co-ordination of administrative power within the bounded nation-state. With the coming of the nation-state, states have an administrative and territorially ordered unity which they did not possess before. This unity cannot remain *purely* administrative however, because the very co-ordination of activities involved presumes elements of cultural homogeneity. The extension of communication cannot occur without the 'conceptual' involvement of the whole community as a knowledgeable citizenry. A nation-state is a 'conceptual community' in a way in which traditional states were not. (1987b: 219, emphasis in original)

Thus, Giddens reiterates Gellner's notion of the need for a shared culture in modern industrial society, but ties this need much more directly to the administrative demands of state power. Giddens sees the rise of the nation-state out of earlier absolutist states in Europe as intertwined with the developments of capitalism and industrialization. Using the memorable image of the nation-state as 'a bordered power-container' (1987b: 120), he stresses several features that set it off from earlier forms of the state. First, territorial borders become much more sharply defined and regulated. In contrast, '[t]raditional states have frontiers, not borders' (1987b: 4). Second, modern states are normally internally pacified, monopolizing the means of violence much more effectively. Third, they administer their citizens' lives much more intensively and uniformly across their territories, dissolving differences between rural and urban ways of life characteristic of more agrarian societies. And fourth, they manage their populations through myriad and increasingly indirect techniques of surveillance. 'The coupling of direct and indirect surveillance (customs officials and frontier guards, plus the central co-ordination of passport information) is one of the distinctive features of the nation-state' (1987b: 120). Nationalism for Giddens is a worldview induced by these instrumentalities of modern citizenship and state sovereignty.

Giddens also sees a dialectic between the growing powers of the nation-state for administration and surveillance within its territory, and the evolution of an international system of nation-states. Internal power relations develop in tandem with external power relations. This dialectic has also been stressed by Charles Tilly and his fellow contributors to *The*

Formation of National States in Western Europe (1975a), which he edited. Central to their account is the economic and, especially, military competition among a multiplicity of Western European states, which forced these states to extract ever more resources from their peasantries to fund such competition. Peasants resisted such exploitation, which drove the competing states to weaken the peasants' position, and expand their tax base, by accelerating the commercialization of agriculture and the growth of trade and industry. In short:

> The formation of standing armies provided the largest single incentive to extraction and the largest single means of state coercion over the long run of European state-making. Recurrently we find a chain of causation running from (1) change or expansion in land armies to (2) new efforts to extract resources from the subject population to (3) the development of new bureaucracies and administrative innovations to (4) resistance from the subject population to (5) renewed coercion to (6) durable increases in the bulk or extractiveness of the state. (Tilly 1975b: 73)

In a concluding essay Tilly proposes a wider historical view that generalizes from the beginnings of the national state in Western Europe to the rest of the world:

> The main rhythm, then, has three beats: (1) the formation and consolidation of the first great national states in commercial and military competitions with each other, accompanied by their economic penetration of the remainder of Europe and important parts of the world outside of Europe: roughly 1500 to 1700; (2) the regrouping of the remainder of Europe into a system of states, accompanied by the extension of European political control into most of the non-European world, save those portions already dominated by substantial political organizations (e.g. China and Japan): roughly 1650 to 1850; (3) the extension of the state system to the rest of the world, both through the acquisition of formal independence by colonies and clients, and through the incorporation of existing powers like China and Japan into the system: roughly 1800 to 1950. If this scheme is correct, the study of European state-making has at least one point of relevance to the politics of the contemporary world: Europeans played the major part in creating the contemporary international state-system, and presumably left the imprints of their peculiar political institutions on it. (Tilly 1975c: 637–8; see also Mayall 1990)

We will look at some challenges to this Europe-centred view of nationalism and the modern state at the start of the next chapter, and explore the relationship between power and nationalism more broadly in Chapters 6 and 7. What the approaches surveyed above share is a concern with how the changes in the nature of society and state in the modern period brought forth new conceptions of authority, legitimacy, sovereignty and citizenship, and new structures and techniques for enforcing them.

Mass Culture: Language and Education

Whereas primordialist approaches to language and nationalism have focused on feelings of authenticity generated within speech communities, modernists have been more concerned with language and communication as evolving technologies with important social effects. As we saw above, the standardization of language and mass literacy, along with a modicum of numeracy and other technical knowledge, and their uniform provision through a state-supported education system, were central to Gellner's conception of nationalism. In the new industrial society

> The employability, dignity, security and self-respect of individuals, typically, and for the majority of men now hinges on their *education*; and the limits of the culture within which they were educated are also the limits of the world within which they can, morally and professionally, breathe. A man's education is by far his most precious investment, and in effect confers his identity on him. Modern man is not loyal to a monarch or a land or a faith, whatever he may say, but to a culture. (1983: 36; emphasis in original)

As we saw in the Introduction (Chapter 1), an early articulator of this perspective was Karl Deutsch, who in applying cybernetics and information theory to politics came to define nationality as a 'wide complementarity of social communication. It consists in the ability to communicate more effectively, and over a wider range of subjects, with members of one large group, than with outsiders' (1953: 97). Deutsch was concerned to define nationality in a manner that was systematically measurable, in terms of the frequency and density of communicative interactions. There are various kinds of community defined by common means and terms of communication – from morse code operators, or technical experts sharing a jargon, to all the speakers of a major world language. But Deutsch was trying to define nations as a crucial level within this range, one where people on average were bound together by common means of communication (language, literacy, communicative rules) and points of reference (topics of conversation, implicit concepts, etc.). Nonetheless, he was aware that in stratified societies patterns of communicative interaction are by no means uniform, and that there was always a potential to develop into, in Disraeli's words, 'two nations . . . the rich and the poor' (Deutsch 1953: 98). Thus he also argued that dominant classes had to provide a focus of social communication to maintain national integration:

> In the political and social struggles of the modern age, *nationality*, then, means an alignment of large numbers of individuals from the middle and lower classes linked to regional centers and leading social groups by channels of social communication and economic intercourse, both indirectly from link to link and directly with the center (1953: 101; emphasis in original)

By far the most influential recent statement on the role of language in nationalism has come from Benedict Anderson (1991). He maintains that, 'What, in a positive sense, made the new [national] communities imaginable was a half-fortuitous, but explosive, interaction between a system of production and productive relations (capitalism), a technology of communications (print), and the fatality of human linguistic diversity' (1991: 43, insertion added). Anderson coins the term 'print-capitalism' to emphasize the link between capitalism and print technology. He understands books, periodicals and newspapers as commodities sold to an expanding market of literate middle-class readers, and publishers as entrepreneurs in this new market environment. In the post-Reformation world older, limited, elite markets for Latin texts were being overtaken by growing demands for religious and secular texts in the vernacular. Written vernaculars were becoming instruments of administration and centralization in the expanding bureaucracies of modern states. There were two key aspects of this process. First, standardization – the privileging of certain dialects in the language continuum, building the print orthographies around their pronunciation and raising that dialect up as the 'model' of the language in question. And second, fixity – by creating a central standard, the natural drift of language is slowed down, and language can be measured against its past forms as represented in print (1991: ch. 3).

In addition to these rather technical aspects in the transformation of language, Anderson highlights an accompanying transformation of worldview. As writing ceased to be an occult practice of the elite, there was a demystification of written language as embodied in Latin, with its association with sacred texts and divine rule. And as large and dispersed populations were bound together by shared reading experiences – whether novels about life in their familiar society, or news reports about foreign wars – they were enabled to think of themselves as members of 'imagined communities' in Anderson's oft-quoted phrase. Communities bound not so much by immediate social interaction, as by horizons of written representation. Thus Anderson treats the nineteenth-century novel as the paradigmatic national literary form (1991: ch. 2).

Michael Mann (1992) has picked up on Anderson's arguments, weaving them into a more general account of developments of economy and state. He recognizes the importance of the growth of 'discursive literacy' (i.e. the ability to read and write non-formulaic texts – signing one's name doesn't count) (1992: 141), and identifies key institutions and media involved in the spread of this practice in the eighteenth and early

---

Box 4.2 Teaching Peasants to be French

Eugen Weber's *Peasants into Frenchmen* (1976) has become one of the touchstones of the nationalism literature. He has shown how long it took for a clear French national identity to really spread through the population of France. Despite the upheavals of the French Revolution and the Napoleonic Empire, at the last quarter of the nineteenth century rural France was still a patchwork of regional languages, dialects and cultures – of peasants economically tied to the land. By the 1860s perhaps half the population still did not speak the standard French of Paris. Weber describes the gradual penetration of a modern, standardized school system into the countryside, and the numerous obstacles it encountered. Fundamental brakes on this process were the poor roads and means of transportation necessary to get rural children to school, and the high demand for child labour keeping children away from school. Regarding the dissemination of Parisian French more specifically, there were other problems: the lack of trained and qualified teachers who commanded the standard language variety themselves; and high levels of adult illiteracy and the exclusion of girls from school, which impeded language reinforcement and reproduction in the home.

In this context draconian methods were often used to try to cultivate the use of standard French. Children caught speaking their native tongue were forced to display a 'token of shame' (a cardboard ticket, stick, peg, ribbon, etc., even holding a brick out at arm's length). 'A child saddled with such a "symbol" kept it until he caught another child not speaking French,

→

nineteenth centuries. These were: the churches, especially Protestant, with their devotional literatures; the state, especially the disciplined armed forces and civil administration; commerce and the growth in contracts, account keeping and marketing; the legal profession; the universities; the printing and publishing industry, especially of periodicals, newspapers and pamphlets; and 'discursive discussion centres', in other words the 'academies, clubs, libraries, salons, taverns and coffeehouses' that stocked many of these reading materials and fostered the discussions in them (1992: 146). Mann singles out commercial capitalism (i.e. capitalism based more on extensive trade than industrialized production) and the expanding militarized state as the prime movers in the spread of discursive literacy, noting that the former was more significant for Britain, the latter more significant for old regimes such as Prussia and Austria, while France was more evenly influenced by these forces. Challenging Gellner's industrialization thesis he argues in a manner that nicely ties together the themes we have examined so far:

> → denounced him, and passed it on' (1976: 313). But it took more than such brutal treatment to make the acquisition of French more appealing to rural people. In time the people began recognize the opportunities that literacy afforded in an expanding market economy, not only in the agrarian sector, but for the next generation achieving upward mobility into state jobs and better opportunities in military careers. Thus education, literacy and standard French became means for rural family prosperity, rather than diversions of precious household labour.
>
> Eventually such standard education began to be perceived not just as pragmatically useful, but as a mark of social status, cultivation and civilization. From this point it became possible to use texts and practices in the classroom to inculcate national values and identity. Children were increasingly exposed to the hexagonal image of France on wall maps, to descriptions of the land in geography texts, to romances of national heroes in history texts and to prescriptions for patriotic behaviour in civic texts. Weber cites an example:
>
>> Society (summary): (1) French society is ruled by just laws, because it is a democratic society. (2) All the French are Equal in their rights; but there are inequalities between us that stem from nature or from wealth. (3) These inequalities cannot disappear. (4) Man works to become rich; if he lacked this hope, work would cease and France would decline. It is therefore necessary that each of us should be able to keep the money he has earned. (1976: 331)

Industrialisation was not a principle cause in this period (it may have been subsequently). It arrived too late and too unevenly. There were two principle causes: on the one hand the emergence of commercial capitalism and its universal social classes; on the other the emergence of the modern state and its professional armed forces and administrators. Conjoined by the fiscal-military pressures exerted by geopolitical rivalry, they produced the politics of popular representation and these formed several varieties of modern nationalism. (1992: 162)

Transformations of Religion

For the rest of this chapter we will briefly consider some sub-themes that relate closely to the arguments explored above. Many observers have commented that the Reformation in Europe, though perhaps not the origin of nationalism, at least appears to have laid some important groundwork. Josep Llobera has argued that competition between ecclesiastical and civil systems for authority and revenues led to the rupture of the Reformation, creating new national churches under the control of monarchs, churches that both challenged external papal power and resisted further fractious radical religious dissent from below, thus helping to consolidate national identities (1994: 134–47). Liah Greenfeld has argued that England formed the first modern nation, through the crucible of the Reformation. Henry VIII led the way in the rejection of papal authority in 1532, and the reformed religion was particularly associated with the rising merchant and artisanal classes, and the newly ennobled members of the aristocracy. As we have already noted, the spread of vernacular Bibles and liturgical ceremonies after the Reformation helped spread literacy and a more uniform ideology. More generally, popular struggles against 'papist' monarchs in the seventeenth century, led by elite parliamentarians observing the new religion, intensified the identification of the defence of Protestantism and the defence of the English nation. These associations were vividly symbolized in the Protestants martyred by Queen Mary, commemorated in Foxe's *Book of Martyrs*, and in such leading Protestant rulers as Elizabeth I and later Cromwell (Greenfeld 1992: ch. 1).

It has also often been noted that the Reformation involved a renewed interest in the Old Testament and a borrowing of much of its imagery for ideological purposes. Not only was the Catholic Church's mediating role between the believer and God broken, making space for the idea of a community of equal believers in the face of God, but the idea of God's 'chosen people', on the model of Israel as the first nation, provided an image of, and template for, the Protestant national community. A notion of fidelity to an original, uncorrupted Christianity became fused with fidelity to the 'nation' struggling against backsliding rulers, and fears of papal subterfuge from without (Hastings 1997: 195–6). The Old Testament language of 'covenants' provided a medium for articulating the complex of bonds and betrayals between peoples and kings in this period (see Box 4.3, p. 86).

It has also often been argued that for all its religious fervour, the Reformation was ultimately the midwife of a more secular world in which religion, if not rejected was at least relegated to the private sphere. But Enlightenment and science are not able to meet the basic human needs for reassurance in the face of uncertainty and mortality (cf. Malinowski 1948), nor provide a focus of social solidarity (cf. Durkheim 1965 [1915]). Thus the nation and nationalism have often been seen as modern replacements for lost religious faith (Hayes 1960), a new receptacle of higher meaning, purpose and sacredness. Anderson begins *Imagined Communities* with the observation that tombs to 'unknown soldiers' (albeit always known to be 'our' co-nationals) are quintessential national symbols. He goes on to say:

> The cultural significance of such monuments becomes even clearer if one tries to imagine, say, a Tomb of the Unknown Marxist or a cenotaph for fallen Liberals. Is a sense of absurdity avoidable? The reason is that neither Marxism nor Liberalism are much concerned with death and immortality. If the nationalist imagining is so concerned, this suggests a strong affinity with religious imaginings. (1991: 10)

Llobera makes the same argument more bluntly:

> It is not only that institutionalised religion (the church) often played an important role in the legitimation of the state and in fostering religious values, but more importantly that nationalism tapped into the same reservoir of ideas, symbols and emotions as religion; in other words, that religion was metamorphosed into nationalism. (1994: 146)

Thus, in this last formulation, however modern nationalism is, it also serves a perennial human need for orientation and meaning. Here we find a curious point of agreement between some primordialists and some modernists. We will return to look at these themes more closely in Chapter 9.

Box 4.3   The National Covenant of Scotland

The Reformation in Scotland, Calvinist and Presbyterian in form, came in two waves in 1560 and 1567, the second having a somewhat broader base than the first, but both led from above, by sectors of the Scottish nobility. By the 1630s, however, the Presbyterian Church (the 'Kirk') had become a pervasive institution in lowland Scotland, where the powers of the government and its magistrates, and the Kirk and its ministers, intertwined (Lynch 2002). The new Kirk was expansionist and proselytizing, and driven by a developing class that included upwardly mobile lairds (lesser nobility), a growing elite of clergy and lawyers, and the burgesses of urban commerce and government. With the move of King James VI/I and his court to London on the union of the Scottish and English crowns in 1603, this matrix of Kirk and urban government became the focus of social power and leadership in Scotland in the absence of a royal presence. When James's son Charles I inherited the throne (1625–49) he sought to consolidate his rule by bringing structures and practices of the Kirk into line with those of the Episcopal Church of England, including the appointment of bishops (rejected in the Presbyterian system) and the use of a more Anglican prayer book and liturgy. There were also threats of royal reappropriation of lands taken from the Catholic Church by the nobility during the Reformation. The leading classes fiercely resisted these incursions on their established power and authority in Scotland, perceiving it as a conflict between the erring religious practices of the Episcopal Church with its 'papist' leanings, and the true reformed religion of Calvinist Presbyterianism in Scotland.

This conflict was played out through the idiom of the covenant. In 1638, in response to Charles's reforms, the Presbyterian elites of Scotland drafted, signed and circulated for further signatures among the populace, the 'National Covenant', which called on all signatories to uphold 'true religion' and oppose 'popery'. They and their followers, particularly when they formed armies to fight in the 'civil wars' (1638–47), were known as 'Covenanters'. Their unfulfilled hope was that Charles would sign, discover the virtues of Presbyterianism and abandon his centralizing project. The covenant, one of the first in a tradition that would last another 200 years in Scotland, was a political device. It asserted a kind of 'contract' between God, the faithful and the king – thus resistance to royal power was cast as an attempt to get the king to join his subjects in their faithful obedience to God. But it was also a powerful metaphor, evoking both the covenants between God and Israelites in the Old Testament, and aspects of the peculiar tradition of 'bonding' in Scotland (c. 1400–1600) by which alliances between equals (nobles, burgesses), or relations of support in exchange for services between lords and followers, were instituted through written 'contracts' called 'bonds' that were signed by the parties concerned. This fusion of a Scottish social institution for regulating power relations with the theological and political struggles of a nationally defined church gave the Kirk a precocious role in defining national identity in early modern Scotland, well before the era of industrialization (see Hearn 2000; Stevenson 1988).

Civil Society

Modernization is closely associated with the development of 'civil society', a term that has enjoyed renewed popularity and been the subject of much debate in recent years. By-passing these debates for the present discussion, we can think of civil society as 'the ensemble of social institutions, associations and organisations, distinct from kinship and the state, through which values, desires and demands are articulated and which often serves to channel these demands toward the state' (Hearn 2000: 19; see also Hearn 2001; Bobbio 1989: 25–6). Thus Breuilly's function-specific institutions of economy and culture, and Mann's array of institutions and media spreading the new discursive literacy can be viewed as exemplifying key agents within civil society. The crucial point here is a general shift from a society in which social roles and group memberships are strongly prescribed and circumscribed, to one in which individuals are freer to identify, associate and combine as they choose. Once again we encounter Gellner's idea of the modern modular individual moving within a shared national culture:

> Modularity, with its moral and intellectual preconditions, makes civil society, and the existence of non-suffocating yet effective segments, possible; but it makes not only for civil, but for nationalist society. Modular man is not universally substitutable: he is substitutable within the cultural boundaries of the idiom in which he has been trained to communicate, to emit and receive messages. (Gellner 1995: 44)

As we have already seen, this new fluidity of individuals and organizations is specifically associated with the growing strength and influence of markets and their associated activities, in the various guises of commerce, industry and capital. It is the market agent, able to establish a contractual relation for the brief duration of an economic exchange, and then move on unencumbered by further obligations, that offers the paradigm for this modularity. Of course, in reality, market activities are hemmed in by laws of contract, state-made currencies, enduring interdependencies among economic actors (e.g. firms and suppliers) and so on. Nonetheless, it is especially the demands of the market, and not simply the human desire for freedom and autonomy, that creates institutional pressures to maximize modularity, creating a whole society on the model of buyers and sellers.

If it is ultimately economic change that brings about this distinctive zone of economic activity, civil society nonetheless creates space for political mobilization, and for the formation of civic associations not specifically concerned with economic goals. The nationalist movements have generally drawn on the organizational resources of civil society – churches, schools, journals, antiquarian societies, associations for the defence and promotion of languages, campaigning groups, etc. – to promote their causes (Hroch 2000; Morton 1996). All complex, stratified societies involve a pyramidal hierarchy of powers, and challenges to power at the top are generally fomented and mobilized in the middle layers. Many a king has been brought to heel by a coalition of noblemen. What is distinctive about modernity and civil society is that the opportunities for such coalitions challenging power above lie not so much in the nodal points of a political structure and the following they can bring with them, as in the much more open social space of association, where the common interests and identities of broad social sectors can be articulated and assembled.

Finally, civil society, like market-based society in general, is closely associated with liberalism and its values – individualism, freedom, and autonomy. It is only an apparent paradox that people in liberal environments sometimes choose to realize their individuality through collectivities, and pursue freedom and autonomy as parts of larger, sometimes nationally defined groups. Liberal values do not prescribe social atomism and disengagement, or association according to some principles but not others. It is precisely their agnosticism as to whether and how individuals form associations that makes them liberal. Thus, the civil societies and attendant values of liberal market societies have proven quite amenable to nationalist mobilization of a variety of types.

Civic versus Ethnic Nationalism

This leads us to the abiding distinction between 'civic' and 'ethnic' forms of nationalism that has been implicit in much of our discussion so far. Early on this difference was couched in terms 'Western' and 'Eastern' forms of nationalism in Europe, but this was a distinction that was understood to have applications beyond Europe. Building on the distinction between pristine and reactive nationalism we have already highlighted, Hans Kohn was one of the first to articulate this difference:

> Nationalism in the West arose in an effort to build a nation in the political reality and the struggles of the present without too much

sentimental regard for the past; nationalists in Central and Eastern Europe created often, out of the myths of the past and the dreams of the future, an ideal fatherland, closely linked with the past, devoid of any immediate connection with the present, and expected to become sometime a political reality . . . While Western nationalism was, in its origin, connected with concepts of individual liberty and rational cosmopolitanism current in the eighteenth century, the later nationalism in Central and Eastern Europe and in Asia easily tended toward a contrary development. Dependent upon, and opposed to, influences from without, this new nationalism, not rooted in a political or social reality, lacked self-assurance; its inferiority complex was often compensated by overemphasis and overconfidence, their own nationalism appearing to nationalists in Germany, Russia, or India as something infinitely deeper than the nationalism of the West, and therefore richer in problems and potentialities. The quest for the meaning of German, Russian, or Indian nationalism, the musing about the 'soul' or the 'mission' of the nation, an endless discussion of its relation to the West, all that became characteristic of this new form of nationalism. (1967: 330–1)

Various writers have drawn the precise line between East and West differently. In an influential essay John Plamenatz has treated the unifying nationalisms of Germany and Italy in the later nineteenth century as Western, as against the Slavs of the Habsburg Empire, and later anti-colonial nationalisms, but the basic contrast is very similar (1976). More recently Rogers Brubaker encapsulated this distinction in his comparison of concepts of citizenship in France and Germany. Viewing this distinction as arising in part out of their interdependent and mutually shaping histories, Brubaker maintains that:

In the French tradition, the nation has been conceived in relation to the institutional and territorial frame of the state. Revolutionary and Republican definitions of nationhood and citizenship – unitarist, universalist, and secular – reinforced what was already in the ancien régime an essentially political understanding of nationhood. (1992: 1)

While in contrast:

The German understanding has been *Volk*-centered and differentialist. Since national feeling developed before the nation-state, the German idea of nation was not originally political, nor was it linked to the abstract idea of citizenship. This prepolitical German nation, this nation in search of a state, was conceived not as the bearer of universal political values, but as an organic, cultural, linguistic or racial community – an irreducibly particular *Volksgemeinschaft*. (1992: 1)

Brubaker is ultimately interested in the implications of these cultural differences, institutionalized in law, for immigration policies in these two countries, observing that the Parisian core of the French state has a long history of assimilating outlying populations both legally and culturally, while the German tradition draws a deeper, 'natural' distinction between Germans and others, and is less equipped for assimilation.

Suffice it to say that this kind of contrast is such a commonplace in the nationalism literature, that it has a tendency to become abstracted from specific historical analyses, especially in less rigorous discussions, and rendered as a universal dichotomy into which all nationalisms can ultimately be placed (Ignatieff 1993). Moreover, for many there is a tendency to view 'Eastern/ethnic' nationalism as the real thing, the essence of nationalism, and 'Western/civic' nationalism as something else altogether – patriotism, state loyalty – but not really nationalism.

But in recent years many writers have tried to suggest that this distinction is problematic and easily overdrawn. As Bernard Yack has pointed out, the idea that some nations are born out of the active consent of their members, as in Ernest Renan's 'daily plebiscite', is obviously false. The vast majority of people are born into and culturally inherit their national traditions. West or East, civic or ethnic, national identity is a condition into which they have been thrown – not one they have chosen (1999: 106–9). More generally, more civic or liberal forms of nationalism are hardly a-cultural but, in fact, have evolved out of a particular culture-history, and generally promote that culture (Nielsen 1999: 127). As Will Kymlicka has argued against Michael Ignatieff (1993) and Will Pfaff (1993), they

overlook the fact that 'civic' nationalism has a cultural component. They say that membership in a civic nation is based, not on descent or culture, but on allegiance to the political principles of democracy and freedom. This is obviously false of native-born Americans, whose citizenship has nothing to do with their political beliefs. They automatically acquire citizenship by descent, and cannot be stripped of it if they turn out to be fundamentalists or fascists. And it is only half-true of immigrants. The American government does require immigrants to swear allegiance to the Constitution, but it also requires them to learn the English language and American history. These legal requirements of gaining citizenship are intended to integrate immigrants into the common culture. (Kymlicka 1999: 133)

David Brown has argued along similar lines that the most important distinction here is not really civic versus ethnic, and the presence or absence of a cultural dimension, but rather liberal (open and tolerant) versus illiberal (closed and intolerant):

> Thus, instead of arguing, as hitherto, that ethnocultural nationalisms are intrinsically illiberal, it may be useful to reformulate the argument. Perhaps it is those nationalisms, whether civic or ethnocultural, which are articulated by insecure élites and which constitute *ressentiment*-based [as in Greenfeld's usage] reactions against others who are perceived as threatening, which consequently become illiberal. By the same token, perhaps civic and ethnocultural nationalisms which begin as protest movements but do not develop their identity primarily in relation to threatening others, and which are articulated by self-confident élites, are most likely to take a liberal form. Feelings of insecurity on both the part of the articulators of nationalist ideologies, and their mass audiences, have the potentiality to transform all nationalisms in collectivist and illiberal directions, irrespective of their civic and ethnocultural mix, depending on how the other and thence the self are depicted. (2000: 67; insertion added)

In this way Brown shifts our attention away from broad-brushed characterizations of nationalisms and towards the specific dynamics of social structural relations and elite leadership. Yack has nicely summed up the problem as stemming from an overestimation of the role of the individual in modern society on the part of liberal theorists:

> The late Ernest Gellner once quipped that Marxists have been forced to come up with a 'wrong address' theory of history in order to explain the success of nationalism: history had a message for classes that somehow got delivered to nations by mistake. Liberal theorists are only beginning to face up to their similar disappointment. History, they believed, had a message for individuals, but that message somehow got delivered by mistake to nations. The age of liberal individualism has also been the age of nationalism; liberal practices have been realized, for the most part, within the framework of national communities. (1999: 115)

Box 4.4 Atatürk – Modernizer of Turkey

As the Ottoman Empire weakened and lost territories across the nineteenth century its rulers (e.g. Mahmud II, 1808–39) attempted military, economic and constitutional reforms, but these were too limited or abortive to satisfy those calling for a modern constitutional state on the European model. After the loss of Greece, Libya, Egypt and the Balkans in the 1912 war, alliance with Germany in the First World War led to defeat and the Treaty of Sèvres (1920), breaking up the remains of the Ottoman Empire and awarding Izmar (Smyrna) to Greece and other parts of the coast of Asia Minor to France and Italy. Mustafa Kemal (1881–1938), a military commander who had distinguished himself in the defence of Gallipoli in 1915, and become increasingly critical of the Sultan's government, led a successful war (1919–22) to drive out the Greeks and topple his own government. The resulting Treaty of Lausanne (1923) established the present borders of Turkey and allowed for a massive exchange of populations between Greece and Turkey.

Later dubbed Atatürk ('father of the Turks'), Kemal instigated an authoritarian programme of westernizing, secularizing and modernizing reforms for the new nation. Reforms included: the replacement of the Islamic with the Gregorian calendar; the replacement of Arabic script with a modified Latin alphabet and the purging of Arabic and Persian words from the Turkish language; banning the wearing of the fez for men, and discouraging the use of the hijab (veil) for women, while encouraging European attire; requiring all Turks to adopt surnames; removing Islamic bans on alcohol; and the establishment of universal state schooling for children of both sexes. Atatürk targeted Islamic institutions, which he saw as a major obstacle to national development. He abolished the caliphate, *shari'a* law, and religious schools (*medrese*) and suppressed dervish orders and brotherhoods. He firmly subordinated religion to the state,

→

Conclusion

Modernization is a central concept for social theory in general, and these theorists have stressed its relevance for understanding nationalism. This is different from the idea of primordialism, which mainly occurs in the literature on ethnicity and nationalism. In nationalism studies modernism forms a more coherent paradigm, bolstered by general notions of social evolution that underpin much modern social theory. In contrast, the idea of primordialism tends to develop through critiques of the limitations of this dominant paradigm, but also lacks, so far, a firm grounding in a broader explanatory paradigm.

As we have seen, there are varying emphases among modernists. All

→
establishing the administration of the mainstream Hanafi school of Sunni Islam, including the training of clerics and Imams, through the Department of Religious Affairs. Along with these reforms his nation-building project encouraged the creation of historical myths about a glorified pre-Islamic history of the Turks, who were identified with the ancient Hittites and thought to have brought civilization to Egypt and Mesopotamia. There was also a consolidation of a legally enforced conception of an ethnic Turkish identity during the 1930s, that privileged ethnic Turks as citizens within the Turkish state, in keeping with similar trends throughout East Central Europe at that time (Çağaptay 2003). And Atatürk secured his programme through measures such as the Maintenance of Order Law (1925), which allowed the government to close down organizations thought to be subversive, a law used effectively against opposing political parties.

Atatürk's legacy for Turkey today is mixed. He endures as an omnipresent national symbol in statues and portraits, on banknotes, in the names of airports and bridges; and many still support the Kemalist project in some form. But the effect of his reforms were probably more limited to urban elites than has sometimes been recognized, his support among soldiers and peasants probably having as much to do with his martial virtues and the defence of Islam against Greeks and infidels. In the later twentieth century both Marxian socialist ideology and religious conservatism, the latter exemplified in the success of the Justice and Development Party (AKP) in the 2002 national elections, have vied with the Kemalist tradition to define Turkish national identity. In times of crisis the Turkish military, seeing itself as the guardian of the Kemalist project, has either imposed military government (1960–5, 1980–3) or strongly intervened in government (1971). This is perhaps Atatürk's most enduring legacy (see Breuilly 1993: 244–7, 270–3; Çağaptay 2003; Canefe 2002; Seton-Watson 1977: 255–60).

would stress economic forces shaping ideological structures, but Gellner and Hobsbawm take particularly materialist positions. Breuilly focuses more on the dynamics of political change, while Anderson highlights fundamental changes in worldview. Mann tends towards a more synthetic view of economic, political and ideological processes. There are many disagreements, but they are nonetheless unified by a general paradigm of profound social and historical transformation over the last 500 years.

The various sub-themes we have encountered also partake of the broader modernization paradigm. The notion of uneven development highlights a relationship of conflict between interdependent societies at different stages in the process of modernization. The civic/ethnic dichotomy similarly encodes a normatively loaded contrast between the 'modern' and the 'backward'. The thesis of secularization, that in the modern world religion would fade or recede into private life, is in a way re-worked in the thesis that nationalism becomes a substitute for religion as the receptacle of ultimate social values. And civil society, understood as a set of institutions and values conducive to liberal, individualistic, market-based ways of life, is usually invoked as an essential element in the process of modernization. In the next chapter we try to get some critical purchase on modernist approaches to the study of nationalism, by problematizing modernization as a paradigm of historical change.

Further Reading

The literature that fits under the heading of modernist theories of nationalism is vast. Central books include: Anderson (1991), Bendix (1964), Breuilly (1993), Deutsch (1953), Gellner (1983), Greenfeld (1992), Hobsbawm (1992), Mann (1993) and Nairn (1981 [1977]). For quicker and more accessible presentations of the core ideas of some of these authors, see: Breuilly (2001), Gellner (1997), Greenfeld (1993) and Mann (1992). Although I have chosen to address them under the heading of 'culture' in Chapter 8, the volumes by Kedourie (1993 [1960]) and Hobsbawm and Ranger (1983) are also central to this literature. Essays by Kamenka (1976) and Plamenatz (1976) also provide key statements.

5
Rethinking Modernism

As with primordialism in Chapter 3, here I will take a broader critical look at the paradigm of modernism, first outlining some main lines of criticism that have been made by others, before offering my own. The critiques I will review first are of three main types. First, there are those who argue that modernists fail to appreciate the historical depth of ethnicities and the way they undergird modern nations (Smith 1988; Hutchinson 2000); second, there are post-colonial critiques that identify a 'Western' and European bias in modernist theories (Parekh 1995; Chatterjee 1996); and finally there is what we might call an internal critique, that worries that modernist arguments have been overconfident and overdrawn (Nairn 1997). After that I will turn again to Ernest Gellner, to explore the way he, in fact, offers two very distinct theories of nationalism, whose logical relationship raises fundamental problems in theorizing the historical origins and trajectory of nationalism. Modernist theorists of nationalism, in fact, offer quite varied explanations of the origins of nationalism, and draw on rather different paradigms of historical change. After exploring these variations I will argue against a conception of modernity as a relatively stable state, and for a reconsideration of the concept of 'uneven development', suggesting that unevenness is not just a rocky step in the path to modernity, but an intensifying condition of the modern world.

Objections Raised

We have already covered the debate between Anthony Smith and John Breuilly about the historical depth of nations, but let's allow the 'reluctant primordialists' a final word. In perhaps his most polemic piece, Smith argues that the modernist theory of nations is not so much a theory as counter-myth to those of nationalist ideologues. He suggests that most social scientists and intelligentsias of the 'first' and 'third' worlds, have structurally conditioned commitments to the very idea of modernity and its radical distinction from 'traditional' society. He regards the 'ironic scepticism' towards the nation that modernists espouse as a way of over-coming a contradiction between their public roles as advocates of modernization and scientific objectivity, and their private realities of particularistic national and ethnic attachments (1988: 6–7). In the same camp, John Hutchinson (2000) argues that modernists traffic in an overly homogenizing and state-centric concept of the nation that by definition occludes the way ethnicities evolve into nations over the long term through waves of ethnic revivalism, in an internal dynamic of competi-tion to define and mobilize aspects of culture and the past. Again, however, I would argue that this disagreement hinges on definitions of ethnicity and nation, not on empirical matters of history.

From a different angle, scholars of post-colonialism have objected to 'the ethnocentric assumptions that inform much of the literature on nationalism' (Parekh 1995: 26). In a manner reminiscent of Elie Kedourie (1993 [1960]), Parekh defines nationalism as a particular strain of philosophy legitimating the modern state as it developed in Europe, one that emhpasizes solidaristic community forged through cultural and linguistic bonds. But Parekh takes Kedourie and others to task for recog-nizing the 'absurdity' of the idea that every nation could have its own state, but failing to condemn the parallel impulse of states to create nations. This

> allows them to assert that nationalism only occurs in 'immature' coun-tries and that the mature and 'civilised' countries of the West are largely free of the virus. As we saw, nationalism has two faces. The state's desire to become a nation is only an obverse of, and neither morally superior to nor less politically harmful than the nation's desire to become a state. (1995: 35)

He goes on to offer the United Kingdom, India and the United States as prime examples of modern states that do not fit the nation-state model because of their ethnic, linguistic and religious plurality, and to note that national groups that enjoy a reasonable amount of recognition within their polities are less inclined to seek their own state. In his view, ethnic homo-geneity is a peculiar resource of (Western) Europe – outside of Europe other means of social categorization are more salient, such as cultural history, language, religion and race, thus hampering attempts to mobilize an ethnic nation (e.g. Hindu nationalism), and leading to pan-nationalist forms based on language in Arab countries and race in African countries. For Parekh, the Eurocentric theory of nationalism has assumed itself to be a universal template, the first emergence of a universal historical trend that the rest of the world must follow. He avers that the process is much more piecemeal than this, that non-European countries selectively adapt elements of this political model, but in ways that are not predetermined by any essential underlying form. For instance he suggests that under Gandhi the Indian independence movement was not inclined to stress historical memory the way European nationalisms often did, because 'memory' has lower epistemological status within traditional Indian thought, being associated with ephemeral fact rather than enduring truth. In sum:

> The colonial nationalist discourse then was necessarily multistranded, multilayered, multilingual, partly autonomous and partly heteronomous, eclectic and provisional, and the post-independence nationalist discourse could hardly be otherwise. If we wish to appreciate its specificity, creative power and moral pathos, we need to study each nationalist movement in its own terms and in its own local language. To start with the assumption that *all* nationalist language is European in origin is not only to praise and blame Europe too much, but also to wholly misunderstand non-Western political history and thought. (1995: 48; emphasis in original)

Along similar lines, Partha Chatterjee (1993) has taken Benedict Anderson to task for arguing, in conventional fashion, that modern nationalism was a pattern established first in Europe, the Americas and Russia, which then provided models that were later adopted in Asia and Africa in their anti-colonial movements. Chatterjee objects that this argument casts those in the post-colonial world as passive consumers of a modernity made elsewhere. On the contrary, he maintains that the modernizing nationalisms of the colonial world were based not on simple imitation of or identification with the West, but on differentiation from it, on establishing an identity in contrast to the West. Standard political stories, for instance of the processes leading to the formation of the Indian National Congress in 1885, obscure a deeper process of cultural transformation and modernization, the real new imagining of the community.

Focusing on the case of India and Bengal in particular, Chatterjee sees this process as based on conceptual oppositions, in which the contrast between the authentic national community and the imposed colonial government is expressed through polarities such as: spiritual/material, inner/outer and essential/inessential. The national community is imagined first by cultural elites as an inner realm of cultural and spiritual essence fundamentally different from the imposed colonial administration. Only later does the modernizing process take on an explicitly political form. He describes how in the mid-nineteenth century the Bengali elite, bilingual in Bengali and English:

> makes it a cultural project to provide its mother tongue with the necessary linguistic equipment to enable it to become an adequate language for 'modern' culture. An entire institutional network of printing presses, publishing houses, newspapers, magazines, and literary societies is created around this time, *outside* the purview of the state and the European missionaries, through which the new language, modern and standardized, is given shape. The bilingual intelligentsia came to think of its own language as belonging to that inner domain of cultural identity, from which the colonial intruder had to be kept out; language therefore became a zone over which the nation first had to declare its sovereignty and then had to transform in order to make it adequate for the modern world. (1993: 7, emphasis in original)

Chatterjee goes on to show how modern forms of Bengali drama, literature and plastic arts draw on indigenous traditions and do not reproduce the aesthetic cannons of these art forms in the West. Ultimately he sees the contemporary problems of the post-colonial world as involving a mismatch between distinctive, non-Western imaginings of national community, and inherited but inadequate Western and European models of the state.

In the 1970s Tom Nairn became a champion of Gellner's modernization theory, albeit from a Marxian point of view and with a special emphasis on the concept of uneven development. But with time he has developed his own reservations about the modernization paradigm, despite broadly supporting it. In a manner similar to Chatterjee, he observes that modernization theory has tended to treat the particularities of ethnicity as passive materials to be re-worked by modernizing nationalists, failing to appreciate the intractable nature of cultural particularity, and how this intractability is precisely what sets the process of nationalism in motion (1997: 8–9). Nairn has also objected that Gellner's bold model has 'had the effect of foreshortening the future', assuming the transition to modernity was more complete than it was, and underestimating 'the enduring pressure of rurality' (1997: 111). The globe remains profoundly 'uneven', and populated by peoples caught between peasant ways of life and processes of proletarianization. This is a point I will return to in the last section. Finally, the Gellnarian approach tended to treat nationalism more as an effect than as a cause, as the by-product of industrialization, perhaps with its own more minor effects, but not as a motor of history (1997: 7). Gellner had argued that the true subject of modern philosophy was industrialization (1959), but Nairn suggests that it is nationalism itself, the various strains of modern philosophy reflecting attempts to make sense of nationally construed realities (1997:17). Like Liah Greenfeld (1992), Nairn sees nations not as side effects of modernization, but as momentous new forms of historical agency that once formed, make history.

The 'Ernest Gellner Problem'

German scholars of the late nineteenth century liked to speak of '*Das Adam Smith problem*', believing that Smith had produced a moral philosophy in his *Theory of Moral Sentiments*, and a theory of political economy in *The Wealth of Nations* that were logically incompatible, the former assuming a natural tendency for sympathy for one's fellow human beings, the other assuming a general propensity for self-interested behaviour (Teichgraeber 1982). While this dichotomy in Adam Smith's work is not as severe as is often thought, it does pose puzzles. In a similar fashion we might speak of an 'Ernest Gellner problem', because we find that he, in fact, had two theories of nationalism, and the logical relationship between them is not entirely clear. On the one hand, Gellner conceives of nations as functional requirements of modern industrialized social life, and nationalism is the process that renders the necessary functional adjustment. On the other hand, the paradigmatic historical process of nationalism for Gellner was a reaction to uneven development, the encounter between Ruritania and Megalomania we saw in the last chapter.

Now these two theories of what happened are not incompatible, and Gellner observes that in some cases people were fairly passively incorporated into the new industrial order, and in others were provoked to mobilize nationally against another dominant nation. But neither are they logically interdependent. One can reasonably imagine a world in which all people are either assimilated into the new functional order or exterminated, with no successful reactionary movements, or one in which all nationalism begins with such reactions, not against new industrial societies, but against exploitative imperial regimes. Obviously Gellner is obliged to tell his bold story in this dual way because it broadly corresponds to the historical record. As a descriptive summary of world history it is very powerful. But as a theoretical whole it is somewhat puzzling, because one gets a sense from Gellner that both these processes – functional integration and reaction to exclusion – are the heart of the matter.

To some degree this 'problem' is solved by the very notion of modernization, as a model of historical time. There seems to be for Gellner, as with many marxists, an unfolding logic to history, driven by technological change. Although he was perfectly capable of questioning the typical ethnocentric story of the rise of the West (1964: 12–13), his entire view of history was framed by the great transition from traditional ancient agrarian states to modern industrial societies. It is this framework of transition from 'tradition' to 'modernity' that narratively binds his two theories together, the one theory characterizing the functional requirements of the new, industrial stage of social evolution, the other characterizing a typical process of transition from traditional to modern society, spurred on by the encounter with modern society. But herein lies the paradox for Gellner's approach: there are two different kinds of nationalism, with fundamentally different causes. For surely there must be some initial transition to this new form of society, but Gellner's transitional type depends on the full-fledged version already existing (for a particularly thorough analysis of the evolution of Gellner's theories, see O'Leary 1998).

Pristine versus Secondary Situations

What Gellner's theory is encountering here is a specific version of a very general problem in historical and evolutionary theory. The anthropologist Morton H. Fried drew attention to the need to distinguish between 'pristine and secondary situations' (1967: 111) in trying to understand social change and transitions from smaller and more egalitarian to larger and more stratified forms of social organization (I summarize this distinction as one between 'simple' and 'complex' forms). A pristine situation is one in which a new social form of greater complexity arises out of a novel set of localized conditions. A secondary situation is one in which contact with a more complex form stimulates simpler forms to change towards that more complex form. Of course, there are many possibilities besides secondary formation in such encounters. The more centralized and powerful society may obliterate or assimilate other groups, or may lock them into a dependent relationship while preventing development towards the more complex form. All these are possibilities, the crucial point, however, is that in such secondary cases the change is not due to endogenous processes, but rather to historically specific external forces. Some societies have stumbled into modern nationhood, while others have had it thrust upon them. Moreover, as history wears on, the pristine situations recede and original instances die out, leaving us with a myriad of secondary formations, and obscuring the initial process of transformation. It is worth noting that this is a more acute conceptual problem for modernists than primordialists, who are less inclined to see the nation as a novel formation.

So how have theorists of nationalism tried to deal with this pristine versus secondary distinction? The answers are more varied and more specific than simply 'it all began in Europe'. Let us survey some of these answers, again beginning with Gellner. For him the substantial congruence of culture and polity was what set the modern world of nationalism off from the cobbled patchwork of traditional agrarian societies and sprawling imperial states. In his final writings (1996b; 1997), he began to use the metaphors of 'marriage' and 'time zones' to convey the spread of nationalism out from its heartland on the European Atlantic seaboard, eastward across Europe into the steppes of Russia. In the first time zone 'the strong dynastic states based on Lisbon, Madrid, Paris and London more or less corresponded to cultural-linguistic zones anyway, even before the logic of the situation, or nationalist theory, decreed that such a correlation should obtain' (1997: 51). By happy or not so happy accident, the bride of 'culture' and the 'groom' of state were already betrothed. This is Gellner's pristine situation, and appears to be a precondition not just for the modern nation, but for industrialization itself. The eastward time zones follow in progressively more troubled secondary formations. In the next zone of Central Europe, the 'erstwhile Holy Roman Empire' that would become Italy and Germany, the bride, fairly widespread high cultures were ready, but the groom had to be laboriously assembled out of the overlapping fragments of princely and papal sovereignty. In Eastern Europe, beneath the carapace of Habsburg and Ottoman empires, the political groom was similarly disassembled, but so was the bride – an ethnic, linguistic and religious patchwork. In the fourth and final zone we come to the Russian empire, a holdover from a pre-national age, prematurely transformed into a modernizing industrial state in 1917, and only truly entering the age of nationalism with the collapse of the USSR. With this schema Gellner sought to summarize how broad circumstances of culture and politics fostered the pristine formation of nationalism at one end, while presenting various waves of secondary formations with particular dilemmas as it radiated east.

In the search for the pristine, Liah Greenfeld is prepared to be much more specific: '[t]he birth of the English nation was not the birth of a nation; it was the birth of the nations, the birth of nationalism' (1992: 23). As we saw in the last chapter, for Greenfeld, nationalism is a matter of ideological innovation led by elites – it is the idea that alters the course of history, not material conditions that call forth the idea. She argues that sixteenth-century England saw a remarkable sustained period of mobility into the aristocracy, which served the political needs of a series of Tudor monarchs, while reconfiguring the country's elites and requiring them to reconstruct their identities in terms that reached down into the wider populace. With the Protestant Reformation and its emphasis on an old testament language of nationhood, the spread of literacy and the English Bible, and the counter-reformational persecutions of Queen Mary I (1553–8), this new elite was supplied with the ideological means to forge an English national identity. She explicitly conceives of the subsequent nationalisms of France, Russia, Germany and the United States as a knock-on series of reactions to the original English instance.

In his critique of the modernists, the late historian Adrian Hastings (1997) agreed with Greenfeld's placing of the origins of nationalism in England, but argued that the beginnings of that nation go much deeper than the sixteenth century, arising out of a long medieval consolidation of the relationship between state and culture in England. He stresses the extensive use of a vernacular literature, and that the Bible provided 'the original model of the nation' (1997: 4). In his account, England saw a precocious confluence of these factors, and subsequent transformations of ethnicities into nations have been driven especially by the spread of Christianity, the Bible and expanding literary vernaculars, fostered partly by missionaries. Thus Hastings might be regarded as an interesting exception to my previous point about primordialists being relatively unconcerned with the pristine/secondary distinction. Here there is a clear pristine case, but with a medieval history.

Benedict Anderson is best known in nationalism studies for coining the term 'imagined communities', spurring scholars to reconsider the ideological nature of nations. But an important and often neglected twist to Anderson's argument is that the key populations first experiencing the interaction of print-capitalism, wider literacy and new needs for identification were not the subjects of old dynastic European states (Britain, France, Spain) often treated as the heartland of nationalism, but the 'creole pioneers' of the Americas. The European-descended governing and middle classes in these lands, anxious about subject indigenous populations beneath them, estranged from social structures and opportunities in their European homelands, literate and mobile and dispersed across vast territories often difficult to traverse, were especially ripe for the consolidation of new identities via the expanding medium of print language. According to Anderson it is they who were the first real innovators of national identities (1991: ch. 4), setting in motion the subsequent waves of change that would wash back over Europe. So here the pristine case, while 'Western' and European descended, is not in Europe, not strictly European.

Anderson's argument points not to one country, but to a set of conditions that affected a series of colonial communities in the Americas. Taking this point further, we need to appreciate that the pristine situation can be conceived not just in terms of a single inno-vating case but also as a systemic transformation driven by relation-ships between separate countries. Anthony Giddens emphasizes, as many others have, the idea that modern states and thus nationalism arose as parts of an interacting system of competing, militarized abso-lutist states in early modern Europe (1987b: 103–16), which drove forward the modernization process by creating demands for new mili-tary technologies, larger and more disciplined armies and navies, and more extensive methods of taxing the populace to fund warfare. More generally Alfred Cobban has argued that the distinctive thing about medieval Europe was its failure to develop a continent-wide empire by conquest, which allowed instead a 'perpetually unstable equilibrium on the system of balance of power' between separate states (1994: 246). Thus, the idea of a national 'right of independence' (i.e. self-determination) evolved out of this geopolitical situation in Europe, common to the countries there but also peculiar to that part of the world (see also Tilly 1975a; Mann 1992).

Though there is a degree of complementarity between these accounts, each highlights a somewhat different set of novel conditions that led to the pristine cases of nation formation. The question is, to what degree are those novel conditions essential to our understanding of nationalism today? Do these conditions give us clues about the very nature of all nationalisms, or only those first cases, later ones simply being adjust-ments to a world in which nations and nationalism have become the norm? Even if the exact forces creating nationalisms have changed, presumably the historical unfolding of those changing forces, and tracing them back to their origins, is essential for understanding nationalism as a process with a beginning and perhaps an end, rather than as a timeless verity.

The Shape of Modernity

One of the characteristic ideological features of the modern age is the tendency to think of history as following a linear plan of development. This tendency reached its peak in the unilinear evolutionism of the nineteenth century. Herbert Spencer (1860) imagined history as a process of complex social forms replacing simple ones on the model of organic evolution. Lewis H. Morgan (1985 [1877]) used the terms 'savagery, barbarism and civilization' to label stages of material technological development, and associated changes in social organization. Morgan influenced Marx and Engels and their model of unfolding 'modes of production' leading to a final stage of communism (Engels 1972 [1884]). Sir James Frazer (1911–15 [1890]) saw science and rationality replacing misunderstanding and superstition. These approaches came in for heavy criticism in the twentieth century, and were shown to be too rigid in many respects, and unable to cope with the actual, multi-stranded variability of human history. Nonetheless, there is a certain overall directionality to human history, and these figures cast a long shadow over later social theory. The theorists of nationalism's modernity that we have been discussing are all subtle and sophisticated thinkers, aware of the errors of nineteenth-century evolutionism. They try to limit themselves to describing empirically identifiable patterns in the historical record. But the very search for patterns, while necessary, can shape our understanding in implicit ways, once these patterns have become habits of thought.

The social evolutionary perspective that still shapes modernist theory can be thought of as containing three main theses, which can be discerned in modernist theories of nationalism. First, that there are specifiable core forces that drive historical change, second, that the broad sweep of human history takes a 'stadial' form, it develops in distinctive stages, and third, that there is a necessary unfolding logic to history – its course is predetermined. As I've suggested, this third thesis of determinism is much weaker in contemporary social theory than it was in many classical nineteenth-century theories. The tendency is to argue that once certain innovations have occurred, they are likely to spread, but that their original occurrence is highly contingent. Nineteenth-century evolutionism often suggested an ontogenic logic, that just as an acorn is genetically designed to become an oak tree, humans (especially white, male, European descended humans) were destined to become more rational, with a greater command over the natural world. This kind of determinism is less present, but the other two theses strongly persist and require some attention.

Consider the different core forces at the heart of the accounts of Gellner, Hobsbawm and Breuilly. For Gellner it is the technology of production that sets the limits and requirements of social organization; with the new technologies of industrial production, new social forms are called forth. As a marxist, Hobsbawm shares in this view, but would also emphasize a dynamic of class conflict; of rising bourgeoisies consolidating their power via the new nation-states, and more marginal petty bourgeoisies struggling to create their own national niches with a modicum of power. Breuilly similarly emphasizes power struggles, but for him this is primarily a matter of the changing institutional forms of the state, and how various groups, not adequately conceived as 'classes' in his opinion, drive forward those transformations in their pursuit of power. Each of these theorists has a somewhat different engine at the heart of their account.

These ideas of core forces do not necessitate thinking of history in terms of distinct stages, but nonetheless are associated with such thinking. There are good empirical reasons for thinking in these terms – measurable quantitative and qualitative step changes – in the case of the modern period, in such things as rates of urbanization, levels of literacy, amounts of energy captured from the environment via fossil fuels and so on. And similar 'jumps' are reasonably associated with the appearances of farming in the neolithic revolution (c. 10,000 years ago) and later the first ancient agrarian states (c. 5,000 years ago). But there is another reason why we think in terms of stages – it makes the welter of history cognitively manageable, abstracting patterns out of ponderous complexity. There is a creative tension between empirical evidence and theoretical needs always shaping our grand views of history, and this should be borne in mind.

The very concept of 'modernity' implies a stadial model, that there was something before that was not modern (traditional society) and that there could be something different after (postmodern society). Moreover, there is a powerful tendency to conceptualize such stages in terms of antitheses. Thus, for Gellner, traditional agrarian society is viewed as static, hierarchical, claustrophobic and bound together by social structure, while modern industrial society is dynamic, egalitarian, open and bound together by culture/language. For Hobsbawm, while having a broadly similar conceptual contrast between what he would more likely call pre-capitalist and capitalist forms of society, the implicit but governing antithesis is between capitalism, in which property is largely private and class interests opposed, and an as yet unrealized future stage of Communism, in which property is collectively managed and social interests unified. And this difference is

evident in their overall arguments. For Gellner the accent is on the enduring difficulties involved in getting everyone over the transitional hump,
and fully into modernity. But once a society has emerged into the modern
era, it has achieved a *stable state*, the final stage (at least from the present
perspective) of history. For Hobsbawm, the culmination of his analysis is
the necessary decline of modernity, to the degree that this is understood
as the period of congruence of capitalism and the nation-state. For him it
is capitalism, understood as *ultimately unstable*, that defines the present
age, and the nation-state and nationalisms are, in the end, transient symp-
toms of its restless development.

Although many would not share Hobsbawm's marxist vision of
history and its potential future, the view that globalization is making the
nation-state obsolete, and that we are presently entering a new phase of
history, is widespread (cf. Guibernau 2001). Such accounts generally
emphasize the globalization of capital, the inability of old nation-states to
manage new, global problems, and the growth of international governing
bodies over the last 50 years as an insipient sign of this transition
(Castells 1997; Held 1996; Ohmae 1996; Strange 1996). But the extent of
these changes has been questioned. Michael Mann (1996) has argued that
the modern state with its 'caged' nations is still very much the dominant
political force, that transnational bodies are relatively weak by comparison, and that nation-statehood is still a primary goal of many political
movements. Not all such formulations of a current transition cast it in
terms of a shift from the modern to the postmodern, but the nation-state is
commonly viewed as the anchor of modernity, its quintessential social
form, so any argument that it is in rapid decline implies that we are on the
cusp of a new historical stage.

I am arguing that our tendency to make sense of history through stadial
models is driven partly by the historical record, partly by our cognitive
need for simplification and partly by our normative perspective, which
either values or devalues the present era in relation to past ones or hypothetical future ones (Fabian 1983). Let me sum up with a contrast. The
typical stadial view of history can be visualized as shown in Figure 5.1
opposite.

History is imagined as a series of plateaux connected by steep transitional periods. As we have said, Gellner has two theories of nationalism,
one for the steep transition, the other for the plateau of modernity. There
are many problems with this kind of picture. It obscures the rise and fall
of great cities, states, empires and civilizations. It falsely suggests, in the
style of classic nineteenth-century unilinear evolutionism, that there is
some predetermined path that all societies must follow. It hides the fact

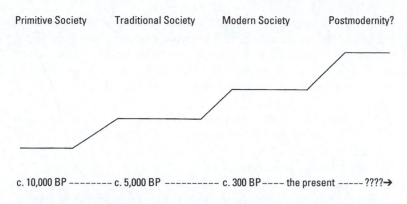

Figure 5.1 The stadial view of history ('BP' = before present)

that societies simultaneously at various 'stages' interact, and that their 'stage' is often an outcome of those interactions, not of some internal development. In fact, it avoids the question of when such interactions mean we must stop thinking in terms of separate societies, and instead conceive a larger social whole, however internally differentiated. All these criticisms have been well rehearsed in contemporary social theory, but nonetheless such a model tends to lurk in the background of much thinking about the development of nationalism.

But if we were to take some other indicators as guides to our visualization of human history, the image might be very different. If we were to take the historical trajectory of the number of people on the planet, the number of them living in cities, the capture and release of physical energy from the environment, the time it takes to transmit a message from one part of the globe to another, and so on, the image would look rather more like Figure 5.2.

Where have our stages gone? What this suggests is not transitions between a series of plateaus, but rather a critical shift within the last few hundred years that has initiated a process of intensification and acceleration, which shows no clear sign of slowing down or stabilizing. While the previous millennia of human existence seems comparatively stable, we must bear in mind this is a matter of certain limits to human material productivity, to the potential size and scale of urban and political units, to our general impact on the environment. Within those limits political and economic systems have expanded and contracted, and crashed against each other, and many of our premodern ancestors would probably not have described their lifetimes as 'stable'.

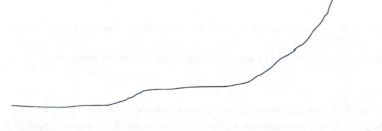

c. 10,000 BP ------- c. 5,000 BP --------- c. 300 BP ---- the present ---- ????➜

Figure 5.2   The accelerating view of history

I am inclined to think of nations and nationalisms as political and cultural forms specific to this period of the last few hundred years – marking the exact 'beginning' would be a somewhat arbitrary and academic exercise. There is clearly a systematic relationship between the intensive and extensive powers of the modern state, the integrating effects of mass culture and the productive power unleashed by modern capitalism (commercial, industrial and financial), and bringing these forces together has been a crucible of power in our age. But the defining characteristic of this age is its instability and restless transformation. The systematic relationships of modernity are constantly being altered by the process of modernity. I am inclined to agree with Michael Mann (1996) that the nation-state is hardly disappearing, and neither is it a static condition. It is rather a highly plastic form within and through which ongoing struggles for power are carried out, struggles which push human history forward at an accelerating rate.

Unfinished Business: Reconsidering Uneven Development

Given this reading of our collective situation, it is worth revisiting the idea of uneven development. What do we mean by this term? It has its origins, and a long, complex history, in the tradition of marxist thought (Bottomore 1983: 498–503), much of which we can by-pass here. The heart of the idea though, is that capitalist competition, contrary to classical economic theory, does not always lead to the uniform spread of the most advanced forms of technology and production, and a general convergence of regions and countries towards a similar model of capitalist production and affluence. Instead, it argues that it is the very interactions between more and less developed regions that gives capitalism much of its dynamic. According to the theory of uneven development, economic processes, in combination with political ones, can mean that countries, regions and sectors become locked into lower levels of development, providing cheap labour and primary products, and thus into subordinate relations with more prosperous and powerful areas. On the other hand, there is sometimes a 'privilege of backwardness', as less developed areas are not committed to forms of production that are becoming obsolete, and can adopt more advanced forms in a single 'leap' forward. Whatever the particular scenario, the underlying principle is that capitalism is competitive, and those with capital will tend to invest and disinvest according to where they can find the greatest profits. While there is some general diffusion of the forms of production and consumption associated with capitalism as it becomes an ever more global process, the effects of capitalism, far from equalizing distributions of wealth and power, intensifies their differential distribution. The rising tide of capitalism does not lift all boats. It lifts a select few much further and more rapidly than most, while many are buffeted by waves and sometimes sunk.

Given its marxist provenance, it is somewhat curious that Gellner gave uneven development such an important role in his own thinking. But as we have seen, his version employed it within the framework of orthodox modernization theory, seeing a general universal trend towards industrialization and affluence, only frustrated in certain circumstances. But whereas the marxian concept has generally been rather limited to economic analyses (but see Roseberry 1989: 215–16), what Gellner drew attention to was the social dynamic, how the perception of differences in prosperity, prestige and power provoked key segments of populations to re-work local ethnic identities and mobilize in national terms. What I am suggesting is that Gellner's recognition of this dynamic is incisive – and it has become one the fundamental ideas of nationalism studies because it is so powerful and widely recognizable in the historical record – but that his desire to confine it to the period of 'transition' to industrialization was an error. Unevenness is a routine and ongoing aspect of our capitalist world, as are the social responses it provokes.

Classically the idea of uneven development was used to grasp relations between developed and underdeveloped countries in the context of global trade and imperialism. Thus the era of capitalism, first commercial and then industrial, is conceived as a shifting sequence of dominant 'core' countries and subordinate regions in the 'periphery' (Frank, 1966; Wallerstein 1974). A recent and more focused example of transnational uneven development can be seen in the shift in the apparel industry in North America following the North American Free Trade Agreement, with much of the production process being relocated from the US to Mexico (Spener *et al.* 2002). However, it can be understood as operating across an array of geographic dimensions (see Harvey 2000: 79–83). Capital investment can move significantly within one country, from more urbanized to what were more rural areas, as with the shift from the old industrial 'rust belt' of the north-east in the US, to the new lighter, industries of the 'sun belt' in the south in the later twentieth century. There is also an intra-urban dynamic, as neighbourhoods in cities, often with distinctive ethnic or racial profiles, receive differential investment, leading to the decay of inner areas and the growth of suburbs (Gotham 2002). And moving in the opposite direction, uneven development is increasingly conceived on a macro scale, encompassing not just relations between countries but whole continents, summed up as the 'North–South divide' of global wealth and poverty (Cohn 2005: 14–15). What all this suggests is that uneven development is a very general process of capitalism, not specific to the analytic level of relations between countries and nations, but that under the right circumstances it can have powerful national effects. Moreover, it may be helpful to pay more attention to the linkages between these levels, which may intensify each other in some instances, and offset each other in others. I will return to this point.

We should also not be too narrow in our thinking about what it is that is unevenly distributed, and how. Politics and economics are interdependent, and it is not so much economy that develops unevenly, as the political economy, the entire array of institutional processes that distribute power. Capital investment takes concrete forms of production, often guided by the state, and one of the consequences of this is that some states have become much more specialized in the production of military technology and capability, the US obviously being the premier in this (Mann 2003), while others have concentrated on the creation of broader welfare provision, as in much of Europe. Within the general condition of prosperity among the advanced capitalist countries, this is an important and consequential uneven development. The literature on nationalism has been especially good at drawing our attention to how the uneven distribution of wealth and power affects perceptions of the world and the self among key populations. When people perceive that they are part of collective distributions of not just wealth, but risk, opportunity, prestige and status, they are more likely to seek ways to either escape into other more fortunate collectivities, or defend and advance the ones in which they are situated. Again this is a general principle, true of class, gender, race, professions and so on, that only take a national form under certain conditions. I am arguing that understanding nationalism involves explaining why this general principle takes that particular form in specific instances.

Josep Llobera has objected to attempts to make capitalism and uneven development the *deus ex machina* of nationalism, thus neglecting the medieval precipitates of modern nations, and the long-term developments of state, civil society and religion (1994: 99–104). Walker Connor has argued that economic disparities are widespread, but do not universally lead to nationalism, and therefore economic explanations of nationalism are at best only partial (1994: 145–64). The argument put forth here is not that uneven development generates nationalism, *in toto*, in the first instance, but rather that uneven development is a general, ongoing condition of modernity, that is usually involved to some degree in processes of nationalism. Nor am I arguing for a narrow economic determinism, but instead that uneven development should be understood as also social in a wider sense, involving perceptions of group identity that are not mere reflections of economic processes, but that do interact with these. As we have seen, Michael Mann (1992) has questioned Gellner's formulation, arguing that industrialism arrives on the scene too late to be the cause of nationalism. But he does attribute nationalism to a competitive dynamic of accumulations of commercial, military and state power in eighteenth- and nineteenth-century Europe, and I think the conception of uneven development offered here is broad enough to be seen as an aspect of that process, before industrial capitalism had truly taken shape.

Let me try to flesh out this view with a couple of cases. Gellner noted that he found it difficult to account for the contemporary nationalist movement in Scotland (1983: 44). Scotland is fully industrialized and shares in a British high culture and language. It had successfully scaled the slopes of modernization in the nineteenth century. According to Gellner's theory the story should be complete and the moderate cultural differences between Scotland and England should not be enough to provoke nationalism. But if we think of uneven development as a continuous and variegated aspect of capitalism, things make more sense. After the First World War, across the twentieth century, Scotland's industrial base suffered decline, as Scottish capital was increasingly invested abroad, and the Scottish economy became the object of a series of remedial economic policies. By the 1960s, when the Scottish National Party was beginning to pick up more support in elections, Scotland was increasingly functioning as a branch-plant economy in which capital investment, usually into new lighter industries such as electronics and chemicals, came from outside the country. At first this tended to supplement the older heavy industries such as ship-building and mining, but by the 1970s and 1980s it was becoming clear that these industries were in deep decline, and that the survival rate of newer industries would be erratic. The joker in the pack was North Sea oil, which appeared in the 1970s to offer the hope of a thriving independent national economy, but it has since become apparent that the financial and technical power to develop this resource lie primarily outside of Scotland, and that a national economy built around a single primary commodity entails serious risks.

This economic story was paralleled by shifts in social and political leadership. Over the twentieth century, with industrial decline and the growth of the modern welfare state, an indigenous combination of industrial and petit bourgeoisies was displaced by a new class of managerial professionals, who increasingly shaped policy and public opinion through key networks and institutions. A broad consensus developed in Scotland, as in much of post-Second World War Europe, around the need for an active role by the state in managing the economy and fostering a social democratic society. A distinctive zone of Scottish civil society, defined by the Scottish Office, local government, trade unions, major businesses, the Scottish legal and educational systems, churches, universities, voluntary organizations, newspapers and other media, helped to articulate this consensus and created a social field that sustained the developing professional and managerial middle class. When the global political economy took its neoliberal turn in the 1970s, leading to calls for the scaling back of the public provisioning and the abandonment of ailing industries by the state, this looked particularly threatening to Scotland's governing classes, whose social leadership was premised on state intervention and ameliorization. The fact that this political economic shift was realized and personified by Margaret Thatcher and a Conservative Party widely seen as English and un-Scottish in Scotland only exacerbated nationalist tensions. It was in this context, through the 1980s and 1990s, that a broad social consensus was built up around the need for a devolved parliament in Scotland to protect the people's national interests and left-of-centre policy preferences.

When one speaks to people in Scotland about these tensions between Scotland and England, one frequently encounters a very important quali-fication – that it is not really England as a whole that is the problem, but rather London and the Home Counties, in other words the core of the British economy with its considerable political and cultural hegemony. While neoliberalism has been inhospitable to old industrial interests in the developed West, it has given advanced financial and commercial interests, and the numerous service industries that revolve around them, a major shot in the arm. The City of London is one of the global centres of such activity. Indeed during the 1980s and 1990s it became common in Britain to speak of the North–South divide that marked off this more prosperous south-eastern core from the rest of the struggling UK econ-omy. Thus the national tensions over social policy and self-determination between Scotland and England were stimulated by and mapped onto, however imprecisely, this historically specific form of uneven develop-ment within the UK (see Hearn 2000, 2002).

The other case I want to consider is that of contemporary Islamism in the Arab world. This term is generally used to designate a political philos-ophy that argues that modern states should be governed according to Islamic principles (*shari'a*) and the social movements associated with this philosophy. The goals of such movements are at once reformist, seeking to restore an earlier and truer Islamic way of life from corrupted traditions, while also seeking to harmonize Islam with many aspects of modernity, such as scientific and technological advances. There have been distinct episodes of such reformism in the Islamic Middle East in the pre-colonial, colonial and post-colonial periods. The majority of contem-porary Islamists follow a *da'wa* approach that seeks to reform society from the bottom up by calling fellow Muslims to follow a purer Islamic way of life. However, an extremist minority of Islamists follow a *jihadi* path that advocates a militant approach to social change by attacking the institutions and personnel of wayward Islamic states and Western powers. In recent years civilians have come to be seen as legitimate targets by some, most notably the Al Qaeda network of organizations under the influence of a *fatwa* issued by Osama bin Laden in 1998. Having said all this, the vast majority of mainstream Muslims, while sharing a critical attitude toward the US, the West and their own govern-ments, disapprove of such violence and are more moderate and tradi-tional in their religious beliefs (Fekry and Nimis 2004: xii–xvi).

Islamism is a response to the conditions of colonialism and Western – today more specifically American – hegemony in the region. It offers a critique of Western values and culture, of foreign political and economic domination, and of states in the region that are seen as co-opted by and subservient to Western powers, and insufficiently governed by *shari'a*. The substantial US military presence in Saudi Arabia, the plight of displaced and subjugated Palestinian people and the perception of Israel as an insertion of US power into the region have been major factors stimulating resentment towards the US and the West. Thus, this religious movement and its goals take hold in a context of lack of control over the politics and economics of the region, and while its goals are ultimately transnational, the specific conflicts to which it responds are often framed by nationalism (cf. Ram 2000; Zubaida 2004).

Contrary to some stereotypes, leading Islamists and their followers tend to come from elite and aspiring, urbanized middle classes, with highly educated professionals often playing a leading role. The two key figures of Al Qaeda, Dr Ayman al-Zawahiri and Osama bin Laden come from aristocratic families. According to the *Encyclopedia of the Orient*:

> Islamism is a phenomenon primarily taking place in cities, and the most prominent members are young people with higher education, often with a modest background and often with parents living in the countryside. Islamists have often a feeling that despite the efforts they have put down in their studies, they have not managed to climb very much socially, that the jobs they were aspiring for are given to people with good social connections, but less qualifications. (Kjeilen 2004)

Thus, here again we encounter the phenomenon of a developing middling class, somewhat caught between different worlds, upwardly mobile but frustrated, and seeking to orient and empower themselves through ideological commitment (Reuter 2002: 10).

Islamism is clearly not the same thing as nationalism, but it articulates with and is pursued through the existing world of nation-states. It is a transnational ideology of religious and social reform that, like nationalism, in practice links issues of social identity and self-government with specific territories. The unevenness it responds to has multiple interdependent dimensions, including economic development in relation to the West, but also the concentration of power in small elites and the state, external geopolitical pressures on the region and the powerful influences of American consumer culture on local ways of life.

Through these two examples I have tried to illustrate the enduring importance of unevenness, and the diversity of its manifestation. Rather than thinking narrowly in terms of the uneven spread of industrialization, we need to think broadly in terms of the uneven distribution of power, although restless capitalism continues to be a central force among others in producing maldistributions of power. This dynamic elicits many responses, only some of which are nationally framed. In the case of Scotland a historic nation embedded within the British state became mobilized around the cause of greater governmental autonomy when faced by an erosion of established local power around the structures of the welfare state. In the case of Islamism, pervasive regional disempowerment of the mass of the population by regional elites, in conjunction with external political and economic forces, has led to a religious reform movement seeking to form a popular base for claiming control over the governments of the region.

Conclusion

I am broadly sympathetic to the modernist approach. While it is interesting to ask where, how and why modern nationalism has been prefigured in earlier times, the material change in our capacities for production, consumption, communication, administration and violence over the last few hundred years has been profound. These heightened capacities must be understood as constituting modern nationalism, even if they have wrought changes on pre-existing ethnicities and polities. As we have seen, the modernist approach poses the question of origins, of pristine and secondary forms of nationalism, a question that has been answered in a variety of ways, more complex than simply holding up Europe as the source of nationalism.

But while favouring the modernist approach, I have also tried to argue that the very idea of modernity is burdened, if often implicitly, by theoretical paradigms which imagine history in the form of distinct sequential stages, each with its own relatively stable and defining characteristics. Far from stability, it is instability in the form of a series of accelerating directional trends, driven especially by capitalism, that characterize modernity. Because of this we need to rethink the concept of uneven development, recognizing it as a more general and ongoing aspect of life under capitalism, rather than as a threshold to a stable modern state.

Further Reading

Smith's article (1988) provides a particularly strong statement of his critique of modernism, an argument rebutted by Zubaida (1989). For a book-length appraisal of modernism by Smith see *Nationalism and Modernism* (1998). Llobera (1994), while broadly modernist, argues for a more long-term view of the European roots of nationalism. Chatterjee (1993) and Parekh (1995) are influential critiques of the Eurocentricity of modernist theories of nationalism. Hall (1998) provides a crucial collection of largely sympathetic critiques of Gellner's grand theory. Particularly valuable in this collection are the chapters by Nicos Mouzelis, Tom Nairn, Brendan O'Leary and Roman Szporluk.

6
Power

It is often argued that nationalism is, in essence, about the pursuit of power (e.g. Breuilly 1993: 1). We turn now to consider approaches to the study of nationalism that have prioritized power relations, some focusing more on the role of the state and nationalism in the creation and pursuit of power, others looking more at the role of elites in popular mobilization. These approaches substantially overlap, of course, but our discussion will move from an emphasis on the former to the latter. We conclude by considering more closely two power-saturated topics deeply intertwined with the study of nationalism: war and class.

There is an affinity between a focus on power and modernist approaches, and most of the theorists considered in this chapter would probably be regarded as modernists. The reason for this might seem obvious, given the considerable powers of the modern state compared to its predecessors. But if one accepts the premise that there have been nations before the modern era, there is no reason why these should not equally be regarded as manifestations of power relations. The fact that the overall systemic power available was less in premodern times does not indicate that power was not a key explanatory variable. However, as we will see, there is a corresponding affinity between what we have loosely labelled primordialism and an emphasis on culture as an explanatory variable. Why the use of the concepts of power and culture should be parcelled out in this way is not as obvious as it may first appear, and the rest of this book seeks to problematize this division of theoretical labour. Power and culture should be twin tools in the analysis of nationalism, not alternative approaches.

Nationalism and the State

In his study of the development of the modern state, Gianfranco Poggi sets up his definition of the state by juxtaposing two theories of 'the business of rule' (1978: ch. 1; cf. Smith 1981: 76–7). The one approach, as formulated by David Easton, treats politics as 'allocation by command', that is, the state is that entity which makes ultimate and binding decisions about how social goods will be distributed (although many distributions are left in practice to custom or market exchange). The other approach, advocated by Carl Schmitt, sees politics as a matter of distinguishing between friend and foe, between 'us' and 'the other' . Whereas Easton's notion of politics implies a stable rule of law for assigning values among citizens, Schmitt's is concerned with the struggles and alliances between states, in a realm of geopolitics fundamentally understood as lawless and unpredictable.

Poggi suggests that we have to borrow from both these formulations to come up with a viable model of the modern state. We might adapt Tom Nairn's characterization of nationalism as 'the modern Janus', which must look into its past to see its future, to note that the state also is Janus-faced, looking both inward to cultivate authority and legitimacy among its members, and outward to jealously guard its interests in an arena of competing states. When trying to think through the relationship between the state and nationalism it is good to keep this fundamental duality always in mind. Poggi also suggests that whereas Schmitt takes for granted the existence of a coherent 'us' to be defended, Easton takes for granted the existence of shared values to be allocated. What both neglect is the process by which common values, and a sense of 'us', are forged in the first place. This too is a fundamental point in understanding the artic-ulations of nations and states.

In a similar vein Michael Mann has identified two schools of theory, developed in the nineteenth and early twentieth centuries, which sought to understand the state in world history. One prioritized economic devel-opment and convergence, either towards universal liberalism or universal communism, with the state expected to shrink or fade away altogether. This school, in its liberal and marxist varieties, was associated with Anglo-French social theory. The other school, associated with German and, for a period, American social thought, prioritized militarism and the pursuit of power among nations, imagined as evolutionary units in a social Darwinian struggle for territorial expansion and supremacy. Neither approach is adequate, but Mann's main point is that the dominant legacy of liberal and marxist theory misleadingly assumes universal patterns of class formation and economic integration, and needs to be tempered by an appreciation of the ways actual class formation is condi-tioned by states and geopolitics (1988: 147–9).

Mann argues that to understand the relationship between states and their nationalized populations, we need to conceptualize three interacting ideal types of class structure:

● *Transnational* – where classes such as capitalists and workers create alliances across state boundaries.

● *International* – where, within the hierarchy of the world's political economy, nation-states act as classes towards one another, engaging in exploitative, clientelistic and oppositional relationships.

● *National* – where class organization and conflict becomes 'caged' within state boundaries, detached from and incompetent in regard to a larger world of geopolitics (1988: 149–50).

According to Mann, liberals and marxists expected *transnational* classes to form and dominate state processes. The militarist school imagined nations more as unified classes engaged in *international* conflicts. But it is the third version, not really grasped by either school, which carries the greatest explanatory weight. Because, in fact, the world we have found ourselves in is one where only small elite classes ever achieve anything like a true transnational status, the vast majority of middle and working classes becoming *nationalist* in orientation. Mann summarizes what happened, and the situation we still largely find ourselves in:

> in the first half of the twentieth century the middle and working classes became national citizens, and were prepared to fight and toil to defend the symbols of their citizenship – monarch, flag, homeland and kith and kin. As modern classes emerged they became predominantly *nationally* organized. As class struggles were regulated and institutionalized, nations emerged and classes developed a certain loyalty to the nation. But, contrary to militarist theory, this was not anchored in international praxis. Nations were not interested or competent in geo-politics. People were still plunged into wars through the private machinations of state elites. (1988: 158, emphasis in original)

Another useful conceptual distinction that Mann employs is between the 'despotic' and 'infrastructural' powers of territorial states. Despotic power refers to the state elite's ability to realize its objectives 'without routine, institutionalized negotiations with civil society groups' (1988: 5). Infrastructural power is 'the capacity of the state to actually penetrate civil society, and to implement logistically political decisions throughout the realm' (1988: 5). The modern state is distinguished by the growth of its infrastructural powers – its ability to pervasively coordinate daily life within its territory through bureaucratic administration, common literacy and mass communication, standardized units of value (e.g. coinage, weights and measures) and market exchange, extensive and integrated systems of transportation and so on. Premodern state forms were generally infrastructurally weak, although they ranged from fractious feudal systems with low levels of despotic power to imperial systems much more able to episodically impose the sovereign's will from the centre. The infrastructural power of modern states on the other hand may work either in service of despotically weak capitalist democracies or despotically strong authoritarian regimes (e.g. Nazi Germany or the Soviet Union). Thus the modern state's capacity to foster national identities rests on these infrastructural powers, but how it does this depends in part on whether power is strongly centralized in the state, or more widely distributed among classes and groups in civil society. These are, of course, ideal types, but they give us some handle on the variegated nature of state power and how it shapes nations.

John Breuilly (1993) has also stressed the relationship between nationalism and the state, developing an elaborate typology for the comparative study of nationalisms. He defines nationalism as an oppositional political movement, justified by nationalist ideology, seeking state power (1993: 9). The form nationalisms take depends on the nature of their goals and the states to which they are opposed. The first (i.e. 'pristine') nationalisms, what Breuilly characterizes as 'preludes' to nationalism proper, developed in opposition to expanding bureaucratic states in England and France. In England a proto-national identity evolved around Protestant ideology and the need for the monarchy to make power compromises with an expanding aristocracy and middle class. In France a revolutionary ideology of citizenship and natural rights was mobilized from below as the state was unable to reform its piecemeal relations with a series of local and provincial powers in the face of an agrarian crisis. Thus, both these proto-nationalisms took the form of internal movements of reform and revolution against a pre-national form of state.

Beyond these more unique early cases, Breuilly classifies nationalisms in regard to two criteria: (1) whether they were opposed to 'non-nation-states' (e.g. modernizing absolutist states and decaying imperial empires) or nation-states proper, and (2) whether their goals aimed at territorial *separation* from the state, institutional and political *reform* of the state, or political and territorial *unification* of a series of separate states. Thus, Breuilly regards the formation of the independent state of Nigeria in 1960 out the former British colony of the same name as a case of separation from a non-nation-state, in that Nigeria was never a part of the British state proper, but rather a colony of an imperial power. The subsequent abortive attempt by the Igbo population of south-east Nigeria to set up an independent Republic of Biafra (1967–70), in response to inter-ethnic violence, would be an example of separation from a nation-state, however newly formed and politically unstable. In Japan's Meiji Restoration (1866–9) an alliance of elites seeking to modernize Japan to secure its political and economic independence from the West toppled the feudal Tokugawa Shogunate, restoring Shinto religion and the emperor in a figurehead role, while also pushing through radical reforms of government on the Western nation-state model. This is a case of a reform movement opposed to a non-nation-state, that is, the former feudal system. By contrast, the fascisms of inter-war Europe, especially in Germany and Italy, represent for Breuilly the rather rare species of reform nationalism opposed to a pre-existing nation-state (1993: 289). While other ideologies (liberalism, conservatism, socialism) mobilize nationalist ideas some of the time, the fascist ideology is peculiarly wedded to the idea of the nation-state. Finally, Breuilly also distinguishes between unification movements such as the Italian *Risorgimento* (c. 1815–71), which sought to assemble a modern nation-state out of the patchwork of principalities and city-states of the Italian peninsula, and Pan-African and Arab nationalisms that have sought, however unsuccessfully, greater political unity among peoples distributed across various post-colonial nation-states.

Within this broad typology of movements, nationalist ideology can serve three different but not mutually exclusive functions. (1) It can *coordinate* the agendas of competing elites, creating a focus around which they can rally and set aside their differences. (2) It can *mobilize* the masses around the national cause. (3) It can *legitimate* the national project in the eyes of outside powers (e.g. Greek nationalists courting British, French and Russian support in their goals to separate from the Ottoman Empire in the 1820s). In contrast to Mann's emphasis on how the infrastructural powers of the state aid the cultivation of national identities and frame middle- and working-class identities in national terms, Breuilly's approach focuses more on nationalist movements and how they are conditioned by the state 'environments' which they mobilize against.

Concerned particularly with understanding the tangled history of Central and Eastern Europe and its new nationalisms in the post-Soviet era, Rogers Brubaker devises a conceptual model for thinking about the dynamics of nationalism within a broader 'political field'. He views nationalist situations as occurring within a 'triadic nexus' of nationalisms,

---

Box 6.1 Secession in Chechnya

There is a long history of conflicts between powers in Chechnya and in Russia/USSR. Largely converted to Islam in the seventeenth and eighteenth centuries, Chechens participated in regional struggles against Russian domination (1834–59), but were incorporated into its empire in 1859. There were regional uprisings against Russia again in the Russo-Turkish War (1877–8) and against the Soviet Union in 1918–20. Chechnya and neighbouring Ingushetia to the west were made an autonomous republic within the Soviet Union in 1936. In 1944, under Stalin, around 500,000 Chechens and Ingush were exiled to Kazakhstan, accused of collaborating with the Nazis. Probably a third of these died, first *en route*, and then under the harsh living conditions where they arrived. The survivors were allowed to return to Chechnya in 1957 under Krushchev.

The political status of Chechnya is currently disputed. Independence from Russia was declared in 1991 by the National Congress led by Dzhokhar Dudaev, but this was not recognized by the Russian Federation or any other state, and in 1992 Ingushetia separated and rejoined the Russian Federation. Although Dudaev was subsequently elected president, the freeness and fairness of elections in Chechnya are generally in question. After an abortive attempt by the Russian military to retake power, Chechnya became increasingly anarchic as rival warlords and mafias vied for power. In 1994 an ill-conceived war with little popular support in Russia was launched by President Boris Yeltsin, which fought the rebel forces to a stalemate, ending in 1996 with a peace agreement and a postponement of resolution of the secession issue. New elections put the more moderate Aslan Maskhadov in the presidency but also brought more radical and strongly separatist Islamists into the government. This marked the development of more moderate and radical wings to the separatist movement. As life in Chechnya again slid into anarchy, Islamist separatists abandoned the government and led a failed raid into neighbouring

→

---

each of which is also understood as a political field of relations (1996: 4–7). Thus, he defines:

- The *nationalizing nationalisms* of new or reconfigured states in which a core ethnocultural nation, previously marginalized, seeks to use state power to consolidate its 'ownership' of the state.
- *Homeland nationalisms*, in which an ethnocultural nation dominant in one state seeks to protect and support the interests of its co-nationals who are a marginalized minority within another (usually neighbouring) state.

→
Dagestan which, followed by a series of terrorist bombings in Russia, triggered the 'second Chechen war' (1999–2002) under Vladimir Putin. In the context of Chechen terrorism in Russia, this war had greater popular support. It was declared over in 2002 but, in fact, occupying and strong-armed Russian forces support a pro-Russian administration, while separatists based in the mountainous southern regions continue to wage a guerrilla war. In 2003 a referendum won substantial support for a new constitutional settlement in which Chechnya has 'wide autonomy' but as part of the Russian Federation. But the brutality of the Russian Military and the Chechen terrorists has also hardened attitudes on either side of the struggle. A new Russian-backed president, Akhmd Kadyrov, was elected that year but killed by a terrorist bomb in 2004.

Chechnya is of strategic and economic importance, as a site of oil production and shipment pipelines, and of key trade routes more generally. Awareness of these strengths no doubt fed into separatist ambitions and Russian claims. The population is far from homogeneous and politically unified. Much of the indigenous power in Chechnya is brokered through the system of clans (*tiepy*), which sometimes articulate with networks of organized crime, and can undercut attempts to create broader national allegiances on the basis of Islamic religion. About a quarter of the population, concentrated in the capital of Grozny, is Russian, and has been more opposed to secession. About two thirds of the population is rurally based, and the country has one of the youngest age profiles in the Russian Federation. Thus, there is a range of competing power bases – clans, religious organizations, ethnicity, urban/rural differences – shaping political unrest and making claims on Chechen identity. In line with norms of international law, Western states have refused to recognize Chechen assertions of independence, while also being critical of Russia's indiscriminate use of military force. Since the 11 September terrorist attacks on the US in 2001, the conflict in Chechnya has been increasingly cast by Moscow as part of an international war on terror, deserving international support (see Bowker 2004).

● *Minority nationalisms*, in which marginalized groups demand state recognition and certain cultural and political rights on the basis of their nationhood.

Typically, national minority movements seek support from and are laid claim to by homeland nationalisms, both of which are in conflict with the nationalizing core nation of the state in which the minority finds itself. To some degree we can see Brubaker's triadic nexus as reformulating well-established terminology for analysing types of nationalism – nation-building, irredentism, seccesionism and so on. But his point is more critical than that. He wants to suggest that we should avoid thinking of this as simply an array of conflict among unproblematically defined national groups. Instead, such groups should be understood as constituted through this very field of political conflicts:

In a context of rampant ethnonationalism, the temptation to adopt a nation-centred perspective is understandable. But the temptation should be resisted. Nationalism is not engendered by nations. It is produced – or better, it is induced – by *political fields* of particular

---

Box 6.2   Yugoslavia – from Construction to Collapse

Dusko Sekulic has posed the question: 'Why was Yugoslavia created and why did it disappear from the map of the world?' (1997: 165). He suggests that conventional explanations, that it was doomed because 'artificially' made by external powers at Versailles following the First World War, and bound to collapse after the death of the dictator Tito in 1980, do not adequately reveal the shifting internal and external balances of geopolitical power at work. Sekulic's explanation stresses 'the importance of the external success of the state for its internal legitimacy' (1997: 167). He traces the rise and fall of Yugoslavia across the twentieth century in light of this assumption.

A brief overview: Formed in 1918, the Kingdom of Serbs, Croats and Slovenes (renamed Yugoslavia in 1929) was dominated by Serbia. It fragmented under Nazi occupation in the Second World War, and was reformed as the Federal People's Republic of Yugoslavia under the leadership of Marshal Tito, whose National Liberation Army had expelled the Axis powers with the aid of the Red Army. Renamed the Socialist Federal Republic of Yugoslavia in 1963, the 'second' Yugoslavia included six constituent republics: Bosnia-Herzegovina, Croatia, Macedonia, Montenegro, Serbia and Slovenia; and two autonomous provinces: Vojvodina and Kosovo. In 1974 a new constitution, responding to political unrest in Croatia in 1970–1, increased the autonomy of republics and provinces. With the 'fall of communism' in 1990, Serbian president Slobodan Milosevic sought to reverse the devolution of power in the 1974 constitution, but soon Slovenia, Croatia (1991), Macedonia and Bosnia-Herzegovina (1992) declared independence. Refusing to accept that the Serbs in these countries (particularly Croatia and Bosnia-Herzegovina) be politically separated from Serbia, Milosevic launched an unsuccessful war to prevent these secessions, finally brought to an end in 1995 by US-sponsored peace talks. The renamed Federal Republic of Yugoslavia now consisted of just Serbia and Montenegro. From 1996 military actions by

→

kinds. Its dynamics are governed by the properties of political fields, not by the properties of collectivities. (1996: 17, emphasis in original)

In Brubaker's model, it is states, not nations, which are the strong forces driving the process. For him nations are institutionalized forms of social practice that take shape in highly contingent ways, more outcomes than agents in the political process. In his treatment of the successor states to the collapsed Soviet Union he emphasizes the ways that minority nationalities in the USSR were codified and reinforced by state policies

---

→

the Kosovo Liberation Army in Serbia's southern province led to violent expulsions of ethnic Albanians in Kosovo by the Yugoslav army, a process ultimately halted by two months of NATO bombing of Serbia and Montenegro, in 1999. Since then Kosovo has been governed by the UN Interim Administration Mission in Kosovo, pending resolution of its future status.

Sekulic puts this chronology into a geopolitical frame. Serbia rose in regional power in the nineteenth century as a result of its successes in winning independence from the Ottoman Empire; as that multi-ethnic Empire fragmented, the expansionist, ethnically defined Serbian state grew in power and status. Aligning with the winning side in the First World War further enhanced its position. By contrast, Croatia, Slovenia and Bosnia-Herzegovina were parts of the decaying Austro-Hungarian Empire, sharing in its defeat in that war. From this weak position, threatened with absorption into Austria and Italy after the war, an alliance of southern Slavs looked attractive. The resulting Serbian-dominated Kingdom, and subsequent incarnations of Yugoslavia, housed two competing visions, one of a greater Serbian nation inclined to centralize power in Belgrade, the other of a federal alliance of Slavic nations. The relative stability of the Tito years (1945–80) was not just a result of his authoritarian state, but also of his ability to situate Yugoslavia geopolitically between the Cold War powers of the USSR and the US, making Yugoslavia relatively prosperous and independent in relation to the USSR, thus enhancing its legitimacy for Yugoslavs. It was not so much Tito's death, as the later collapse of the USSR, and the changed environment of Europe, that destabilized the Yugoslav balance of power. Now that Western European states no longer had territorial pretensions, and were clearly stable and prosperous, leaving Yugoslavia and aligning with Europe made sense for those in the western parts of Yugoslavia. In this new context it was Serbian power and status and the vision of a greater Serbia submerged in the Yugoslavian state, that was declining, and prone to extreme measures to reassert itself.

which treated national minorities as relevant statistical and legal categories, and reinforced national languages, intelligentsias and elites as part
of a strategy of governance (see also Slezkine 1996; Verdery 1996).
Thus, the infrastructural power of the state, as Mann would put it,
fostered, preserved and strengthened an array of nationalities under the
framework of the Soviet Union.

Brubaker's injunctions to shift our focus from 'nations as actors' to the
'fields of power' within which they interact should also remind us to question the homogeneous category of the nation-state. It has often been pointed
out that very few cases even approximate the ideal model of 'one nation/one
state' but, more than this, states vary radically in size, power and influence,
and these differences condition the development of nationalisms both within
and between states. Is the nationalism we perceive in a major economic and
military power such as the US really comparable to that found in the much
weaker and more sharply stratified states of Latin America? How do we
compare the economically focused nationalism of a micro-state such as
Singapore to that of an industrializing behemoth like China? It is not just that
nations take shape within the framework of states, but those states are highly
varied in their size and power, and are situated in a complex inter-state
system of conflicts, interdependencies, alliances, clientelistic relations and
such. These vast differences in geopolitical power can skew our perception,
as during the height of the Cold War when the nationalist dimension of various anti-colonial struggles was often downplayed by Western scholars who
viewed events within the frame of an ideological struggle between
American capitalist liberalism and Soviet communism. If we accept Mann's
thesis that infrastructural power is a key instrument of nation-building, then
this implies a gradation from sub-Saharan states such as Somalia or the
Congo, where infrastructural power is very weak (though forms of ethnic
social organization may be very strong), through intermediate cases, such as
most states of Latin America, on up to the dominant states of the North
today, where infrastructural power is highly developed (Mann 2002: 2–3).
By this criterion the conventional image of a world full of theoretically
autonomous and comparable (let alone culturally homogeneous) nation-
states, is rendered deeply problematic.

This brings us back to the inner and outer faces of the state identified
by Poggi. Though each state must face in both directions, there develops
a global division of labour, whereby hard geopolitics, the defining of
'friends and foes', is managed and led by the major powers, with minor
states aligning themselves according to their circumstances, while being
ultimately more concerned with the cultivation of nationhood through the
'allocation of values' on the inner slope of the state. With any given case

of nationalism there are basic questions to be asked about the degree to which it is oriented to one, or the other, or both of these faces. Does it primarily seek control over the allocation of values within its territory? Does it aim to expand its territory and resources? Does it aim to cultivate domestic support by vanquishing external (or internal) enemies? These are very different purposes, entailing very different kinds of nationalism.

Elites and Popular Mobilization

Many approaches have paid particular attention to the process by which social and political leaders, elites, foster a popular following for their national cause. Before considering some examples, we should remind ourselves that the term 'elites' is relative, covering a wide array of social positions, from those with predominant influence over the state and its economy, to those with leadership roles within certain institutions (e.g. religious), areas of practice (e.g. the arts), or populations (e.g. ethnic groups), or more often some complex combination of these. Thus the elites of nationalist movements, especially separatist ones, are often in subordinate, 'non-elite' roles in relation to the larger socio-political structures they find themselves in.

A recurring theme in the study of nationalism is the idea that changes in governmental structures initiate crises and opportunities for certain elite or proto-elite groups. Using a 'rational choice' framework for his analysis, Michael Hechter (2000) argues that elite groups pursue their structurally determined interests through the mobilization of larger collective identities. In the case of nationalisms those larger identities are defined in cultural terms, and frequently reinforced when the cultural groups tend to occupy a distinctive niche in the economy – that is, when there is what Hechter calls a 'cultural division of labour' (2000: ch. 6). He suggests that it is not necessarily control over the state which is the key object of nationalist struggle, but rather the somewhat looser entity he calls 'the governance unit': '*that territorial unit that is responsible for providing the bulk of social order and other collective goods – including protection from confiscation, justice and welfare to its members*' (2000: 9, italics in original). States are governance units, but not all governance units are states. For much of human history, states have rested on top of a plethora of such governance units (e.g. the *millet* system of the Ottoman Empire), governing indirectly through them. But with the rise of the modern centralized bureaucratic state from the late eighteenth century there has been a trend to dismantling them and replacing them with forms of much more direct rule from the centre. For Hechter it is this shift that has provided the initial and continuing stimulus to nationalism in the modern era. Thus, he suggests that local elites associated with cultural groups and their governance units will, if possible, tend to mobilize people on the basis of national identity when their power is threatened by a strengthening central state, or will seize opportunities to increase their power if the central state is in decline (2000: 30).

Anthony Smith's early work placed considerable emphasis on the role of elites (1981: ch. 6), although in recent years he has come to see this as misplaced (1998: 190). For Smith the general ideological context for elite mobilization of nationality is a crisis of legitimacy engendered by the rise of the 'scientific state', driven forward by inter-state competition, which legitimates its rule over society in rational-legal terms and increasingly governs by bureaucratic means. This challenges traditional modes of authority, usually based on religion, and also generates new, expanding generations of 'intelligentsia' by which he means 'all who possess some form of further or higher education and use their educational diplomas to gain a livelihood through vocational activity' (1981: 108). In short, they are professionals committed to principles of expertise, rationality and meritocracy, pursuing advancement through the expanding institutions of the modern state and society.

Smith suggests that members of this developing strata of society frequently found themselves frustrated and then radicalized by three factors: (1) overproduction of their own kind, leading to periodic surpluses of professionals unable to validate their status by appropriate employment; (2) resistance from an older generation of bureaucrats whose position was based not on education, but on an identification with the authority of the state and its rulers; and crucially (3) more-or-less overt discrimination against the new intelligentsia on the basis of cultural difference. Faced by these 'blockages', and inspired by the ethnic revivalism of key intellectuals, the intelligentsia were especially prone to realign their identities with the ethnic communities from which they came and their histories. Creating alliances with other social groups as circumstances permitted – entrepreneurs, lower clergy, workers, peasants – the intelligentsia sought to solve its problems of advancement by cultivating nationalist movements that would create amenable states, or at least 'governance units'. Both Smith and Hechter allow that the personal material interests that motivate members of these interstitial strata come mixed with value orientations in which the nation is a higher good. In different ways they both conceptualize the dynamic of nationalist mobilization in terms of the power problematic of insecure, intermediate elites or potential elites, moved to assimilate their specific structural frustrations to those of a wider ethnic community. While they see this dynamic as originating with the rise of the modern 'scientific' state, it is a characteristic pattern that is repeated, with variations of course, in later national movements such as the post-Second World War anti-colonial nationalisms of the developing world and the neonationalisms of the Western democracies.

Miroslav Hroch has paid special attention to the dynamics of early nationalist movements in the smaller nations of Central and Eastern Europe in the nineteenth century (2000) and made comparisons with recent post-Soviet nationalisms in that region (1996). In a fairly standard fashion, he maintains that nationalist movements require certain basic conditions: some cultural and historical antecedents, such as a linguistic tradition and institutional remnants of earlier periods of greater political autonomy; the stimulus of new levels of social mobility and communication; and a specific context of political conflict and crisis. Hroch is especially known for formulating a three-phase model of the development of nationalist movements.

- *Phase A* is a period of scholarly enquiry and cultural revival led by intellectuals and artists, the 'intelligentsia'.
- In *Phase B* the movement broadens out into a range of activists with a more clearly defined political project of national agitation.
- In *Phase C* a mass movement develops encompassing the full social and class structure of the national group.

According to Hroch, there is no one class or social group that constitutes the basis of a nationalist movement, but he does emphasize the leading role of the intelligentsia in getting the process started, and of more educated professionals in broadening the movement in its later phases. Part of the significance of this point is that the movements he is concerned with generally arose in agrarian contexts before industrialization (*pace* Gellner), and thus industrial class relations *per se* cannot be used to analyse the process of mobilization. More important for him than industrialization is the transition from absolutist to constitutional regimes in this period. His model of phases needs to be viewed against the backdrop of that transition. In some cases the transition from *Phase B* to *Phase C* was combined with the upheavals of constitutional reform and a growing labour movement. This was the case in the national agitations of the Czechs and the Magyars around the revolutions of 1848. In some cases the transition to *Phase C* was delayed until after the transition to a constitutional regime, held in check either by low levels of economic development (Lithuania, Latvia, Slovenia, Croatia) or political oppression, such as the Magyarization of Slovakia after 1867, or the Russification of the Ukraine. Some movements, particularly those of Serbia, Greece and Bulgaria under the Ottoman Empire, entered into *Phase B* under the old regime, producing patterns of armed insurrection. Finally, there are those cases associated with a more developed, capitalist Western Europe, where movements developed entirely under constitutional conditions. Patterns of development are particularly variable in this type, but there is a tendency here according to Hroch for movements to develop more slowly perhaps never reaching *Phase C*, which he suggests is the case for Scotland, Wales and Brittany. The general image suggested by Hroch's model of movement phases and regime transitions is one in which the building pressure of expanding social mobilization comes up against and responds to the resistance of the archaic regime, or capitalizes on the indeterminacy of political and social upheaval. By the same token, constitutional regimes are more effective at dissipating opposition, accommodating movements and cultivating legitimacy. They can absorb the pressures of nationalist agitation more effectively.

Hechter, Smith and Hroch offer analyses that tend to treat elites as a key structural component in a larger social dynamic. Others, however, such as Paul Brass and Jack Snyder, have focused more specifically on the agency and tactics of elites in the instrumental pursuit of their ends. Elites play a darker and more malevolent role in their accounts. As we saw in Chapter 3, Brass (1991) places great emphasis on the role of elite competition in the production and reproduction of ethnicity and national-ism through the manipulation of symbolism. Certain conditions, of course, have to obtain for elites to engage in the political manipulation of ethnic symbols – there must be some raw ethnic materials to work with, and means of generalized mass communication across class divisions. Given these conditions, ethnic and national identities are likely to be intensified by intra-ethnic competition between elite groups to control local societies, by inter-ethnic competition between elites to control new economic and political opportunities afforded by modernization, or by a combination of both. The presence of institutional infrastructures through which and in regard to which elites can operate, whether pre-existing or in formation, is also crucial:

> In early modernising societies, a high degree of communal mobilisa-tion will be achieved most easily in two types of situations: (*a*) where there is a local religious elite in command of temples, shrines, or churches and the lands and trusts attached to them and a network of religious schools; or (*b*) where the local language has been recognised

by the state authorities as *both* a legitimate medium of education and administration, thereby providing the native intelligentsia with both material and cultural rewards to offer to new social groups aspiring to education and new opportunities. (1991: 64)

These infrastructures help explain why, and in which cases, religion and language are so often salient categories for ethnic identities. Brass also highlights characteristic sets of tensions between competing elites, particularly between (1) alien conquerors, (2) native aristocracies (landlords) and (3) religious elites. Thus, an indigenous landholding elite, if they have not been co-opted or replaced, may try to mobilize peasants and oppose an alien conquering elite. Indigenous religious elites may oppose another religion imposed or favoured by alien conquerors, leading to inter-ethnic conflict between religious elites within a given region. The native aristocracy may collaborate, orienting itself religiously and/or culturally to the alien conquerors, leading to conflicts between it and indigenous religious elites, seen as the true representatives of the people. Finally, indigenous religious elites, fortified by extensive religious organizations, may oppose alien aristocracies *in situ*, when they have also become the local landed class, displacing the native aristocracy. Each actual case is more complex than these abstract scenarios suggest, but they give a sense of some of the major cleavages that have frequently precipitated ethnic and nationalist mobilization. Brass's main point, however, is that it is these kinds of intra-elite conflicts that set in motion the processes by which ethnic and national identities become sharpened, and certain key symbols move to the fore-ground, becoming shibboleths of national identity.

In his book *From Voting to Violence* (2000) Jack Snyder seeks to counter the view that nationalism only occurs where democracy is absent, and to show why the new post-1989 wave of transitions to democracy, like earlier democratic transitions, have been particularly prone to take the form of exclusivist nationalism. He dismisses the view that the collapse of Soviet state structures has unleashed deep ethnic rivalries, arguing instead that the early phases of democratization provide an ideological environment particularly favourable for the cultivation of national identities, and susceptible to abuse by unscrupulous elites. He begins by highlighting the fact that *democracy* – rule by the people, is often elided in practice with *nationalism* – rule in the name of the people: 'This ambiguity between rule by the people and rule in the name of a people constitutes one of the main attractions of nationalist doctrine to elites who seek to rule undemocratically in an era of rising demands for a mass role in politics' (2000: 24).

Box 6.3 Ethnic Outbidding in Sri Lanka

Sri Lanka (Ceylon before 1972) provides a case study of the dangers of majoritarian politics. The Sinhalese, predominantly Theraveda Buddhists, constitute the majority population (around 75 per cent), while the Tamils, predominantly Hindu and concentrated in the northern and eastern provinces, constitute the largest minority (around 18 per cent). These groups coexisted relatively peacefully on the island for over a thousand years. The island became a British crown colony in 1802, achieving independence in 1948. Under British rule from the mid-nineteenth century greater numbers of Tamils were brought to Ceylon from southern India to be plantation workers. The British tended to favour the minority Tamils, who by 1948 were disproportionately represented in the civil and judicial services, and as university students.

    Despite early agreements by ethnic political leaders to see both the Sinhala and Tamil languages officially recognized in the new country, in 1956 the Sinhalese-dominated government made Sinhala the one official language of Ceylon, appealing to popular resentments and with strong support from Buddhist clergy and Sinhalese nationalist organizations. Non-violent protests and anti-Tamil riots in which at least 150 Tamils were killed (DeVotta 2005: 149) soon followed. Subsequent agreements (in 1957 and 1965) between ethnic political parties on either side to moderate communal tensions by introducing a degree of language recognition and administrative devolution in the Tamil-dominated provinces, were undermined by Sinhalese opposition parties raising fears of the political fragmentation of Sri Lanka. During the 1960s and 1970s Tamils became used to an abusive and oppressive military presence in the north, as new legislation continued to favour Buddhism and the Sinhalese. In 1978 a new constitution was established which made Tamil a national language, and introduced a new electoral system designed to increase Tamil representation, but also to secure a permanent majority for the party then in power. Tamil demands for autonomy were not addressed. In 1983 Tamil rebels ambushed and killed thirteen soldiers, provoking anti-Tamil

→

The context in which elites are most able to abuse this distinction is in the early, incomplete phases of democratization. Mature democracies are characterized by free, fair, and regular elections, constitutional guarantees of citizenship rights and constraints on the actions of state officials, freedom of speech and association and, very crucially for Snyder, a professionalized media that widely represents diverse views in society (2000: 26). These institutional features are also bolstered by long habit, custom and convention in mature democracies, making their value part of a widespread common sense. In the early stages of

→

riots in which up to 2,000 Tamils may have been killed, and thousands of businesses and houses were burned (DeVotta 2005:153). Subsequent events escalated into a full civil war that persisted until the current cease-fire and peace process, mediated by Norway, beginning in 2001.

The Liberation Tigers of Tamil Eelam (LTTE), founded in 1976, are led by the militarily skilled and charismatic Velupillai Prabakharan. The LTTE has eliminated or absorbed most other Tamil organizations, and dominates life and politics in the Tamil provinces, especially in the rural areas. In its early years it probably received some support from India, but more recently funding has tended to come from a Tamil diaspora in Canada, Europe and Australia. Although proscribed as a terrorist organization by the US, Britain, India, Australia and Malaysia, it is nonetheless recognized as a necessary party to the current peace negotiations, due to its *de facto* power. The LTTE has become widely known for the tactic of suicide bombings carried out by 'Black Tigers', especially since it was used to assassinate Indian Prime Minister Rajiv Gandhi in 1991. Women have been active militants in the Tiger forces, and especially favoured for suicide bombing missions. This extreme level of commitment and sacrifice appears to have developed in a context where Tamil youth have become deeply disenchanted with their life prospects and bitter about communal sufferings, and are drawn into a cult-like organization that offers intense validation in exchange for such sacrifices (Reuter 2002: 155–63).

Applying an 'historical institutionalist' approach Neil DeVotta (2005) argues that this political situation has arisen out of a process of 'ethnic outbidding'. By this he means that since independence the political parties representing the Sinhalese majority have usually competed with each other to appeal to show the most favour to the Sinhalese and least conciliation to the Tamils, as a strategy for winning power. Cross-ethnic attempts by elites to moderate the social tensions (as in 1957 and 1965) have been repeatedly undercut by this electoral dynamic. DeVotta sees this as a key example of the need for institutional mechanisms to safeguard minority rights in systems where ethnic majorities are routinely translated into electoral majorities (see also Horowitz 1985).

democratization state societies will acquire some but not all of these features, while retaining non-democratic ones from the past. It is this mixture that is particularly volatile, especially when media institutions have been liberalized, released from tight state controls, but elections and constitutional constraints are not yet entrenched, and patterns of voluntary association have not developed to cut across other (e.g. ethnic) social cleavages.

Snyder explains nationalism, understood especially as ethnic chauvinism tending towards violence, as an effect of 'elite persuasion':

Democratization produces nationalism when powerful groups within the nation not only need to harness popular energies to the tasks of war and economic development, but they also want to avoid surrendering real political authority to the average citizen. For those elites, nationalism is a convenient doctrine that justifies a partial form of democracy, in which an elite rules in the name of the nation yet may not be fully accountable to its people. Under conditions of partial democratization elites can often use their control over the levers of government, the economy, and the mass media to promote nationalist ideas, and thus set the agenda for the debate. Nationalist conflicts arise as a by-product of elites' efforts to persuade the people to accept divisive nationalist ideas. (2000: 32)

The efficacy of elite persuasion depends on what he calls the 'marketplace of ideas' (2000: 56–66; see also Snyder and Ballentine 1996), in other words, the channels of mass communication through which ideas are disseminated and debated. In the early stages of democratization such 'markets' are prone to crucial imperfections, namely: (1) major media and sources of information are likely to be controlled by elite groups; (2) the public is likely to be more sharply divided into segments exposed to only one point of view in the media; (3) journalists will have a less developed sense of professional autonomy and self-regulation; and (4) institutions that scrutinize public debate will be relatively weak. More generally the ease or volatility of democratization is conditioned by the ability (or not) of elites to adapt their interests to the new institutional environment of democracy, thereby maintaining their social position, and by how well established institutions of representation are at the time that political participation begins to expand. As a rule, higher *per capita* wealth, a more developed middle class and historically early democratization, as in Britain, are conducive to a smoother transition, while the opposite, as in pre-First World War Serbia, tends towards ethnic conflict.

War

Snyder's concerns draw our attention to the darker side of nationalism and its potential for ethnic violence and war. Warfare and other forms of coordinated violence are perennial themes in human history, engaged between 'clans, villages, city-states, empires and kingdoms' (Smith 1981: 74) long before nation-states existed. But as Michael Howard observes, nations as we know them evolved partly out of patterns of warfare between earlier forms of polity:

These wars, in many cases, had been fought not between peoples but between princes asserting juridical claims to what they regarded as their personal property; but they were none the less decisive in the creation of these coherent political units out of which 'nations' were to evolve. (1994: 255)

Moreover, the rise of the modern nation-state changed the fundamental complexion of war. As we have already seen, inter-state militarist rivalry in Europe from about the eighteenth century on was a major stimulus to state expenditure, centralization and need for popular legitimacy (Tilly 1975b; Mann 1988: 104–10; Giddens 1987b: 103–16). Mann describes a general shift from an early modern form of 'limited warfare', for example, the Seven Years' War between Britain and France (1756–63) and the Austro-Prussian War (1866–7), in which warfare was planned and prosecuted by elites and their clients for fairly well-defined geopolitical reasons and with relatively little direct participation by the mass of society, to full-scale 'citizen warfare' beginning with the First World War, in which masses of untrained citizens had to be turned into soldiers, and warfare had increasing impacts on civilian populations. The striking thing about the warfare of modern nation-states, as Mann puts it, is that '*war is appalling, but popular*' (1988: 172, emphasis in original). According to Mann, this is not due to collective fear and irrationality of the masses, or the machinations of threatened industrialists or reactionary traditional elites. Instead, these wars, especially the First World War, were engaged by the masses, especially the new middle classes, with enthusiasm, because people believed in the progressive nature of their nations, and that they were worth 'defending':

From about the 1860s to 1914, middle class experience was one of progress – not just of material progress, though this was marked, but political and cultural too. The middle class became house-owners, servant-employers, voters, jurors, literate participators in national culture and commercial markets – these were all solid achievements, summing up to the first mass-participatory societies seen anywhere since the Roman Republic. There were two variant forms. In continental Europe, nationalism from 1789 onwards had first been a domestic ideology of citizen rights for male householders. In countries like Britain and the United States, where these rights were achieved relatively early, nationalism was less an overt ideology than an implicit sense of identity, stake and community in the nation. In both, the aggressive and militarist nationalism which began to appear in the last

---

Box 6.4 Mobilizing the Confederacy in the American Civil War

The generally accepted name of the 'American Civil War' (1861–5) is curious when one considers that it was not an internecine war over control of a single state and territory, but a war to prevent a distinct territory from seceding. As Susan-Mary Grant (1998) has observed, this war has come to be remembered as an iconic 'salvation drama' of American nation-building, often belying the way it was understood by participants at the time. The war was precipitated by a shift of political power away from the southern states dominated by cotton plantation agriculture cultivated by black slave labour, and towards the more industrialized and commercial north-eastern states based on wage labour and immigration. As new states continued to join the Union, 'free states' increasingly outnumbered 'slave states'. At the same time there were growing tensions over protectionist tariffs that favoured the northern over the southern economy. The new Republican Party (established 1854) opposed the expansion of slavery in the West, and was successful in mobilizing anti-slavery sentiments in the North. When their candidate Abraham Lincoln won the presidency (1861–5), southern states lost their long-standing control of the Congress, Senate and Presidency, and began to secede one by one, eleven in all by June 1861, to form the Confederate States of America (CSA). Initially an attempt by the North to retake federal forts in the South, by 1862 full-scale war had developed, and Lincoln had committed himself to the complete abolition of slavery in the Emancipation Proclamation (passed in 1863). The South enjoyed superior military leadership for the first two years, but eventually the industrial superiority of the North was decisive. They were better able to produce arms and munitions, had a navy able to effectively blockade Confederate ports, had better railroad links, a larger population replenished by immigration, and well-established governing

→

---

decade of the nineteenth century was built on top of the notion of a progressive, prosperous bourgeois nation in control of its own destiny. (1988: 174)

Mann goes on to suggest that in the nuclear age such militarism is complicated by the risk of all-out destruction. The United States has in recent decades preferred 'spectator-sport militarism' in which wars are carried on by proxy by the citizens of client states, or are kept short with low body counts. The divergence of the Vietnam War from this model led to serious problems of domestic political legitimacy, and it remains to be seen whether the US will successfully extricate itself from military conflicts in the Middle East initiated with the War in Iraq. The science and means of warfare continue to evolve and change its dynamics, but the links between

→ structures. The CSA's failure to enlist foreign support also weakened its cause.

At the start of the war only one in four white families in the CSA owned slaves – slavery was mainly an economic benefit to the plantation-owning cotton aristocracy. Considering this, Geoffrey Taubman (1997) has asked why so many non-slaveholders, largely yeoman farmers, enthusiastically fought for the cause. While southern yeomen derived advantages from cotton-driven prosperity, patron–client relations with the slave-owning class and superior social status in relation to slaves, nonetheless the slave owners monopolized the best lands and political offices, impeded economic development and possibilities for entry into that class by yeoman were shrinking. Thus, there was no simple unity of interests between the two classes. It is also notable that in the years leading up to the war, attempts to mobilize support for slave-holding interests and possible secession were largely confined to the slave-owning class, having little popular appeal. Taubman argues that people are more likely to take serious risks, such as warfare, to defend themselves against *losses* and to preserve the status quo, than they are to obtain potential *gains*. He suggests that CSA president Jefferson Davis had a sense of this principle, and quite consciously discursively reframed the conflict away from one of losses for the slave-owning elite, or dubious benefits of expanded slavery for yeoman, and instead cast the war as a defence of core American values of individual liberty, freedom and independence established in the American Revolution (1775–83), and now threatened by a federal North seeking to centralize power. Davis likened the southern secessionists to the early American rebels opposing British colonial rule, calling for the defence of a collective honour and autonomy of southerners, not the sectional interests of slave owners. This language apparently struck a deep chord in many young men of the yeoman class, inspiring them to enlist, especially in the first years of the war.

warfare, its expense, domestic political legitimacy, and national identity continue to be strong. Smith, always relatively sceptical about political explanations of nationalism, nonetheless has often noted the importance of war for national and ethnic identities, not surprisingly tracing this process back into premodern times. As he puts it: 'Historically, protracted wars have been the crucible in which ethnic consciousness has been crystallised' (1981: 75). He suggests that there are four main reasons why war has this effect: (1) the mobilization of men and resources, especially in 'more infantry-based and interdependent fighting formations' (1981: 77) creates social solidarity in the face of ethnic others; (2) war propaganda and the deployment of positive (us) and negative (the enemy) stereotypes sharpens such distinctions; (3) inter-state wars are usually fought over territory, tending to delineate and align spatial and social boundaries; and, finally, in line with the arguments of Mann and others (4) inter-state wars promote the centralization and institutionalization of power, requiring 'a distinctive internal ordering of its population, thus turning it into a community with a sense of its historic identity' (1981: 78).

The preceding remarks again point us back to the interdependence of the 'inner' and 'outer' faces of the state and their dialectical development. So far I have highlighted the way inter-state warfare promotes the forma-tion of national identities, and national identities provide a key resource for war-making. However, nationalist or inter-ethnic violence also occurs within states between ethnic groups contending for control of the state. As Horowitz has observed, although militarization and military service can have a socially integrating effect, in many places in Africa and Asia recruitment to the armed forces is ethnically skewed (remember the case of Fiji outlined in Box 1.1, p. 2), thus reinforcing ethnic cleavages and putting a crucial means of political self-help in the hands of one group:

> In an ethnically divided society, domination of any powerful institu-tion by a single ethnic group constitutes a danger that that institution will be used for ethnic purposes. Split domination – an arrangement in which the key institutions of the society are dominated by different ethnic groups – may provide the basis for a bargain to stabilize this balance of power by recognizing ethnic spheres of influence. More often, however, split domination is unstable, particularly when one ethnic group controls the armed forces and another dominates the civilian regime. Each of these institutions is a potential master to the other. In the absence of highly skilful bargaining or preventative arrangements, the civilian regime stands in danger of military over-throw. (Horowitz 1985: 457)

Mann (2001) has attempted a preliminary explanation of 'murderous ethnic cleansing', the most acute form of violent ethnic rivalry. The factors and possibilities are highly complex, but his analysis indicates that situations resembling Brubaker's 'triadic nexus' of nationalizing, homeland and minority nationalisms, in which ethnic groups are locked in competition over power and resources, are the most likely to be tipped over into ethnic cleansing. In states housing larger numbers of ethnic groups, none with a clear majority, tensions are more likely to be diffused and less likely to escalate. But where the number of substantial ethnic groups is fewer, and some have co-ethnics in command of neighbouring states, ethnic strife is more likely to come to a head. Add to this political and territorial instability, as with Germany after the First World War and

Yugoslavia after the collapse of the USSR, and circumstances are ripe for such extreme ethnic violence.

Class

As Josep Llobera has argued (1994: 123–6), marxist claims to the effect that nationalism is a by-product of capitalist class interests, a trick played on the proletariat by the bourgeoisie, do not bear up under close scrutiny. In some cases class stratification tends to coincide with and reinforce ethnic cleavages, as with the Tutsi and Hutu in Rwanda, but in others, especially more economically developed countries, class differences largely cut across national cleavages. For instance, Scots and English in the UK occupy largely similar class structures (McCrone 2001: ch. 3). But it would be a mistake to totally disregard class relations in the consideration of nationalisms just because they don't follow any universal pattern. Moreover, it is particularly simple dualistic or at best tripartite models of class (bourgeoisie/petty bourgeoisie/proletariat) that are unhelpful here. As we have already seen, more nuanced (and weberian) notions of complex layerings of classes and class fractions, some with senses of group identity and status rivalry with other groups, can provide useful analytic tools for understanding and comparing actual cases (see Seton-Watson 1977: ch. 11).

Breuilly (1993: ch. 1) begins his book on nationalism by denying that there is any single, consistent underlying relationship between class relations on the one hand, and nationalist movements on the other:

> Nevertheless, in nationalist movements as in all other political movements, there are social and economic interests. One can identify some typical relationships between broad social groups and nationalism, though I would stress that these do not exhaust all possible and actual relationships and do not in any sense 'explain' nationalism. (1993: 19).

The 'typical relationships' Breuilly surveys include: (1) Nobility of middling ranks, more attached to populations on their territorial domains, mobilizing national sentiments and a larger, poorer nobility against great magnates. This happened in Poland and Hungary in the nineteenth century, and among the middling samurai of Japan, leading to the Meiji Restoration. (2) Where a clergy wielding religious authority finds itself opposed to the established state it could mobilize the faithful, often peasants, in nationalist terms, as with the Irish in Britain and the Romanians of Transylvania, whose Uniate and Greek Orthodox churches were not recognized under the Habsburg Empire. (3) Although business interests tend to take a passive or resistant role to nationalist agitation, where there is a small, territorially defined business class whose interests are threatened by the central state, they may put their weight behind nationalism, as in Catalonia and the Basque Country in the early twentieth century. (4) Ethnically defined petite bourgeoisies (craftsmen, small merchants, shopkeepers), concentrated in towns and cities, played a key role in mobilizing sentiments in the nationalisms of nineteenth-century East-Central Europe, and in some twentieth-century colonial societies. For instance, Czech craftsmen and shopkeepers led nationalist boycotts against larger scale German businesses in Bohemia and Moravia. (5) Organized labour often became aligned with anti-colonial nationalist struggles in the mid-twentieth century, providing key leadership, resources and presence in capital cities. Movements in Tanganyika, Guinea, Nairobi, Tunisia and South Africa each show variations on this theme. (6) In colonial contexts it is also the case that segments of the peasantry may align with nationalist elites if this helps them to circumvent the control of rival local segments collaborating with the colonial political economy. (7) As we have seen, some quotient of professionals and intellectuals have an almost ubiquitous presence in nationalist movements, their ideological, communicative and, sometimes, legal skills and privileged status being almost indispensable for effective mobilization. As this sampling suggests, the upshot of Breuilly's scepticism about the overall explanatory power of 'class' is not that we should disregard it entirely, but that the relevant class processes have to be specified in each case (and there will be some similarities among some cases).

Hroch (1998) has defended himself against the charge made by Gellner (1994) that he attempts to reduce nationalist movements to class politics. Hroch avers that he has always been careful to stress the multiple causes and conditions that lead to nationalism, and to use a somewhat looser language of 'classes and groups' to offset any reductionist class-based reading of his arguments (1998: 100–1). Defining class in more strictly marxian terms than Breuilly, as 'those social groups which are distinguished by the nature of the ownership of productive forces' (1998: 101), Hroch acknowledges that this is only one of several potentially 'nationally relevant conflicts of interest'. Nonetheless the major axes of conflict that he sums up clearly articulate on the ground with specific historical concatenations of class and status:

Especially it was the conflict between new university graduates coming from a non-dominant ethnic group and a closed elite from the ruling nation keeping an hereditary grip on leading positions in the state. Further, I pointed to the tension between craftsmen belonging to the non-dominant group and the large traders and manufacturers belonging to the dominant nation. To these instances may be added the tension between the towns and the countryside, between the centre and the provinces, and so forth. Ultimately the struggle for positions of power may also be considered an interesting conflict. (1998: 100).

Once again the key role of that peculiar class fraction, the 'intelligentsia', is emphasized. Moreover, Hroch's *Phase C* (see above) is defined in terms of the movement achieving support across a range of classes and class fractions. Thus, while no one class is *the* agent of nationalism, class structure is basic to his definition of a fully fledged national movement.

Mann's concepts of international, transnational and national classes outlined at the beginning of this chapter are fairly abstract devices for thinking about how classes and nations evolved together, entwined, as the products of 'modernizing churches, commercial capitalism, militarism, and the rise of the modern state' (1993: 249). He has also concerned himself with more fine-grained concepts of class. In particular, he has argued that the growth of the modern middle class since the late nineteenth century has been a defining feature of the nation-states we find ourselves in to this day. He identifies three key fractions:

1. The *petite bourgeoisie*: proprietors of small, familial business.
2. *Careerists*: wage or salaried employees moving up corporate and bureaucratic hierarchies.
3. *Professionals*: 'learned', collectively organized occupations licensed by the state. (1993: 549)

These groups, which overlap in some cases, are seen as bound together by their participation through employment and self-employment in the hierarchies of capitalism and the state, in markets and bureaucracies, whether private businesses or public agencies. These broadly shared situations are bolstered by privileged patterns of consumption, the 'ability to turn income into small investment capital' (1993: 589), and a privileged position in the expanding sphere of citizenship rights. This middle class has largely sided with capitalists in their struggles with labour, but

The middle class cannot be reduced to mere loyal retainers of capitalism and regimes. At the beginning of the twentieth century it was also the main reinforcer of the nation-state. Moreover, two subfractions – state careerists and highly educated careerists and professionals – were the main carriers of distinct and varied statist nationalisms. (1993: 589)

Illustrating this point by examining the most thoroughly studied case, inter-war Germany and the rise of fascism, Mann is at pains to show that it is not the petite bourgeoisie, so often accused of status insecurity and a predilection to seek refuge in authoritarian leadership, but rather those fractions of the middle class most deeply ensconced in the institutions of the state, that are the most inclined to become deeply committed to nationalist projects. Again, for these groups it is not fear but enthusiasm for and belief in the liberating value of their nation-states that motivates support for nationalist projects.

From these examples we can surmise that while the analysis of class relations is no magic bullet for understanding nationalism, neither is it something that can be ignored. We can also detect a broad and incomplete historical trajectory between two paradigmatic situations. In the first, characteristic of nineteenth-century Europe, traditional elites encounter nationalist movements led by small but developing middle classes, or other interstitial mid-level elites, who may have some success incorporating much larger populations of peasants and proletarians into their project. In broad outline, twentieth-century anti-colonial nationalisms have echoed this form. In the second, after the rise of Mann's 'middle-class nation', in the wealthy, 'post-industrial' countries of the North, the educated middle classes have radically expanded. Here the pivotal middle-class fractions and sub-elites that might be playing a lead role in nationalisms, such as those found in Flanders, Scotland, Quebec and Catalonia, are immersed in the larger middle classes born of capitalist prosperity and enlarged welfare states. The dynamic is not as sharply outlined, but economic interests and class processes are still discernable. Considering the cases of Quebec and Scotland, Michael Keating notes that trade unions have tended to back the new nationalisms in those countries, while also maintaining intra-class alliances with other unions in Canada and Britain respectively. Big business, to some degree controlled outside of the countries in question, has been hostile, suspicious of the redistributive policies of nationalists and anything that might impede open markets (2001: 266). In a recent study of social and economic change in Scotland since 1980 Paterson *et al.* (2004) remark:

The class of professionals and managers now makes up over one-third of the population. This has happened in a time when Scotland has resumed some democratic control of its own politics, and the two processes may in fact not be unconnected. The professional class came to support an elected parliament during the 1980s and 1990s, as they became alienated from the policies of the Conservative government. Their openness to these new ideas may be partly due to their own diverse origins in the upward mobility of the post-war years. Now that the parliament is in place, they are the leaders of the civic institutions with which it has to negotiate if it is to achieve anything in the way of policy or of public debate. (2004: 101)

This middle class consists of Mann's 'careerists and professionals', who appear to still be in the vanguard of nationalist politics, albeit in more moderate and incremental forms, in the advanced economies of the powerful states of the North.

Conclusion

This chapter has surveyed major discussions of nationalism and power processes found in the literature. Various themes have emerged. First, that there is a complex dialectic between the inner and outer faces of the state shaping national sentiments and identities. Being national means both making claims on one's state and fellow citizens, and being divided from and sometimes in conflict with the nationals of other states. How this works will depend on the power and size of the state one finds oneself in, which is highly variable. States, and configurations of states, frame oppositional nationalist politics. Such movements take the forms that they do partly in response to the state powers they must engage. Second, a nationalist movement does not arise spontaneously out of a population; such movements are always cultivated and coordinated by groups relatively elite in relation to the people they mobilize. Some researchers focus primarily on the social conditions that make this process of movement expansion possible. Others have been more concerned with the dynamic by which the motives and interests of smaller groups are generalized and 'geared up' into a broader movement, often seeing this as a process of instrumental, self-interested manipulation by elites. Third, warfare and violence have been a perennial part of nationalism, both creating and strengthening national sentiments, and providing a key resource for modern militarism and nation-building. Finally, while there are no simple regularities between nationalism and class relations, neither is class dispensable for any fine-grained understanding of nationalist dynamics.

In the next chapter we will think more specifically about the concept of power and its implications for our understanding of nationalism, arguing that the roles of states, elites, classes and other groups, need to be framed within a more general concept of power as social organization.

Further Reading

Poggi (1978) remains an excellent short introduction to the nature of the modern state. For state-focused assessments of nationalism Bendix (1978), Breuilly (1993, 2001), Brubaker (1996) and Mann (1993, 1988) are core readings. For placing nationalism in the context of evolving international relations see Mayall (1990) and Tilly (1975a). Tarrow (1994) is a very helpful introduction to the nature and dynamics of social and political movements in general, which complements key studies of nationalist elites and mobilization such as Brass (1991), Hechter (2000), Hroch (2000, 1996) and Snyder (2000). The significance of war for nationalism runs through many of the readings just cited, but Smith (1981) and Mann (1988) are good places to start, and Bessinger (2001) and Brubaker and Laitin (1998) provide recent comprehensive discussions of ethnicity and violence. On class see especially Hroch (1998) and Mann (1993: ch. 16).

7
Rethinking Power

In the last chapter we considered various power-centred approaches to the study of nationalism. Here I want to begin by developing a more explicit conceptualization of power in general, and its significance for nationalism. While special attention to the power of states and elites is clearly warranted, the thrust of this chapter is to situate these aspects of nationalism within a broader conception of power as inherent in all forms of social organization. This will help sensitize us to how the powers latent in all social relations become manifestly organized in nationalist terms under certain conditions. The chapter goes on to explore the way nationalism articulates with other social processes that are often sidelined by our attention to states and elites. I look at: cities as primary sites of nation-formation; gender relations as part of the infrastructure of national power; and the politics of stable democratic regimes as the routinization, rather than the overcoming, of nationalism. In each case I aim to show how nationalism articulates with other aspects of social organization, drawing on and influencing their inherent powers.

Power and Organization

It is sometimes forgotten that Max Weber's influential definition of power as 'the probability that one actor within a social relationship will be in a position to carry out his own will despite resistance, regardless of the basis on which this probability rests' (1978: 53) comes in the middle of a discussion of the nature and types of social organization (1978: 48–62). Though the language sounds very individualistic, it is clear that for Weber power is most significantly a property of social organizations. I follow Weber and several other more contemporary thinkers (Beetham 1991; Mann 1986a; Poggi 2001; Wrong 2002; Clegg 1989) in emphasizing this connection. The anthropologist Eric Wolf wryly commented in a late essay on power that the concept of social organization, once a mainstay of the social sciences, is out of fashion: 'We structure and are structured, we transact, we play out metaphors, but the whole question of organization has fallen into abeyance' (1990: 590–1). I share Wolf's sense that organization needs to be reinstated at the centre of our social analyses – particularly when we are trying to understand power. While we often conceptualize power on the model of encounters between individual actors, human agency, our power, develops and is realized primarily through forms of social organization. As Stewart Clegg has argued:

> organization may constitute a form of collective agency and . . . there is no reason to make this a second-rate form of agency compared to that of the problematic human subject. Where organization achieves agency it is an accomplishment, just as it is for the individual but more so, because it involves the stabilization of power relations across an organizational field of action, and thus between many subjectivities, rather than simply within one embodied locus of subjectivities. (1989: 188)

An important conceptual distinction pervades the literature on power, that between 'power to' and 'power over' (Morriss 2002: 32–5). We speak both of the power to do things, power as an ability or capacity to effect change, and of power over others, to direct and control their actions. This is also sometimes phrased as the difference between our 'collective' power to achieve shared ends, and power's 'distributive' aspect, its tendency take shape unevenly, privileging some and subordinating others. As Michael Mann notes:

> the relationship between the two is dialectical. In pursuit of their goals, humans enter into cooperative, collective power relations with one another. But in implementing collective goals, social organization and a division of labor are set up. Organization and division of function carry an inherent tendency to distributive power, deriving from supervision and coordination. (1986a: 6–7)

Mann is one of the few to explicitly situate his concepts of nations and nationalism within a general theory of power, and the perspective advanced here is similar and broadly complementary to his (see also Poggi 2001 and Clegg 1989: Ch. 9). His monumental project, however, has been to trace the evolving history of major sources of social power from the neolithic up to the present. My purpose here is more circumscribed, to abstract and highlight general aspects of power that I see as recurring in the literature on nationalism, rendering these as more explicit tools of conceptual analysis. The main thing I want to suggest is that each case of nationalism will have its own distinctive organizational composition, which defines its power dynamics and possibilities.

Centralized versus Diffuse Social Organization

We can distinguish between two organizational tendencies (cf. Mann 1986a: 7–9; Wrong 2002: 14–20). At one extreme there are formal organizations that have highly centralized command structures and rules of authority, sharp definitions of membership and high levels of commitment and compliance from members. Most formal organizations, however, exhibit these features in more moderate forms. Typical examples are armies, political parties, churches and sects, business enterprises and, of course, the state. At the other extreme people are organized by diffuse and extensive social institutions that serve human needs, but lack the bounded quality of formal organizations and any clear locus of authority. They are often experienced as 'natural', seeming to govern human behaviour from nowhere, and to evolve, expand and contract organically, without conscious human direction. Premier examples of this kind of social organization are languages and markets. Actual cases of nationalism are conditioned by the particular combination and dynamics of more formal organizations and more diffuse and extensive fields of social relations within which they develop, and upon which often they capitalize. Sects mobilize within fields of religious believers, government agencies codify and regulate languages, trade unions strike within national and international markets, and so on.

Organizational Embedding

Organizations of any size, because of the functional division of labour that Mann highlights, are made up of other embedded levels of organization. A nationalist project may take hold in some part of a larger organization and then spread to influence the whole, or become contained in the part. Thus, the lesser clergy at the parish level may mobilize against the church hierarchy, a department in a university may try to influence the institution's policy on teaching languages or history and an internal pressure group may try to shift a political party's policy on the devolution of government to the national level, or on its attitude to immigration. The state itself needs to be viewed as an organization of organizations, a complex of many parts, each with its own organizational capacities and powers, and potentials to work with or against the whole.

Organizational Articulations

The key point is that how a nationalist movement fares is substantially determined by the organizational opportunities it encounters, and the possibilities for mobilizing larger organizations through sub-organizations, and for articulating organizations across different spheres of activity. A nationalist movement may operate primarily within one sphere but a powerful movement will tend to cut across and combine, generating a more complex array of organizational powers that penetrate society more broadly and deeply. These are well-known aspects of how social movements work within organizational fields (Tarrow 1994) applied to the case of nationalism.

Created versus Found Organizations

Following on from the previous point, it is useful to distinguish between 'created' and 'found' forms of organization embedded in the modern state. Thus, the functional differentiation of the state *creates* new, professionalized agencies: militaries, police, education and healthcare systems, public transportation systems and levels of local/regional government. These units can become bases for nationalist mobilization and struggles to define national identity. Thus, as we saw with Donald Horowitz (1985: ch. 11), militaries in weaker states may initiate coups to back nationalist projects, especially when they become dominated by one ethnic group. More generally, large state institutions tend to become aligned with differing visions of the nation, thus in the US the armed forces are associated with conservative politics, and the educational institutions with more liberal politics, differences in ideology that ultimately have bearing on notions of national identity. Now for *found* organizations. Michael Hechter's (2000) model of far-flung imperial polities that governed by 'indirect rule' being replaced by modern states exercising forms of 'direct rule' is instructive. What he calls 'governance units', relatively culturally coherent quasi-polities, are the objects of this shift from indirect rule to direct rule, and are an example of what I mean by 'found' organizations, that existed prior to or at one time territorially outside the modern state, but were incorporated. In settler states like the US and Australia, forms of local and regional government are created, on a fairly uniform template, as the state territorially expands (eliminating or marginalizing indigenous populations and their political institutions in the process). But in other cases, such as Catalonia in Spain and Scotland in Britain, the smaller pre-existing polity was incorporated, reconstituted in the process in some ways, but not in others. Here the modernizing state simply makes a virtue of a given field of organizational power, aligning and subordinating it to itself. But forms of social organization can function in different ways according to their circumstances (Steward 1972: 91–2). Embedded forms of organization, whether found or created, can provide the means for realizing the central state's power in one era, while becoming the basis for resistance to that power in another.

Interstitial Positions Within Social Hierarchies

This question of sub-levels of organization accords with a theme we have encountered repeatedly throughout this book – the crucial importance of interstitial positions within social hierarchies (Hearn 2001: 345–8). We have seen how often the leadership of frustrated lower-level elites and middle classes has figured prominently in the development of nationalism. Those interstitial positions are given form and power possibilities by the specific array of organizations that are available or can be generated. I am underscoring a point widely accepted in the literatures on social movements and nationalism but in a sense so obvious that it is too easily forgotten. Jack Snyder has put it well:

> Effective institutions and unifying ideas are indispensable for collective action in a large group like a nation, but they are difficult and costly to provide. To overcome these difficulties nationalists need an institutional base from which to build a constituency. These nationalists need to start from some smaller group that already has the habit of mutually beneficial cooperation, which can serve as the kernel for wider collective action. People studying collective action in settings of high risk and cost (e.g. revolutions, rebellions, and resistance movements) have found that the inclination to shirk is most often overcome by mobilisation through small-scale social networks of people who trust each other. Their trust is based on a history of interactions in other activities. History shows that the small-group kernel for nationalist collective action may come from almost any group: the ruling dynasty of the prenational regime, the dominant faction of a region, a cohesive and privileged economic group, a religious or cultural elite, a part of the military officer corps, intellectuals sharing a common education or outlook, prominent figures in an ethnic group, or the leaders of a powerful clan. (2000: 50; see also Hechter 2000: 125; Wrong 2002: ch. 7)

Snyder's concluding list concerns something more like the classes, class fractions and groups we discussed in the last chapter; however, I think it is implicit but obvious that these will normally be constituted through particular compositions of formal and informal organizations. There are two points to be drawn out here. First, that Snyder's notion of small groups as the taproot of trust relationships clearly echoes the argument I was making in my critical comments on primordialism in Chapter 3. The affective ties that arise out of propinquity are a key resource for nationalism, but they are not simply sentimental dispositions lodged in human nature, they are inherent aspects of intimate social settings. Second, it takes power to make power. Political mobilization, as a rule, gets generated within the intermediate layers of social hierarchies, among precisely those populations that have enough power, that is, organization, to mount a viable bid for more, and yet not enough to be satisfied or secure in their social position. Correspondingly, these layers of society, the middling classes, are crucial as legitimacy brokers within the larger organization of power, embodied by the state and society. They can focus dissent, but they can also be the prime champions of their nation-state. Those at the bottom layers of the social hierarchy are normally too disorganized, do not command enough leverage, to effectively disrupt power relations, apart from volatile moments of systemic crisis. Even in those extreme cases, movement leadership usually comes from higher up the social hierarchy. Those at the bottom are, as Mann puts it, 'organizationally outflanked' (1986a: 7–8). It is the middle classes in complex modern societies, with their specialized skills, greater resources and more stable organizations, that are in the position to tip the balance of power in favour either of those above, or those below. When territorially and culturally defined populations to which those middle classes are experientially attached are what lie 'below', there is a latent degree of organization to potentially be mobilized.

Means, Opportunity and Motive

If we make an analogy to the proverbial detective solving a crime, this discussion has been more about 'means' and 'opportunity', and less about 'motive'. The basic argument is that we need to attend to the disposition of power within interacting fields of social organization, the particular patterns of means and opportunity, to understand why nationalisms unfold the way they do. As for 'motive', this perspective can only offer a very general answer. Humans naturally seek control over their own lives, to maximize and enhance their power by investing themselves in particular forms of social organization. Why this is sometimes done through national-ism rather than some other kind of 'ism' (or no 'ism' at all) is something that has to be answered on a case by case basis, although part of the answer is surely that in a world full of nationalisms, people are forced to follow suit. But my main point here is that I don't believe there is any primary human motive towards nationalism or ethnicity, or to have one's identity realized in these terms. A highly general need for power is at the root of most human endeavour, and it is the historically particular means and opportunities that present themselves for realizing this general need, that give shape and speci-ficity, sometimes nationalist, to this need. Power understood in this manner is not the problem or preserve of elites and states, however much these shape it, but of the human populations more generally. To understand nationalism in specific cases we need to trace the dynamics of power-making through-out an interacting complex of organizational forms.

Cities

The heavy emphasis we have seen placed on modernization and the state tends to obscure the more specific role of urban social organization in the rise of nationalism (see McNeill 1974; Tilly 1994). In his essay 'The Curse of Rurality: Limits of Modernization Theory' (1998) Tom Nairn examines the career of Pol Pot and the pathological ethnic nationalism of the Khmer Rouge in Cambodia in the late 1970s, which killed at least 1.5 million people. The Khmer Rouge's millenarian communist project was to re-mould the peasantry into an ethnically pure peasant nation, via ethnic cleansing, and to destroy the seditious influences of urban life. For a few brief but extremely violent years a powerful state drove forward its project: city populations were decanted into the countryside, intellectuals persecuted, banks blown up and cathedrals disassembled, and city life was ruthlessly demonized. Vietnam invaded in 1978, soon toppling the Pol Pot regime and occupying the country amid civil war for the next ten years. Tenuous but more democratic government has been established in the 1990s. Leaving aside the complex causes of this terrible episode, one thing it underscores is the impossibility of genuinely rural nationalism. However much Romantics and later Communists might dress up their nationalist projects in peasant garb and root them in the countryside, cities, as the primary places of wealth creation, self-organization and middle class formation, are an essential and core element in the making of nations. Pol Pot set about destroying the only population that could cultivate a viable nation-state.

What the Pol Pot regime destroyed was that crucial phenomena for nationalism that we discussed in Chapter 4 – civil society (or at least Cambodia's weakly developed version of it). Civil society is a form of social organization connected to cities and markets (Wirth 1995 [1938]: 76–8). We have noted that more or less explicitly nationalist organizations operate within this more fluid, associational environment. But we also need to appreciate that such associations were enabled by the entire nexus of national urban life, often spanning across class boundaries, and involving myriad interests around politics, sports, leisure, religion, temperance and so on (Hohenberg and Lees 1985: 278–9). The idea of the nation was sustained by this dense network of urban associations, not explicitly concerned with nationhood, but always available as channels for the communication of nationalist ideas and sentiments. The broader organizing discourses of nationhood, both as a general political principle and in regard to specific countries, could find concrete expression through these more formal organizations. Their power did not simply emanate from the state and the elites, but permeated the sinews of self-organization that sustained the middle-class nation. In recent years there has been much debate about whether this associational dynamic in urban life, often called 'social capital', is declining (Coleman 1988; Putnam 1995; Edwards *et al.* 2001). This question obviously has bearing, perhaps as much as those about globalization, on whether nationalisms gain their legitimacy and mobilize populations differently today than they have in the past.

It is well established that the decline of medieval European feudalism was linked to the rise of the power of towns (Poggi 1978: 36–42) that progressively outflanked rural feudal power relations (Clegg 1989: 242–51). As John A. Hall observes:

Historians agree that Max Weber *was* correct in the more materialist part of his theory concerning the rise of the West, namely in his contention that only in Europe did the city gain full autonomy. Only here did cities possess their *own* governments and armies rather than being controlled by the arbitrary rule of mandarins. It has been argued that it is the depth of market penetration throughout European society that ensured the ultimate success of the market principle, and that it is this which made cities so important. Nevertheless, it would be a mistake to deny the extraordinary importance of the European city. It invented a new civilization, that of the Renaissance, whose political theory contributed vitally to the rest of European history. It provided a space in which the merchant was politically powerful, and in which bourgeois values could gell and solidify. We live in the world created by this civilization. (Hall 1986: 136, emphasis in original)

The key points here are first, that cities increasingly became the primary sites of social power in the early modern period, and second, that the idea of self-governing, spatially defined collective identities that would become characteristic of nationalism took shape first in these urban contexts (cf. Armstrong 1982: ch. 4). The Renaissance revival of civic republican ideas in the Italian city-states, drawn from classic texts of Cicero and others, spread throughout Europe, eventually shaping Enlightenment thought. As Nairn has noted, the intelligentsias of seventeenth- and eighteenth-century Europe

dwelt in a world which had existed long *before* that of the reigning monarchies and the religions which they increasingly opposed. They lived, that is, in the partly mythic domain of Greco-Roman Antiquity, and enjoyed a common high culture measured primarily in terms of familiarity with Aristotle, Stoicism and the chronicles of Republican Rome. (1997: 124, emphasis in original)

As he goes on to say, from their perspective, a world of self-governing city-states and other micro-polities, for instance on the model of the Republic of Genoa which had regained its independence in 1746, was entirely plausible (1997: 127). Martin Thom (1995) and Maurizio Viroli (1995) have both explored the evolution of these notions of civic patriotism that helped justify the powers and autonomy of rising urban spaces and their cultures. However, to Thom and Viroli's dismay, the big guns of the forming nation-states did soon win out, and they also chart how this civic republican ideology both fed into later liberal nationalist projects, and morphed into its opposite, the romantic, ethnic and rurally oriented nationalisms of the nineteenth century. The latter was a reaction to the former, its bucolic images spurred by the ambivalence felt by those provincial intelligentsias being forced to play catch-up with great urban centres such as Paris, London and Vienna. But it was the earlier idea of the self-governing city that offered the first incarnation of the idea of nationalism we know today.

Having said this, it is not simply a matter of urban/civic versus rural/ethnic types of nationalism. I have already suggested in Chapter 4 that this is too crude a dichotomy. All nationalisms pose the problem – how to ideologically enrobe the cities crucial to their development in larger territories, that include rural places and folk that may find those cities alienating and resist their claims. Indeed many of the most 'civic' and 'liberal' nationalisms have struggled to square this circle, projecting a national identity driven by cities onto the countryside. In his celebrated study of this process in English literature, *The Country and the City* (1973), Raymond Williams observed:

> It is significant, for example, that the common image of the country is now an image of the past, and the common image of the city an image of the future. That leaves, if we isolate them, an undefined present. The pull of the idea of the country is towards old ways, human ways, natural ways. The pull of the idea of the city is towards progress, modernisation, development. In what is then a tension, a present experienced as tension, we use the contrast of country and city to ratify an unresolved division and conflict of impulses, which it might be better to face in its own terms. (1973: 297)

This resembles strikingly our familiar motif of the Janus face of nationalism. It is the dilemma of the new national bourgeoisies of the nineteenth century struggling to build new national identities. In a wonderful study of the formation of a nationally conscious middle class in Oscarian Sweden (i.e. late Victorian, from the reign of King Oscar II, 1872–1907) Jonas Frykman and Orvar Löfgren (1987) have focused on this rural–urban dialectic of imagination. Seeing themselves as a progressive force for order and rationality, the Oscarian middle classes defined themselves against what they saw as a degenerate and prodigal aristocracy, a threatening and undisciplined working class and a disappearing peasantry, once regarded with contempt, but increasingly viewed as a national repository of authenticity and naturalness:

> The life-style of the Oscarian bourgeoisie came to be defined in terms of a national culture, which also had to do with the sharpened class conflicts of the late nineteenth century. For the new elite, it seemed as if the nation was about to be torn apart, and there was a search for symbolic expressions of national solidarity, above the world of class strife. The love of a common peasant heritage and the Swedish landscape was supposed to bind the nation together. This was the period of the erection of national monuments, the building of folk museums, the celebration of national jubilees, and the writing of patriotic songs. (1987: 268–9)

Thus, the culture of the Swedish middle class was generalized as the 'national' culture, appropriating and subordinating the cultures of other classes in the process. The middle class's organizational strength was translated into an organizing ideology of the nation. The scenario is typical of that nation-building era in Europe. In the advanced capitalist countries of today, the peasants are gone, and the distinction between working and middle classes has become blurred. With modern transportation and communications the boundaries between rural and urban are also less distinct in some ways. We are perhaps more prepared to treat our great cities as national symbols, while the habit of representing the nation through icons of nature within the national territory persists. No answer can be formulated here, but it would be worth inquiring into the current state of the rural–urban dialectic in the imagining of contemporary nations (cf. Hearn 2003).

Lest it seem that this is simply all old news about the rise of modernity, let me reiterate Hall's point above – this urban-shaped world is our world. Economic power is a crucial aspect of power in the modern era, and economic power is primarily driven by cities. Jane Jacobs (1985) has argued that modern macroeconomics, from the mercantilists right through Adam Smith and his current heirs, has too often been based on the false assumption that it is the nation-state that is the decisive unit of analysis for understanding wealth creation (leaving aside the microeconomics of individuals and firms). She argues that it is cities that are the key agents and drivers of economic development, not nations (or more precisely, states). She advocates recalibrating policies of import-substitution once directed at 'underdeveloped countries' to cities in general, especially those in decline. For her, vibrant economies depend on cities producing goods for regional markets, creating work for smaller nearby urban centres in their tow, and new demands for importable goods from other cities further afield. Instead, she argues, current states too often become committed to 'transactions of decline' in which capital cities prosper through the governmental task of managing the decline of ailing urban economies through subsidies, sometimes mollifying separatist sentiments by this means. The number, size and distributions of cities in any nation-state is obviously significant for her analysis, networks of interdependent cities being more stable and resistant to business cycles than any single urban economy on its own. Thus, there are consequential differences between states like the US with a vast network of cities, the UK with one highly dominant urban core, or Singapore, which is virtually all city. Nairn (1996: 277–9), not surprisingly as an advocate of the 'break up of Britain', has picked up on her solution to the unmanageability of national economies – allow large nation-states to dissolve, bestowing sovereignty, and responsibility for economic policy, on cities and their regions. Jacobs grasps the unlikelihood of this scenario, but poses it as the logical prescription based on her analysis. Her book was written in the mid-1980s amid the worries of terminal 'stagflation' in advanced economies, and that shapes her argument. But the basic point for us, regardless of whether city-focused economic policies can better deal with macroeconomic instabilities, is that modern power lies predominantly in cities. The implication is that the fates and fortunes of states are actually those of cities, or networks of cities (cf. Tilly 1994: 12), whose populations come to imagine themselves and their fellows in their rural hinterlands, that network and the territory it occupies, as nations.

In this context it is worth noting how much cities have become a key focus of attention for understanding processes of uneven development (see Savage and Warde 2000; Sassen 2000), which I have argued is a constant potential stimulus to nationalism. As long as states are the designated champions of urban economies, then the shifting inequalities in power among cities across the globe will be translated into international rivalries in the economic domain, and sometimes beyond, and into competing strategies from within the nation of how to remedy the problem, which will carry differing inflections of national identity. When regions within states find their urban strength waning in relation to more powerful urban centres within the same state, then calls for greater political autonomy for that region/nation become more likely. I suggested at the end of Chapter 5 that this was part of the explanation for devolution in Scotland. And conversely, when one region considers that its strength is sapped by less developed parts of the country, as with the Italian north (Lombardy) in relation to the south, some push for political autonomy is also likely. Slovakia and Croatia's early exits from Yugoslavia probably also fit this pattern. Finally, there are, of course, rebellious and revolutionary nationalisms that, given the exigencies of armed struggle, must base themselves in rural hinterlands, often seeking peasant support. But the leadership of such movements normally have a more urban provenance (like the Paris-educated Pol Pot), and the objectives must involve retaking the cities, to begin the project of nation-building in earnest. In sum, if cities are both the key sites for the creation of national identities and the ultimate drivers of uneven economic development, then the importance of the urban organization of power in making nationalism is further underscored.

Gender

Increasing attention has been paid to the relationship between gender and nationalism over the past twenty years (see Yuval-Davis 2001). This is valuable for two reasons. First, it corrects the strong tendency to neglect and obscure the actual historical role of women in nationalist movements, resulting from male biases in the leaderships of those movements and among academic researchers. Second, inquiring into the gender dimension of nationalism forces us to grapple with some of the complexities of how nationalist power gets socially organized. A substantial portion of this literature has been more specifically concerned with evaluating the compatibility or not of feminist and nationalist projects, especially in 'third world' contexts (see Jayawardena 1986; McClintock 1996; West 1997). I will not try to engage that discussion here, but the core dilemma it addresses, whether nationalism can be a vehicle for women's empowerment or only subverts it, is an underlying theme in what follows. The inherent difficulty of enquiring into the gender/nationalism relationship must be stressed. All complex societies have structured gender relations that are also a part of their broader systems of social stratification. We can identify some historical and ethnographic social settings where there is minimal gender hierarchy, especially among foragers, and also in horticultural societies where property and status is passed through the female line and men move to live close to their wives' families upon marriage. But nationalism has generally taken hold in societies where there was already some form of patriarchy, a gender hierarchy that favours men. It seizes upon pre-existing gendered forms of social stratification, sometimes reinforcing, sometimes altering, sometimes ameliorating, depending on the context. Nationalism is not simply a projection of gender relations, but like other social processes, it is empirically always bound up with them. It is easy to see that they are interconnected, much more difficult to characterize the relationship as a whole.

Much of this literature has been concerned with women (and men) 'as signifiers of ethnic/national differences – as a focus and symbol in the ideological discourses used in the construction, reproduction and transformation of ethnic national categories' (Anthias and Yuval-Davis 1989: 7). The familiar gendering of nations as 'motherlands' and 'fatherlands', and personification in such characters as Britannia and John Bull in the UK, or Marianne of France, spring to mind. More deeply, beyond such explicit symbolizations, embodied notions of gender get mobilized by nationalist discourses. Michel Huysseune (2000) has explored the use of a masculinist discourse by the separatist movement *Lega Nord* in northern Italy. This discourse operates within an ideological opposition of a weak, indigent and feminized South and a virile, hard-working and masculine North. It has a more populist appeal than the stilted intellectual language of experts and leading politicians, and articulates with other widely familiar conceptual polarities: Europe/Africa, modern/backward and so on. Huysseune suggests that through this discourse the *Lega Nord* is able to present itself as, on the one hand, a force for progress and gender equality in keeping with EU ideals, while also implicitly reinforcing a patriarchal vision of social leadership in the North. Considering the early Irish state after independence in 1922, Tricia Cusack (2000) has shown how visual and literary representations of women cast them as peasants, natural mothers and carriers of tradition rooted in the past, while men were allowed to wear the forward-looking face of nationalism. 'Thus women's participation in Irish public life was delimited in the name of traditional values (ethnic nationalism) while men claimed to advance the civic state' (2000: 558). Nationalism abounds with such gendered discourses. In extreme cases such representations of gender relations are known to take the form of bodily violence, such as the rape of non-Serb women by Bosnian Serbs (Yuval-Davis 1997: 109–10). Wendy Bracewell (2000) has examined the meaning of rape for Serbian nationalism in Kosovo. In the 1980s, against the background of growing Albanian/Serb tensions is Kosovo, there developed in Serbia's press and public discourse a kind of moral panic about the rape of Serbian women by Albanian men in Kosovo. (There was no reliable evidence to indicate any actual changes in the frequency of rape in Kosovo during that time.) Bracewell argues that this rape discourse expressed a general crisis in Serbian masculinity, brought on by political and economic instability, unemployment and changing gender roles, a condition which Serbian nationalism offered to remedy by restoring masculine strength. She quotes a leading Serbian nationalist intellectual: ' "a Serb is a man who is not a man unless he is also a Serb" ' (2000: 577).

These examples highlight how nationalism gets represented through gender relations. For the rest of this section, in keeping with the chapter, I want to focus more on gender as social organization, rather than as symbol. I will look at three broad contexts, which, of course, interpenetrate. First, I will look at the state's historical role in fusing nationalism and patriarchy, while also altering their relationship. Then I will look at the bourgeois family household and sexuality as a key site of socialization. And, finally, I will consider the variable ways that gender gets mobilized in nationalist movements.

The classic nation-states of Europe developed within systems of patriarchy. Mann (1986b) has described an evolution in the last few centuries from fairly pure forms of patriarchy where all public political roles were held by men and women were confined to a domestic sphere within family and lineage structures, to a milder form of patriarchy where women are still partly tied to the private sphere, but also participate more fully in public life. The catch, as we know, is that women earn less than men for the same kind of work and have not been joined by men in most of the labour of the domestic sphere, especially child-rearing. Manuel Castells (1997: ch. 4) has gone so far as to argue that globalization is heralding the 'end of patriarchalism', which parallels his argument about the declining power of the nation-state. Sylvia Walby (2000) is unsatisfied with this developmental model of women gaining equality with men by escaping the confines of the domestic and entering the public. She suggests we think in terms of two gender regimes – a domestic gender regime – and a public gender regime. Gender relations, whether equal, or much more likely, unequal, can be institutionalized both through kinship and household, and through the state and the market. Movement from one sphere to another is not a guarantee of greater equality. She notes, in line with Mann and Castells, that for the past 100 years the 'West' has been shifting from a domestic to a public gender regime as the demands of capitalism and the logic of the liberal state tend to move men's and women's social roles closer together, and cause public policy to penetrate more deeply into private life. But:

> This process of transformation from a domestic to a public gender regime is uneven, between countries and between regions, over both space and time. This has meant that there are different forms of gender regimes in different countries, although there has been a transition in most of the western world in the form of gender regime. In some locations some of the domains have been transformed more rapidly than others, creating variations in the forms of gender regime. (Walby 2000: 529)

Walby's 'two regime' model is designed to bring out case-by-case differences, allowing for the possibility of a variety of different domestic and public gender regimes, in a variety of combinations. Nonetheless, in keeping with Mann's version, the winding story of women's political progress in the 'West' has often been about struggling to be included in the definition of the public nation, to become equal citizens. The historian Glenda Sluga (1998, 2000) illustrates how rough a journey this has been. She recounts how in the years just after the French Revolution there was some opening up for women to participate in a public debate about their national citizenship. Olympe de Gouges published her 'Declaration of the Rights of Women' in 1791, but by 1793, amid worsening crisis, 'the political activity of women was officially and legally suppressed' (1998:

90) and de Gouges was sent to the guillotine. Jacobin republican men argued that the proper role of women was to be 'orderly' and support their patriot husbands as wives and mothers. By the time of Napoleon this view had hardened:

> In the *Code Napoleon* familial male/female relations were central to the authority and development of the power of the modern nation-state. The Code enshrined national control of a range of practices associated with the private sphere, including birth, marriage and the education of children. The Code applied different conditions of citizenship to men and women. For example, marriage to a French woman did not guarantee citizenship, however, all children born of a French father in a foreign country were French. The foreign woman who married a Frenchman became French, but a Frenchwoman assumed the nationality of her husband. (1998: 94)

Sluga shows that the same principles were at work over 100 years later in the decade after the First World War, when

> fifteen European states, including all the *new* European states, introduced new laws requiring that female nationals marrying an alien lost their nationality. If the husband's nation did not allow alien wives to assume the nationality of their husbands, they became stateless. (2000: 511–12, emphasis in original)

This highlights the patriarchal definition of citizenship in Europe well into the twentieth century, leaving aside the slow and hard battle for equal rights with men (voting, property, etc.) by women who were recognized as nationals. More generally Sluga's aim is to demonstrate how in the post-Second World War peace process and negotiations of the League of Nations, the move towards greater international recognition of ethnic/national groups was linked to a tendency to treat women's rights as an issue to be addressed at the national level (in a sense replicating the public/domestic divide at a higher level).

One of the main themes in the work of Michel Foucault (1990: 140–1) was the idea of 'bio-politics': that since the eighteenth century states have become particularly concerned with the management of their populations as a biological resource, 'with matters of life and death, with birth and propagation, with health and illness, both physical and mental, and with the processes that sustain or retard the optimization of the life of the population' (Dean 2003: 329). As Nira Yuval-Davis points out, women have often been the main targets of state policies regarding the biological reproduction of the nation. On the one hand, they are pressured to reproduce populations (especially men) depleted by war and disaster, or conversely to abstain from reproduction when there are fears of overpopulation straining national resources and capacities. On the other, they are made the object of eugenicist policies, such as the involuntary sterilization of women seen as not fit to reproduce, as was done to some black women in the US South between the 1920s and 1970s (2001: 123–5). It is also worth noting the special role of women as a supply of un- and underpaid labour to the nation-states. Women contribute to the 'bio-power' of the state by absorbing much of the cost of biological and social reproduction in child-rearing. Moreover, they have frequently served as a 'reserve army of labour', especially during wartime, as illustrated by the famous American Second World War icon of 'Rosie the Riveter' – representing women temporarily 'masculinized' as they moved into wartime factory production jobs they were previously thought unsuited for, only to be refeminized after the war. Thus, in Mann's terms, women have been doubly caged by the nation-state, once as nationals and again as women. The organizational power of states has been partly based on the patriarchal organization of their social power, often justified in terms of the good of the nation (cf. Lazar 2001; Verdery 1996: ch. 3)

While gender ideology was being shaped from the top down, it was also crucially being formed from the middle out – through the codification and dissemination of bourgeois sex roles and norms of respectability. George Mosse (1985b) explored the profound shift in mores from the late eighteenth to the late nineteenth century. As we have seen, the European middle classes of the nineteenth century struggled to define themselves and the nation against the classes above and below them. This was done especially through notions of 'decency' and 'respectability', the controlled and decorous management of the appetites, and sexual passions in particular. Mosse weaves together the condemnation of masturbation and nonheterosexual practices, the elevation of Greek sculpture as a paradigm of desexualized beauty, and new-found prudery in literary subjects, as parts of a set of values and manners that demonstrated the middle class's exemplary self-command. This was combined with gender stereotypes: 'masculinity meant depth and seriousness, while the feminine was shallow and frivolous' (Mosse 1985b: 17), which situated men in overall control of this ethos of control. During this period the bourgeois family took on a special responsibility for socializing the population, first its own children and then, by example and instruction, those of other classes, in the ways of discipline, respect for authority and love of the nation. As Mosse remarks,

The prevailing sentiment was that the family was a cheap and efficient surrogate for the state, controlling the passions at their source. Clearly the family was the policeman on the beat, an indispensable agent of sexual control as directed by physicians (more often than not, the family doctor), educators, and the nation itself. Any threat to its survival endangered the nation's future. (1985b: 20)

While the structure of the nuclear family had a deep history in Europe, it had hitherto been more embedded in community-wide patterns of kinship and sex roles. Structural transformations of the larger kin and community context, brought on by industrialization and urbanization, underwrote this new privileging of the (often idealized rather than real-ized) married couple and their bourgeois family. Returning to the case of Sweden, Löfgren describes the uneasy reception of these bourgeois mores as they seeped into the rural areas:

One sign of the new togetherness of the loving couple, which may seem unimportant but had great symbolic significance, was revealed in the altered seating arrangements in parish churches. Men and women had previously been separated, in a pattern that communicated a solidarity within each sex and cut across boundaries of kith and kin. Among the new urban bourgeoisie this arrangement was abandoned for a new one: the wife left the other women and came to sit at her husband's side. The first instances of this rearrangement provoked strong reactions from the peasants. Usually it was visiting townspeo-ple or upper-class couples who introduced the pattern: 'It was the quality folks that started this, like the gentry: anybody else would have been embarrassed to sit beside a man, but it caught on', one peasant women recollects. (Frykman and Löfgren 1987: 99–100)

Let me conclude this section by considering three different examples of women's participation in nationalist movements, asking what might account for different patterns of participation. In an influential essay Anne McClintock (1996) compares the developments of Afrikaner nationalism and the black nationalism of the African National Congress (ANC), with an eye on gender. What emerges from her account is a contrast, within a common overarching frame of patriarchal gender rela-tions. Afrikaner national identity was forged in the decades after their defeat in the Anglo-Boer War (1899–1902), drawing together the rural, mostly agriculturally based patchwork of Dutch-descended people into a more ideologically and linguistically defined group. A standard

Afrikaans language was developed. In 1918 the all-male secret society the *Broederband* (the Brotherhood) was founded to foster Afrikaner solidarity. And in 1938, the *Tweede Trek* (the Second Trek) re-enacted the Great Trek of a hundred years earlier, when thousands of Boer's had migrated eastward to occupy new lands, and escape British colonial authority. The *Tweede Trek* was a pivotal nation-building ritual, in which the image of the stalwart patriarchal Boer family travelling in covered wagons became iconic. McClintock suggests that 'Lacking control of the institutions of modernity, Afrikaners mobilized through the one institution with which they were intimate and over which they still held precarious control: the family' (1996: 275). In this process the Afrikaner women were drawn into the domestically confined role of *volksmoeders* (mothers of the nation), guardians of culture and language, and embodying the sufferings of their community in the Anglo-Boer War, when many women and their children were concentrated into camps by the British, where disease was often rampant and mortality high. There was a degree of importance and empowerment attached to this role within Afrikaner nationalism, but it was largely inward-looking and symbolic.

The ANC was formed in 1912 to articulate grievances regarding the exclusion of blacks from the political negotiations forming the Union of South Africa in 1910. In the early years the wives of male members were made 'auxiliary members' with duties to provide shelter and entertainment to the male delegates. But by 1943 the ANC granted women full voting rights and formed a Women's League. This growing role in the core organization was linked to the fact that black women were being explicitly politicized through their resistance to the state's efforts to control their mobility in pursuit of work through the use of passes required to move from one area to another. Major women's protest marches against these policies in 1918 and 1956, resulting in arrests, imprisonment and hard labour, were key events in demonstrating their militancy and radicalizing their demands. While maternal images of black African women were part of the ANC language, by the 1970s women had made themselves recognized as an active element in the public nationalist struggle. As McClintock puts it, 'African women nationalists, unlike their Afrikaner counterparts, have transformed and infused the ideology of motherhood with an insurrectionary cast' (1996: 279). In short, despite their shared patriarchal frameworks, these two historically intertwined nationalisms presented women with very different possibilities and demands for participation, based on very different problems of the organization and pursuit of power.

In a very different context, Deborah Elliston (2000) has explored the gender dynamic of contemporary nationalism in the Society Islands of French Polynesia. Since the 1980s there has developed a movement for independence from France (based partly on objections to France's use of one of the islands' atolls as a nuclear testing ground) that has made considerable electoral and ideological progress. The support for the movement however, comes predominantly from men, especially those between the ages of fifteen and thirty. Women have largely stayed aloof. Given that in these islands gender relations are relatively egalitarian, and women have traditionally enjoyed substantial social power, we might expect women to be more involved. Elliston explains this gendered skew of nationalist sentiments in terms of differences in how men and women are socially and spatially integrated into society. Although there are no matrilineal rules of land tenure, a pattern has developed since the nineteenth century whereby women tend to be the titleholders of kin-group lands, and titles tend to pass down the female line. Young women maintain strong ties to their natal households and their larger kin groups, associated with specific lands. A woman may move away from home for long periods to work in the city, but her own room will be preserved for her in her household of origin, a practice not paralleled in the case of young men. It is the custom for young men to travel about the islands in their formative years before marriage, staying with friends and more distant kin, exchanging casual labour for room and board. Many young men end up in the capital city of Papeete on Tahiti Island, doing occasional work and living a fairly footloose life. Thus, while young women are firmly attached to the place where they were born, involved in household income and decision-making and trained to become household heads, young men experience years of shifting residence, structural dependence, and peripherality to decision-making in their natal households. Elliston argues that:

> The generalized place nationalists use to forge their movement is more persuasive for young men than young women because they practice different modes of belonging to places. While the practices and meanings of place differences serve to animate nationalist calls – enabling them to posit 'Tahiti and her Islands' as the place in relation to which nationalist collectivity should be forged – gendered and generationally differentiated modes of belonging qualify and compromise the persuasiveness and possibilities of this place-based alliance. (2000: 197)

This example suggests that not only are the forms of participation in nationalism often gendered, but also the very relevance of nationalism may be affected by the broader social organization of gender differences in some cases.

Democracy as Routinized Nationalism

In the Introduction (Chapter 1) I suggested that nationalism is not just the pursuit of statehood – well-established states and their populations continually engage in nationalism. The time has come to elaborate this point. We know that ruling elites and states, whether authoritarian or democratic, engage in ideological projects of nation building to give themselves political legitimacy. And we recognize that this process will be renewed in phases, according to political circumstances. But I want to argue that in stable democratic regimes this process of nationalism is very deeply embedded in civil society and electoral systems, and not simply an elite- or state-led process. It is part of the normal functioning of democratic regimes.

My view runs against much of the literature. Donald Horowitz (1985) has emphasized the differences between ethnic politics, based on notions of kin-based group membership, and liberal democratic politics, based on the ideal of free individuals choosing their political memberships. Where the former principles are strong, creating social cleavages between ethnic groups, attempts to operate the latter principles, as through democratic elections, will be deranged. Horowitz's extensive analysis of these situations rests on a mostly implicit contrast with the 'normal' politics of liberal democratic regimes, where voting is shaped by personal rather than collective interests and choices. This focus on individualism tends to underestimate the continuing role of nationalism in the democratic process. Jack Snyder (2000), as we have seen, identifies nationalism with incomplete democratization, suggesting that as democracy becomes more fully developed and deeply institutionalized, nationalism as such recedes into the background. In John Breuilly's (1993) analytic framework nationalism is a form of oppositional politics, usually opposed to something that is not a nation-state, such as colonies and empires. For him, the whole purpose of nationalism as an ideology is to erase the distinction between state and society by making the cultural group and its state congruent – nationalism simply is the pursuit of that goal. But once it has been achieved, whether by separation, unification, or reforming the *ancien régime*, the reasons for nationalism evaporate.

In the Introduction (Chapter 1) I also offered this working definition of nationalism: as the making of combined claims, on behalf of a population, to *identity*, to *jurisdiction* and to *territory*. What probably comes first to mind with this definition is the image of a culturally defined population, largely occupying a region within a larger state territory, calling for greater political autonomy and perhaps independence. But the definition is deliberately broad to allow for the fact that nationalism can be at play even when contention is not over territory, but rather over what notions of national identity and/or proper government will be in force within a given territorial domain, which may itself be relatively unproblematic. It also allows for the fact that liberal democracy, as a political form, is sufficiently open-ended to engender considerable disensus and conflict over conceptions of national identity and proper government. Liberal democracies do not so much transcend nationalism, as domesticate it, routinizing its dynamic by channelling it through core political institutions. On the one hand, nationalism is seriously altered by this context, de-fanged for the most part, and rendered less dangerous. But on the other hand, it is an indispensable aspect of the state's ongoing need for legitimacy and inevitable competition between social groups to define the wider society of which they are members.

Nationalism is a basic part of how relatively stable democracies legitimate and re-legitimate themselves. David Beetham (1991) has argued that the legitimation of modern states has three aspects: (1) legitimation through formal acts of consent by the governed, such as voting – when voter turn-out is low, legitimacy may be threatened; (2) conformity of political actors to legal rules – for example, rigging elections is illegitimate; and (3) the justification of rules in terms of shared beliefs – if the rules are not in sync with people's values, standards and normative expectations, legitimacy will suffer (1991: 15–20). It is the third of these aspects that particularly concerns us here. Liberal democracies are premised on a high degree of tolerance for diversity of belief and opinion, as long as conflicts generated by this diversity are acted out within the 'rules of the game'. But while the fundamentals of the constitutional structure may enjoy wide and deep legitimacy, disagreements over a range of policies – immigration, minority rights, language policy, patterns of economic redistribution, reproductive rights, access to arms, church–state relation – may become intense, with implications not only for legislation, but for constitutions as well. Though some disputes such as these are engaged as 'single issues', many have a tendency to become aggregated and aligned in unifying worldviews. To this extent, what is at stake is contending visions of how a population within a given territory should be governed, and such visions are normally underwritten by a certain conception of the population's common *identity*, embodied in shared beliefs and values, what Rogers Smith (2003) has called 'stories of peoplehood'.

The dynamics of association in civil society, and of participation in the party political system, provide the mechanisms by which competing 'stories' of the nation struggle with each other, and are promoted. The state must continually reach down into this process of contentious national identity-building to renew its legitimacy. Norberto Bobbio has defined civil society as

> The place where, especially in periods of institutional crisis, *de facto* powers are formed that aim at obtaining their own legitimacy even at the expense of legitimate power; where, in other words, the processes of delegitimation and relegitimation take place. This forms the basis of the frequent assertion that the solution of a grave crisis threatening the survival of a political system must be sought first and foremost in civil society where it is possible to find new sources of legitimation and therefore new sources of consensus. (1989: 26)

Even when problems of legitimacy for the political system are not 'grave', the process of democratic politics looks much like this. Sara Diamond's (1995) study of right-wing movements in the US since the Second World War describes how a diverse array of groups, movements and causes on the right have coalesced over the decades into a powerful and effective political base for the conservative right and the Republican Party. Over the years, issues of anti-communism, racist segregationism, moral traditionalism, evangelical and fundamentalist Christianity and neoconservativism have interweaved, at times opposing and other times supporting the state. In recent years it has been the highly effective grass-roots organizing of the evangelical Christian movement through its church networks, in alliance with a more elite neoconservative intellectual movement embedded in the Republican Party and associated think tanks, that have consolidated a base of political support for the current president George W. Bush. The fruit of this alliance is the agenda of a nation guided by Christian values and forcefully promoting democracy around the world. A similar story, though currently less successful, could be told about mobilization on the US left, aligning anti-poverty, civil rights, anti-militarism movements, and gaining for a period from the strains on political legitimacy engendered by the Vietnam War and the Watergate scandal. Precisely because they tend towards stronger programmes of ideological conformity, movements on the conservative right may be more successful than those on the liberal left in generating

an 'imagined community', but an imagining of the nation, and its relations to other nations, is what is at stake on both sides.

Bobbio also makes the useful observation that political parties are
ambiguously placed between state and civil society (1989: 25). On the
one hand, they are the organizations officially sanctioned by the state to
field candidates, win votes and form governments; on the other, they are
successful only insofar as they can build up constituency support from
below, outside of the state proper. They function like dredges that reach
down from the state into society, gathering legitimacy and transferring it
back onto the state. Parties long in government, burdened by the realities
and compromises of actual power, will often appear to lose touch with the
common people, while those out of government will be able to more
easily present themselves as representatives of the estranged masses.
These comments obviously apply especially well to two-party systems.
The main point, however, is that political parties by their nature compete
to win votes and, especially with the post-industrial decline of more
clearly class-based party politics, they do this by making claims to represent the entire national population, defining its interests and values in
terms of the party's interests and values. In this way, far from transcending nationalism, normal democratic party politics keeps national identity
on a constant 'slow boil'. Nationalism is an essential resource for the
maintenance of legitimacy in democratic regimes, which harness and
contain its frequently dangerous energies, while also utilizing them. So
just as Ernest Gellner argued that nationalism is the demand to be ruled
by those co-ethnic with oneself, I am suggesting that it is also at work in
the demand to be ruled by people who share one's moral values and
beliefs.

Michael Billig's influential thesis of 'banal nationalism' (1995) is
celebrated for its attention to the mundane ways in which national identity is reinforced by a myriad of small daily practices in which it is
implicit. But his larger point should not be lost and is similar to my own.
Nationalism is not just residual background noise in democratic regimes,
it is a key legitimizing resource that can be activated and brought into the
foreground, for example, during times of war and other social crises. In
the US today, the anxieties raised by the terrorist attacks of September
2001, the solidarity engendered by the commitments of war and the translation of a morally conservative Christian agenda into a successful legitimizing national discourse rooted in civil society has led to ideological
polarization between left and right. A friend in California recently sent
me a humorous email, in the form of a letter to President Bush, declaring
the secession of California and the other Democratic-voting states from

the US, and gloating over the cultural capital they would take with them. Another such email was simply an image of North America, with boundaries redrawn to unify the Democratic voting states with Canada, leaving a rump of southern and midwestern states called 'Jesusland'. These things will not happen but all humour requires a basis in truth. I have been trying to identify that basis.

Conclusion

This chapter has not presented a theory of nationalism as such, but rather outlined some guiding principles for the study of power, emphasizing their particular relevance to the study of nationalism. This is because I view nationalism as a particular, largely modern way of pursuing power, one that both arises out of, and seizes upon, other dimensions of the social organization of power. I focused on cities, gender, and democratic politics as ways of illustrating these articulations of modes of social organization, which have ramifications for how the power of nationalism is realized. As I have said, I see the social quest for power as the normal mode of human affairs, one that is transhistorical and behind most human processes. Although people can be motivated by nationalism, and it can become an effective social force, ultimately that 'force' is rooted in the fundamental need for power, and nationalism is more the form that the pursuit of power takes under certain conditions than a cause *sui generis*.

Further Reading

The most important statement articulating an organizational conception of power that bears upon questions of nationalism is found in Mann (1986a: ch. 1). Other key works developing an organizational view of power include: Beetham (1991), Poggi (2001), Wolf (1999) and Wrong (2002). On the significance of urbanism for nationalism start with Armstrong (1982: ch. 4), Jacobs (1985) and Nairn (1997: chs 5 & 7). Several of the studies discussed in this chapter come from a very good special issue of *Nations and Nationalism* on gender (2000, volume 6, part 4). Walby's valuable discussion of patriarchy there is developed at greater length in Walby (1990). Lazar (2001) and Verdery (1996: ch. 3) provide contrasting case studies of the state's nationalist agenda for gender relations and biological reproduction in Singapore and Eastern Europe respectively. Yuval-Davis (1997) provides a general introduction to the topic of gender and nationalism.

8
Culture

In this last of our expository chapters, we look at 'culture' as an analytic lens for understanding nationalism, again surveying some influential approaches. Primordialist themes of the power of symbols of descent, territory and language to create and evoke emotional bonds and national identities clearly resonate with notions of culture. So in a sense we are coming full circle to where the book began. But primordialism usually implies assumptions about the psychologically deep-seated nature of nationalist sentiments, and about the relatively stable and enduring nature of culture, assumptions that need not be part of a cultural analysis. Therefore, I think it is appropriate to treat the concept of culture separately. I stress, however, that the concept of culture shades into that of ideology, and that we must, in fact, imagine a continuum between cultural and ideological analyses. I begin by offering a fairly standard concept of culture to orient what follows. In the next chapter I will problematize this 'standard' concept of culture, arguing for one more closely related to the idea of organizational power explored in Chapter 7.

A Concept of Culture (and Ideology)

Anthropologists have claimed 'culture' as a central concept for much of the history of their discipline, and their definitions have had a wide influence in the social sciences and humanities, so that is where I start. The concept has broadly come to denote the sum of mental phenomena that orient and structure life in social groups. It is usually emphasized that culture is always learned, not biologically inherited, and that it consists of knowledge one must possess in order to pass as an accepted member of a social group. Thus, culture is not a private affair – it is by definition shared, however imperfectly, with other people. Symbols are often cited as the key medium for transmitting culture. A further caveat is usually offered: we are all equally endowed with culture as a general human capacity, individuals and groups cannot be ranked from 'uncultured' to 'cultured'. It is worth noting this because of Ernest Gellner's (1983) argument that

170

nationalism involves the generalization of a 'high culture'. Gellner did not mean that nationalism bestows culture on those who did not have it before, but rather that the culture of elite groups, and especially their language and literacy, spreads and replaces, or at least supplements, other 'folk' cultures sufficiently to create a certain ideological unity around the idea of the nation.

Clifford Geertz has probably been the most widely influential anthropological theorist of culture in recent decades, so it makes sense to turn to him for a representative definition of culture: 'an historically transmitted pattern of meanings embodied in symbols, a system of inherited conceptions expressed in symbolic forms by means of which men communicate, perpetuate, and develop their knowledge about and attitudes toward life' (Geertz 1973: 89). Later in the same essay Geertz goes on to argue that culturally patterned sets of symbols have a special dual nature. They function simultaneously as 'models of' reality, representing what is, and as 'models for' reality, guiding appropriate social action in that reality (1973: 93–4). This unity of descriptive and prescriptive functions is often seen as basic to the nature of culture. This prescriptive aspect of cultural symbols points us, however, to the close affinity between the notions of culture and ideology. Often, when we use the term ideology we mean more specifically 'political ideology'. As Andrew Heywood observes:

> Coming into existence in the early nineteenth century, political ideologies are a kind of 'world view', made up of a collection of doctrines, theories and principles which claim to interpret the present and offer a view of a desired future. These more or less systematic sets of ideas provide the basis for some kind of organised social action; they may defend the existing order, advocate its reform and improvement, or propose its revolutionary overthrow and replacement. (Heywood 1994: 7–8)

It has often been noted that the peculiar thing about nationalism in this narrow sense of political ideology is its promiscuous ability to combine with other such ideologies – liberalism, socialism, conservatism, fascism and so on (Benner 2001; Freeden 1998). Heywood goes on to note that this narrow political sense of ideology is embedded within and linked to larger and more diffuse networks of ideas. In fact, ideology is often used in a much broader sense to characterize society-wide patterns of thought, in ways that make it almost indistinguishable from the concept of culture (e.g. Wuthnow 1987). Similarly, some employ a concept of culture so infused with a concern for power relations that it becomes difficult to distinguish from the concept of ideology (e.g. Sider 1986). Mindful of the analytical difficulties that can arise from this kind of blurring, Eric Wolf draws a distinction in his own writing between 'ideas' and 'ideology':

> The term 'ideas' is intended to cover the entire range of mental constructs rendered manifest in public representations, populating all human domains. I believe that ideology needs to be used more restrictively, in that 'ideologies' suggest unified schemes or configurations developed to underwrite or manifest power. Equating all ideation with ideology masks the ways in which ideas come to be linked to power. (Wolf 1999: 4)

The various scholars discussed below can be seen as roughly defining a continuum from more cultural to more ideological conceptions of the governing patterns of symbols and ideas at play in nationalism. They can also be seen as progressing from a concern with more 'naturalized' to more 'politicized' roles for ideas, bearing in mind that for many the whole point of ideology is that it renders inherently political ideas in naturalized terms. Under the covering headings of 'ethno-symbolism' and 'ideology', the following discussion progresses along both continua at the same time, from culture to ideology, and from naturalized to politicized ideas and symbols.

Ethno-symbolism

In Chapter 2 we encountered Anthony Smith's arguments about the deeper ethnic roots of modern nations. Here we examine his concept of culture and how it shapes his idea of *ethnies*, nations and their historical continuity. In the 1990s Smith began labelling his approach 'ethno-symbolic'. Reflecting on the development of his ideas he remarks:

> Given the many economic and political ruptures between pre-modern and modern collective cultural identities in the same area, any continuity between *ethnie* and nation had to be located in the cultural and symbolic spheres. This in turn led to the adoption of the term 'ethno-symbolism' for an approach that sought to establish relations between the different kinds of collective cultural identity by focussing on elements of myth, memory, value, symbol, and tradition that tended to change more slowly, and were more flexible in meaning, than the processes in other domains. (2004: 196)

Smith uses this term to identify both his own work and that of John Armstrong and John Hutchinson, which we will consider below. This approach relies on something like Geertz's conception of culture offered above. Smith describes *ethnies* and nations as being composed out of 'myth-symbol complexes' and more specifically '*mythomoteurs*', a term he adopts from Armstrong (1982: 8–9). The former is the looser term for the ideational repertoires of given cultures, while *mythomoteur* more specifically designates a 'constitutive political myth' (Smith 1986: 58) that defines identity in relation to a specific polity while also legitimating it. *Mythomoteurs* come in various broad types. Dynastic *mythomoteurs* attach to 'the office of the ruler and by extension to the ruling house and dynasty' (1986: 58). Typical of both the ancient imperial polities of the Middle East (e.g. Egypt, Sumer, Assyria) and the medieval kingdoms of Europe (e.g. under Charlemagne), such *mythomoteurs* are generally fused with religion, connecting dynastic lineages to ancestral religious figures, and infusing the dynastic dominion with an aura of sacredness, and its inhabitants and their ruler with a chosen role in realizing the divine will. Communal *mythomoteurs* 'are nurtured by other strata and focus on an image of the whole community rather than a privileged lineage or state institution' (1986: 61). Here Smith contrasts two forms. A more political form, exemplified by the Hellenic city-states of the fifth century BC, in which cultural pride revolving around a pan-Hellenic religious pantheon, shared heroic myths and linguistic continuity was focused in individual city-states with their local deities, political institutions and aesthetic achievements. And a more religious form, in which collective identity revolves around a special relationship between a people and their God. Prime examples include the Jews and the Armenians. After long periods of episodic kingdom building, from the destruction of the first temple and the Babylonian exile (586 BC) the history of the Jews became one repeatedly politically destabilized by large, predatory neighbouring empires. In this context the role of the priesthood, the prophets and subsequently the rabbis and synagogues, and of the law of the Torah, with its boundary-preserving rules of intermarriage, circumcision and dietary laws, served to reinforce communal identity. According to Smith:

> When the Synagogue took over the functions of the Temple, the democratisation of religious self-conceptions was complete; the rabbi was a teacher and an expounder of the *Torah*, not an intermediary, and the Oral Law, embodied in the Mishnah, was designed for the whole community of believers. Similarly, any restoration of the Exile became increasingly geo-communal rather than geo-political: it

involved the return of the whole community of Israel to Zion, its sacred centre, more than the restoration of the rule of the house of David in Palestine, and the Messianic era was centred less on the person or agency of the anointed one than on the universal justice and peace which Israel's restoration would bring. Priestly and prophetic denunciation of the institution of monarchy had paved the way for a theocratic and communal conception of the basic *mythomoteur* of the Jewish people. (1986: 64)

Part of Smith's point here is that these *mythomoteurs* are flexible and evolving, and that the Jewish communal-religious type evolved out of an earlier, more dynastic type, under the vagaries of historical circumstances. He suggests a similar development of the Hellenic communal-political *mythomoteur* into a more communal-religious one under the Ottoman Empire as the Greeks became a *millet* (an ethno-religious population with a distinctive legal and administrative status under the system of Ottoman rule) socially organized especially by the Patriarchate of the Greek Orthodox Church.

Obviously these dynastic and communal *mythomoteurs* tend to correspond with Smith's two types of *ethnies*: lateral and vertical. Smith tends to draw his examples from the premodern historical record, but it is possible to extend his model to the present day. Recent Serbian nationalism has drawn on the myth of the defeat of Prince Lazar on the fields of Kosovo, defending Orthodox Christianity against Islam. Even an ethnically complex settler society such as the United States draws on certain legitimating myths, as a pioneering entrepreneurial people, with a special historical mission to promote religious freedom and democracy, unified through purifying crises such as the American Civil War in which the stain of slavery was cleansed (albeit very imperfectly). However, we can also identify counter-streams of myth, either because the perspective of the present allows us a fuller view of things, or because liberal democracies must necessarily tell themselves more contradictory stories, or both. Thus, for example, notions of the US as embodying principles of religious tolerance sit uneasily with concurrent notions of it as a specifically Christian and Protestant country, although both link back to the story of Puritan pilgrims landing at Plymouth Rock (cf. Cauthen 2004: 26–30). Smith does seem to see real limits to how far *mythomoteurs* can be extended. He casts a sceptical eye on the building of a unifying identity for the new Europe, arguing that much of its myth-history resources are too tied to specific parts of Europe, and to no longer acceptable ideas of religious and imperial mission:

Here lies the new Europe's true dilemma: a choice between unaccept-
able historical myths and memories on the one hand, and on the other
a patchwork, memoryless scientific 'culture' held together solely by
the political will and economic interest that are so often subject to
change. In between there lies the hope of discovering that 'family of
cultures' . . . through which over several generations some loose,
overarching political identity and community might gradually be
forged. (1999: 245)

Two other themes that permeate Smith's work are the ideas of 'golden
ages' and 'chosen peoples' in the symbolic construction of communal
identity. Smith stresses that *ethnie* and nation-building frequently draw
on notions of an ideal period in the community's past, characterized by
heroic figures and great cultural achievements (1986: 191–200). A typical example of the modern recovery/reconstruction of a golden age is
found in the Finnish *Kalevala*, a collection of ballads and poems assembled and combined in 1835, which inspired contemporary artists and
intellectuals, estranged by Swedish cultural and Russian political domination in the later nineteenth century, with its tales of heroic ancestral
deeds (Smith 1991: 66). These golden ages are not simply treasured
objects of collective memory, but serve important functions. They articulate the defining moral and aesthetic standards of the cultural group;
they provide hope and inspiration for moral regeneration and national
rebirth; they indicate, through lineal heritage, the inherent capacity of the
group to recapture its glorious past; and they provide guidance for action
in the present, justifying people's sacrifices for the national cause (Smith
1999: 263–4).

A long-standing but growing interest in Smith's work is the idea of
'ethnic election', or more specifically, chosen peoples (1992; 2003a). In
short, religious traditions frequently supply an ideational template for the
imagining of the nation and its purpose. He does not argue that nations
and nationalisms should be regarded as the direct causal outcomes of pre-
existing religious traditions, but rather that such religions have supplied
crucial cultural resources for such projects. Key among these are: (1) a
sense of being chosen by the deity for a worldly mission; (2) having a
divinely appointed sacred relationship to a specific territory; and (3) a
belief in the regenerative power of individual and collective sacrifice
(2003a: 255). In modern nationalisms these ingredients may either be
fused within a religious nationalism, where a particular faith and nation
coincide, or a more secularized nation may simply inherit these ideological forms from its more religious past, preserving them while filling them

Box 8.1 Symbolizing the New Republic of South Africa

In 1990, after four decades of apartheid, the National Party government of South Africa yielded to internal and international pressures and began relinquishing power. The African National Congress (ANC) won an overwhelming majority in the first multi-racial elections in 1994 and proceeded to reform the constitution and government as a multi-ethnic parliamentary democracy. The new republic of 44.8 million people rivals India in its diversity: with eleven official languages and eight non-official ones; about three quarters of the population being some variety of Protestant Christian, other religions including traditional animism, Islam, Hinduism, Judaism and Buddhism; and respondents categorizing themselves in the 2001 census as African/Black (79 per cent), White (9.6 per cent), Coloured (i.e. 'mixed race' people of the Cape, speaking Afrikaans, 8.9 per cent), and Indian/Asian (2.5 per cent).

Along with diversity there are profound inequalities and economic and social problems. A substantial portion of the black majority lives in extreme poverty, especially in rural areas, while much of the white minority lives in relative middle-class comfort, many of the wealthiest living in suburban, gated communities, especially around Johannesburg. Despite economic growth there is 40 per cent unemployment, violent crime rates are very high, international drug trafficking is rife and around 21.5 per cent of the population were estimated to be HIV positive in 2004. Achieving a new national unity under these conditions is a serious challenge.

In April 2000 the Republic adopted a new Coat of Arms and motto to express this challenge.

The anthropologist Alan Barnard (2004) has analysed the symbolism involved and how it attempts to grapple with the diversity of the South African people. The image of the two figures holding hands on the shield is derived from the an ancient work of Khoisan rock art, and is chosen because the Khoisan are, according to official description, 'the oldest known inhabitants of the land', thus symbolizing a generic indigeneity for all South African peoples. The original image has been abstracted by removing a bow and arrow, some body decoration, and male genitalia, and then duplicating and 'flipping' the original single figure to create the image of two people coming together. The motto underneath, '*!Ke e: /xarra //ke*', is officially translated as 'Diverse people unite'. The motto is written in /Xam, an extinct language distantly related to modern Khoisan languages. Barnard observes that this neatly avoids privileging any of the 'living' official languages,

→

with more secular-nationalist content. Once again, ancient Israel provides a highly influential model of the elect nation, sometimes filtered though Christianity. While distancing himself from any historical-causal analysis, Smith nonetheless strongly suggests that we have to account for the persistence of nations over the *longue durée* in terms of such

Figure 8.1   The South African Coat of Arms

again invoking a kind of 'virtual primordiality' for the present republic. The motto began as the English phrase 'diverse people unite', echoing other national mottos such as the US's '*E pluribus unum*', 'From many, one', as well a Marx and Engels 'Workers of all nations, unite', which was then translated into the extinct /Xam. The resulting phrase is ambiguous and can be read in several ways. Barnard suggests the alternatives: 'People of different origins are joining together', or 'People who differ in opinion are talking to one another'. This more subtle rendering may better capture the challenges that South Africa's people are now facing.

symbolic processes, and that the strength and resilience of nations will tend to depend on them.

Smith situates these key symbolic processes – *mythomoteurs*, golden ages, chosenness – within a general context of symbolic activity that concretely sustain them: rituals, commemorations, festivals, monuments, sacred places, emblems, flags, coins, hymns and so on. He is very aware that these symbolic ideas need to be routinely and popularly enacted and encountered to have a role in the creation and maintenance of ethnic and national identities. He is also adamant that while such symbolic processes clearly serve the instrumental needs of political leaders, this is not an adequate explanation for their existence:

> What it misses, however, is even more important: the ways in which such myths and symbols, values and memories, *shape* the nation-to-be. They are not simply 'instruments' of leaders and elites of the day, not even of whole communities. They are potent signs and explanations, they have capacities for generating emotion in successive generations, they possess explosive power that goes far beyond the 'rational' uses which elites and social scientists deem appropriate. Evoking an heroic past is like playing with fire, as the history of all too many *ethnie* and nations locked in conflict today, can tell. The fires generated by these mythical pasts burn for several generations, long after the events that first stimulated their acceptance. It is for this reason that some attention must be devoted to the forms of ancient myths, and the symbolism of holy places, in the present construction of nations. One may learn as much about the 'spirit' and 'shape' of modern nations by an investigation of their myths of golden ages and their poetry of nature, as by any analysis of social institutions and class formation. (1986: 201, emphasis in original)

Smith's intellectual shift from a somewhat more modernist, intelligentsia-focused analysis to the perspective summarized above was significantly stimulated by John Armstrong's book *Nations Before Nationalism* (1982). Whereas Smith searches the globe for variations on his ideal types, Armstrong works more in the style of a grand narrative, describing a complex layering and transformation of social institutions over the *longue durée*. He prefers to analyse ethnicity and nationalism as sets of features shaped especially though their interactive relations. Drawing on the work of the anthropologist Fredrik Barth (1969), he sees ethnicity as primarily a matter of 'attitudes' that ethnic groups have towards each other. Group identities are defined by symbolic contrasts and oppositions with other groups, and it is the marking of social boundaries through symbolic differences that is the definitive feature of ethnicity, rather than any enduring demographic or cultural 'content' of the group. Having said this, Armstrong defines nations, ethnicities and 'supraethnicities' (1982: 285) based on religious adherence, in terms of characteristic sets of myths and symbols that do the effective boundary work, so there is a kind of defining content implied by his interactive framework.

Armstrong's sweeping history of Eurasia is difficult to summarize and I can only do so schematically here. Two great divergences in religious social formations lie at the base of his account. First, he sees the division between Eastern and Western Christian civilizations, the former unifying the roles of emperor and head of the church, the latter separating these roles between secular rulers and the papacy, as having resounding consequences. Second, he sees Christianity and Islam as encoding cultural ideas about social organization into their ideological structures that were dominant in regions where they eventually took hold. Thus, Christianity has an elective affinity with sedentary ways of life that nostalgically imagine paradise on the model of a settled, cultivated terrain, while Islam has a historical affiliation with nomadic ways of life, imagining paradise on the model of the dessert oasis, and society in terms of genealogical relations rather than shared occupation of territory. He argues that these deep patterns of imagining society and its ideal past are strongly associated with these two religions, even if sedentarism and nomadism did not always, especially with the passage of time, characterize populations following these faiths.

On this base of religious, macro-ethnic patterns he identifies two other determining patterns: urbanism and empire. Armstrong argues that long-term patterns of urbanism have been consequential for the formation of ethnicities:

> In classifying the impact of different types of cities upon ethnicity, three salient criteria can be identified: (a) strong civic consciousness, expressed in the symbolism of architectonic unity as well as in more direct social participation; (b) territorial extension of the city, by legal jurisdiction and by residence of the elites, to a surrounding rural district; and (c) sharply separated ethnoreligious elements, often distinguished by residential segregation but always identified by other boundary mechanisms such as distinct legal codes. (1982: 127)

He explores various combinations of the relative presence or absence of these criteria, but most telling is the contrast between the characteristic northern West European city and the Polish and Hungarian cities of central Eastern Europe. In the former there was strong civic consciousness of a burgher class, lacking territorial extension to the countryside and ethnic segmentation. This proved an ideal seedbed for modern nationalist ideas (see the discussion of 'cities' in Chapter 7). In the latter, weak civic consciousness (social leadership was rurally located in the gentry) and lack of territorial extension, combined with ethnic segmentation, tended to produce intense ethnic divisions. On top of this urban dynamic lay an imperial one. This is where the idea of the *mythomoteur* comes into play for Armstrong. Whereas Smith tends to generalize this concept to the self-imaginings of all ethnic groups, for Armstrong it is closely linked to the legitimation of a polity in the strict sense. Armstrong's *mythomoteurs* are manifold and evolving ideological structures, but crucial components include, for the Islamic polity: universal theocracy, and the principle of *ghazi* (struggle against the infidel); for the Christian polity, leaving aside significant variations between East and West: the polity as the 'terrestrial reflection' of the divine plan, and *ante-muralism* (seeing the polity as the front-line of defence of Christendom). The diffusion of these *mythomoteurs* over broad imperial areas is shaped by administrative centralization and the integration, through such things as 'architecture, rubrics, and insignia' (1982: 164), of smaller polities and urban centres with the imperial capital. The later chapters of the book explore the roles of language and more specific religious organizations in further honing these larger patterns into the smaller scale ethnicities and nationalities we recognize today. But these are primarily refinements of the main thrust of the argument, which is laid out at the level of world religions and empires.

John Hutchinson shares Smith and Armstrong's belief in the substantial ethnic foundations of modern nations (Hutchinson 2000). He makes a strong distinction in his writings between 'cultural' and 'political' forms of nationalism (1987a: 12–15). Both forms are in a sense 'political', having objectives and strategies for achieving them, but they differ in what those objectives are:

> Political nationalists have as their objective the achievement of a representative national state that will guarantee to its members uniform citizenship rights. They tend to organize on legal-rational lines, forming centralized apparatuses in order to mobilize different groups against the existing polity and to direct them to this unitary end . . . The aim of cultural nationalists is rather the moral regeneration of the historic community, or, in other words, the re-creation of their distinctive national civilization. Since a civilization is a spontaneous social order, it cannot be constructed like a state from above, but only resuscitated from the bottom up. (1987a: 15–16)

Hutchinson suggests a kind of dialectic or 'cycle' between these two forms. Cultural nationalists inevitably encounter state power and need to commit themselves to more activist forms of politics to affect the state and realize their aims, but political nationalist movements in turn are prone to bureaucratic routinization and can engender social divisiveness if the project fails to make progress. Under these conditions they will need to turn back to the cultural nationalists for re-legitimation. Hutchinson's primary empirical focus for these ideas has been Ireland in the nineteenth and twentieth centuries. He stresses that this cyclical pattern is generated by modern states with open, non-repressive political spheres in which people are relatively free to mobilize (1987b: 499).

His ultimate concern, however, is with cultural nationalism, and countering the idea that such nationalisms are by definition retrograde, conservative and backward-looking. Despite their concern with the recovery of the national past, he argues that such movements need to be understood as just as modernizing as political forms, as being 'evolutionary' rather than 'primitivist' in their objectives: 'Cultural nationalists act as *moral innovators*, establishing ideological movements at times of social crisis in order to transform the belief-systems of communities, and provide models of socio-political development that guide their modernizing strategies' (1987a: 30–1, emphasis in original).

Hutchinson sees cultural nationalists as characteristically rejecting both traditionalism and modernism, or rather trying to blend them in service of a national communalism that articulates distinctive national values in an evolving world of nations. In contrast to the idea that national cultures are instrumentally 'invented' (see below) or constructed by elites, he suggests that older myths and symbols are overlain with new ones by cultural nationalists in times of intense crisis, such as the Irish war of independence. Thus, his image of the cultural heritage of the nation is an archaeological one of an accumulation of layers of myths and symbols deposited in periods of intense national-symbolic activity (2004). His notion of cultural nationalism is deeply imbued with a weberian idea of charisma, in which social leaders don't simply pursue valued ends, but rather reorganize values.

More recently Hutchinson has been concerned to develop the theme of nations as 'zones of conflict' (2001). Far from homogeneous communities, he conceptualizes nations as complex entities divided by ethnic, regional and class identities, and drawing on competing repertoires of myths and symbols. Countering the Gellnerian image of nations unified by generalized high cultures, he suggests that:

State modernization is an important factor in the formation of national cultures, but not as is generally assumed in creating the cultural homogeneity necessary for a common citizenship. It ignites competing ethnic traditions with their different visions of community, and recurring conflicts that generate an exploration of different strategies by which nations can negotiate contingencies. This once again reinforces the dynamic aspect of ethno-national cultures and the pluralities within nations that gives them resources through which to overcome crises. (2001: 93–4)

All three of these 'ethno-symbolists' allow a place for politics in their conceptions of culture. In different ways they treat culture as a necessary resource for politics, with Hutchinson going somewhat further in conceiving conflict to be internal to the cultural process. But they are also concerned to conceptualize culture as a relatively autonomous process, in no way reducible to politics, and with a remarkable capacity for persistence across time.

Ideology

In this section we continue to look at the ideational dimension of nationalism, but in contrast to the ethno-symbolists, who tend to favour 'culture' as a way of conceiving of this ideation, here we consider approaches where ideas are understood more as 'ideology'. But just as the last section moved from more implicit to more explicit invocations of the relationship between culture and politics, this section moves from the more implicit to the more explicit manifestations of nationalism as ideology.

Michael Billig's striking notion of *Banal Nationalism* (1995) has been quite influential in recent years. His core aim is to help us understand nationalism better by drawing our attention away from its explicit and 'hot' forms, such as the wars of the 1990s in the disintegrating Yugoslavia, and towards its implicit and 'cool' forms, the banal and everyday invocations of nations and national identity that go unnoticed. He summarizes his argument by noting the difference between someone who salutes a flag, acknowledging national allegiance in a public ritual, and how we respond to a photograph in a magazine of that person's patriotic salute (1995: 40–1). He argues that it is a mistake to see only the original act of saluting as an event encoding ideology, because our implicit understanding of the photograph in the magazine involves us, however slightly, in the ideological acceptance of a world of nations and nation-alisms. And while we may encounter and participate in explicit events such as the salute rarely or even never, most of us engage in the implicit world of national symbols all the time. For every patriotically waved flag we encounter, many more sit quietly in the background, unnoticed, but still reminding us of our nationhood. Thus, for him nationalism is not simply something we believe in (or not), but something we become habit-uated to: 'Daily, the nation is indicated, or "flagged", in the lives of its citizenry. Nationalism, far from being an intermittent mood in estab-lished nations, is the endemic condition' (1995: 6). His point here relates closely to the one I was making Chapter 7 about the way liberal democ-racies routinize rather than transcend nationalism.

Banal Nationalism is also a critique of theories of social identity that understand it as the outcome of a process of self-categorization in search of a positive self-image (1995: 65–70). Such an approach, for instance, would explain a strong national identity paired with the demonization of some other national group as a way of building up self-worth by commit-ting to a like-minded group whose positive valuation is inherently based on a contrast with the devalued other. While Billig is not denying that this happens, he objects that what this approach fails to explain is why the categories are there, how the categorizing gets done and why the cate-gories endure. His notion of banal nationalism is meant to answer some of these questions. Basic to his argument is the idea that national identity is not simply a cognitive schema that sits in the mind, latent until some situation (a football match, a terrorist attack) activates it (1995: 69). Rather it is built into the entire cognitive and discursive environment (cf. Mavratsas 1999). One of the analytic tools he uses to bring this argument into focus is the linguistic concept of 'deixis': the way language refers indirectly to its context, in ways that assume and reinforce a common understanding of that context between those who utter and those who hear or read those utterances. He observes how the talk of politicians and newspaper articles, constantly using tiny words like 'we' 'us' 'here' 'the people' and so on, imply shared nationhood without directly referring to nationalism. By extension, the sports pages and even the weather report can be understood as banal, deictic enactments of naturalized national identity.

Finally, Billig's book also has another target – American nationalism. Banal nationalism, by definition, goes unnoticed, and Billig is very concerned that current discourses of nationalism tend to focus only on the 'hot' varieties associated with places like Serbia and Rwanda, ignoring the nationalism of the powerful nation-states because it is not associated with internal ethnic violence. He argues that it is curious that at a time when American economic and military power imposes itself around the world, academic discourses of globalization and postmodernity should loudly herald the demise of the nation-state and unifying national identities (1995: ch. 6). In fact, Billig argues, the emerging global culture has a distinctively American hue and thus, for Americans, including academic advocates of postmodernism (1995: ch. 7), there is an inability to recognize their own nationalism, which they universalize and confuse with the world at large. Having made this point about the invisibility of one's own

---

Box 8.2   The Naming of Streets by Arab-Palestinians

Drawing inspiration from Michael Billig (1995), Maoz Azaryahu and Rebecca Kook (2002) explore the role of street naming in encoding national identities and histories into the everyday urban environment. They examine three Arab-Palestinian communities: in Haifa and Jerusalem before the establishment of the state of Israel in 1948 and in the Israeli town of Umm el Fahm in the 1990s. In each case, in different ways, local elites inscribe aspects of the politics and identities of Arab-Palestinians in that time and place.

For administrative reasons the British Mandate government in Palestine (1922–48) began directing both Jewish and Arab municipalities to name streets in the 1920s. In Haifa there were separate Arab and Jewish neighbourhoods and thus the process of street naming begun in 1934 allowed leaders from each community to name streets in their 'own' areas. Names in the Arab neighbourhoods tended to commemorate figures from the golden age of Arab-Muslim culture: philosophers, geographers, poets and military leaders. Only two street names commemorated Arab-Christians. Many of the street names referred to places outside the British Mandate, in Saudi Arabia, Lebanon, Iraq and Trans-Jordan. Thus, the identity of Haifa Arabs was being situated within pan-Arab horizons. The naming of one street after Omar Al Mukhtar (1858–1931), executed by Italian colonial authorities for leading a rebellion in Libya, and another after Salah al-Din (Saladin), who liberated Jerusalem from the Crusaders, put an accent on resistance to the European presence in this pan-Arab sphere.

Jerusalem from the 1920s reflected the stronger hand of the British authorities, as it was the seat of colonial government. Names were preferred that commemorated the history of the city, especially around the Crusades, rather than ethnic or religious communities. In 1938 a Street Naming Committee was established with representatives from the Christian, Muslim and Jewish communities. For those zones of the city that were predominantly Arab and Jewish, Arab and Jewish members on the committee were respectively invited to propose names. The Committee tended to follow the Mandate government's injunctions to

→

nationalism for those of the powerful nations, Billig is also saying that at the right moment the banal nationalism of the US becomes highly explicit. His book stressed the activation of latent American nationalism in the 1991 Gulf War, a point since further underscored by the 'War on Terror'.

The historian of Germany, George Mosse, has been an important influence on Smith (2003a:14–15), especially in regard to Smith's ideas about 'chosen peoples'. In a series of writings Mosse explored the new mass politics of nationalism, premised on the idea of popular sovereignty

---

→

highlight Jerusalem's particular history, but with some latitude to appeal to the populations of each ethnic/religious zone. As in Haifa, Arab street names commemorated cultural heroes of the Arab-Muslim world. Because of the complex inter-communal negotiations through the Committee, the resulting street names were relatively depoliticized, although some logical choices, such as Saladin again, inevitably carried political overtones.

The third case, Umm el Fahm, had achieved the status of an Israeli town in 1985, and then the Islamic movement won municipal elections in 1988. Here the map of a new and growing town became a surface on which to project an explicitly ideological worldview in one fell swoop. The theme of early Islamic history is again emphasized, but with perhaps a greater role for religious leaders in particular. Four street names refer to the Muslim conquest in Spain, and the authors suggest that this invokes a notion of the Arab-Islamic world at the height of its expansion, and that a subtle metaphor between Spain and Palestine as territories lost to Islam is perhaps being made. From more recent history, Omar Al Mukhtar is again remembered, as well as 'Izz al-Din al-Qassam (1882–1935), an early advocate of militant struggle against British colonial government and the Zionist project, who was killed in a gun battle with British forces. Al-Qassam became the first Palestinian martyr to the cause, his name later being appropriated by terrorist squads of the Palestinian Islamic Jihad. In this instance, the encompassing political confrontation becomes manifest in the choice of names. The authors note that in the case of streets named after other cities, the themes appear to be cities containing key Muslim shrines (Jerusalem and Hebron), and cities 'lost' to Israel (Haifa, Yaffa/Jaffa and Sarafend).

Azaryahu and Kook sum up the differences between the three cases thus: in Jerusalem street names were made to celebrate 'local history rather than national myths', in Haifa a more 'pan-Arab model of identity' is suggested, and in the 1990s in Umm el Fahm a more 'pan-Islamic version of Arab-Palestinian identity' is celebrated (2002: 211). In each locale, in a particular historical moment and context, visions of collective history and identity are written into the urban nomenclature.

set in motion by the French Revolution (1991: ch. 1). Two ideas running through his writings tend to frame his analysis. On the one hand, he argues that the symbolic language of nationalism is a secularized version of religious 'liturgy' (1976) – it both draws on religious idioms and echoes its ritual form. On the other hand, he emphasizes the 'style' and 'aesthetics' of nationalism. This is partly a matter of the role of artists of all types in the creation of nationalist symbolism and myths, but also of the way in which the masses themselves relate to those symbols, as exemplifications of 'beauty'. Mosse argues that it is a mistake to try to understand fascism and National Socialism as rational political theory:

> The fascists themselves described their political thought as an 'attitude' rather than a system; it was, in fact, a theology which provided the framework for national worship. As such, its rites and liturgies were central, an integral part of a political theory which was not dependent on the appeal of the written word. Nazi and other fascist leaders stressed the spoken word, but even here, speeches fulfilled a liturgical function rather than presenting a didactic exposition of the ideology. The spoken word itself was integrated into the cultic rites, and what was actually said was, in the end, of less importance than the setting and the rites which surrounded such speeches. (1991: 9–10)

It is worth noting that Mosse does not make a strong distinction between 'culture' and 'ideology' in his work, which is perhaps not surprising given a subject matter in which these two concepts so deeply interpenetrate. He argues that the concept of 'propaganda', while obviously playing a role, is too narrow to capture the process he is describing, the long, organic growth of a popular liturgical political style from the Napoleonic Wars up to the Third Reich (1991: 10–11).

A prime example of the fusion of religious ideas and imagery with the secular liturgy of nationalism is found in what Mosse calls 'the cult of the fallen soldier' (1990: ch. 5), a European-wide phenomenon, but one highly elaborated in the countries that lost the First World War, especially Germany. In this process the personal loss of a brother, husband or friend in war, became publicly and personally represented as martyrdom and sacrifice for a greater national good. This understanding was reinforced by monuments, cemeteries and ceremonies to the war dead, and paintings and postcards in which dying soldiers were portrayed reclining in the arms of Christ. Fallen soldiers embodied youth, beauty and manliness, which was sacrificed for the nation. After the war the popular trope of the war dead, rising from their graves to redeem the *Volk*, was reiterated in essays, pamphlets and plays: 'Familiar ghost stories were infused with themes of Christian resurrection to explain away the finality of death on the battle-field and to give hope to a defeated nation' (1990: 78).

Developing his aesthetic theme, Mosse charts an evolving concept of beauty in Germany in the eighteenth and nineteenth centuries, fusing Greek classicism and Germanic romanticism (1991: ch. 2). What came to be central to the 'new politics' was the idea of festive occasions and expe-riences that 'uplift' those present, moving them from their banal and mundane existences into a transcendent realm. National monuments strategically located in natural settings became 'sacred spaces', key sites for such cultic experiences. In these events: 'the "people" were not considered merely as a gathering of individuals, but exemplified an idea of the beauty of soul which was projected upon the outward world' (1991: 45). Mosse acknowledges that post-Second World War this litur-gical aesthetic has lost much of its power to enchant, both within Germany and beyond. But he suggests that the basic human longings for order and transcendence are constant, and that under the right conditions of disappointment with political and social institutions, the attraction of aestheticized solutions to social problems can be rekindled (1991: 215–16).

Eric Hobsbawm (1992) regards nationalism primarily as an ideology, taking its full shape in the later ninetenth century, which insists, follow-ing Gellner, on the congruence of the nation and the state. He sees it as arising partly to compensate for the loss of more traditional, localized forms of community under modernization (1992: 46), and in its most extreme forms, such us German fascism, developing after the First World War:

It was plainly something that filled the void left by failure, impotence, and the apparent inability of other ideologies, political projects and programmes to realize men's hopes. It was the utopia of those who had lost the old utopias of the Age of Enlightenment, the programme of those who had lost faith in other programmes, the prop of those who had lost the support of older political and social certainties. (1992: 144)

Nonetheless, Hobsbawm accepts that nationalism exists not only *in extremis*, but also as part of the normalized worldview of citizens of modern nation-states. Much like Mann, he sees the modern period as producing a fusion of national and class identities in practice (1992: 145). Understanding how this fusion came about requires consideration of how nationalism is 'constructed essentially from above', but in ways which latch onto the 'assumptions, hopes, needs, longings and interests of ordinary people' below (1992: 10). Thus, where Smith sees *ethnies*, Hobsbawm recognizes 'popular proto-nationalism' (1992: ch. 2), in a patchwork of overlapping symbolic repertoires drawn from religion, political history and especially language. But for him the very point is the lack of coherence between these various sets of symbols and individual ethnic groups. Thus, the 'deliberate ideological engineering' (1992: 92) of nation-building governments had to work with this uneven mixture of sentiments and symbols, moulding them into serviceable identities.

It is here that the influential thesis explored in the editied volume *The Invention of Tradition* (Hobsbawm and Ranger 1983) comes in:

> 'Invented tradition' is taken to mean a set of practices, normally governed by overtly or tacitly accepted rules and of a ritual or symbolic nature, which seeks to inculcate certain values and norms of behaviour by repetition, which automatically implies continuity with the past. (Hobsbawm 1983a: 1)

Hobsbawm is quick to distinguish between this sense of 'tradition' and 'custom' on the one hand, and 'convention' on the other. A custom is a social practice legitimated by long precedence, however much it may have evolved in the process. Marriage today is often a very different institution from what it was a couple of generations ago, but it is still the same custom. A convention is simply a routine way of doing something, legitimated by its efficiency in achieving the desired end, such as rules for traffic. But with traditions the link between the practical and the symbolic is broken, allowing the sign to become fully symbolic: 'the wigs of lawyers could hardly acquire their modern significance until other people stopped wearing wigs' (1983a: 4). Hobsbawm suggests that traditions have probably been invented in all ages but that, paradoxically, they are likely to proliferate precisely when a society is undergoing rapid change. Thus it is precisely the modernity of the nation-state that compels it to fabricate attachments to a deeper history.

In his survey of this process in Europe between 1870 and 1914 (Hobsbawm 1983b), certain typical forms of invented traditions recur: public ceremonies and rituals (holidays, commemorations, professionalizing sports); public monuments (statues, memorials, civic buildings); codifications of national history, civics and geography in primary education texts and lessons; national personas (Marianne, Deutsche Michel) and heroes (William Wallace, Joan of Arc). Within this almost 'universal'

grammar of invented national traditions Hobsbawm discerns some interesting variations (treating the US as an honorary part of Europe in this
instance). In the Third Republic of France (1874–1914) centrist elites laid
claim to the symbols of the Revolution of 1789, the tricolour, Bastille
Day celebrations begun in 1880, circumventing the use of these symbols
by more radical and socialist elements. The French state's new traditions
centred on rather generic symbols of the event of the Revolution, avoiding the complexities and divisions of history before and after 1789. Key
figures of the Revolution – Robespierre, Mirabeau, Danton – were
avoided as symbols because of their associations with party factions. By
contrast, the USA, a country of immigrant working classes, developed a
cult of the founding fathers with associated rituals (the Fourth of July,
Thanksgiving Day) that was unproblematic because it bore little relationship to these people's actual historical experiences. Immigrant groups
were further assimilated by nationalizing ethnic holidays (St Patrick's
Day, Columbus Day), and by the inculcation of flag worship in public
schools. The (Second) German Empire (1871–1918), with no political
definition or unity before 1871, was more inclined than France to invent
a catalogue of deep historical symbols, drawing on Teutonic mythology,
folklore and nature images such as the German Oak. Hobsbawm suggests
that this symbolic vocabulary was also suited to defining proletarian
socialists and Jews as urbanized aliens in relation to 'the great masses of
the lower middle class, handicraftsmen, and peasants who felt threatened
by both' (1983b: 279). Finally, in Britain the monarchy provided a key
symbol of historical continuity in changing times, especially through
events such as Queen Victoria's jubilees of 1887 and 1897. He suggests
that 'the revival of royal ritualism was seen as a necessary counterweight
to the dangers of popular democracy' (1983b: 282). Thus, in each of these
cases the specific repertoire of symbols attached to the more generalized
template of invented traditions was partly determined by axes of social
division, and the need of national ruling classes to integrate and co-opt
social groups that threatened their power.

Probably the most strict rendering of nationalism as ideology is that
offered by Elie Kedourie (1993 [1960]). Like Mosse, he conceives of
nationalism as a 'politics in a new style' initiated around the beginning of
the nineteenth century, but unlike Mosse, he sees nationalism as reason
gone awry, rather than aesthetics abused. He approaches nationalism as a
problem in the history of European ideas, an ideology developed in the
realms of philosophy and political theory, and misapplied to the practical
realities of governance. The basic context for this ideological formation
was the alienation felt by subjects, and particularly intellectuals of the

---

Box 8.3 Mexico – Pre-Hispanic Archaeology and the Virgin of Guadalupe

D. A. Brading (2001) has traced the development of nationalist invocations of the past in Mexico's history. The insurgency against Spain that
began in 1810 involved a popular rhetoric in which insurgent leaders were
compared to the late Aztec rulers Monctezuma and Cauthémoc fighting
the sixteenth-century conquistadors. The Creole leadership of the royalist
army that defeated the insurgents nonetheless soon adopted their rhetoric
of a pre-Hispanic Mexican nation awakened. However, this view was
reversed from the mid-nineteenth century when the Liberals rose to power
under the presidency of Benito Juarez (1858–72), with a Europhile, anti-
clerical modernizing programme of republican patriotism that regarded
the Indian populations and the pre-Hispanic past as backward. From the
1880s this view began to soften and Aztec symbols and mestizo (mixed
Indian and Spanish decent) identity began to be celebrated. But it was with
the Mexican Revolution (1910–20), with its peasant mobilization, that
mestizos came to be regarded as the literal embodiment of the nation, and
archaeology and the pre-Hispanic past became an integral part of Mexican
nationalism.

Brading focuses on the work of the Mexican archaeologist Manuel
Gamio (1883–1960), a student of the American anthropologist Franz
Boas. He led various innovative excavations of pre-Hispanic urban
centres, most notably of the ruined Toltec city of Teotihuacan near Mexico
City. Gamio curiously combined *indigenismo* and assimilationism in his
attitude towards indigenous culture. On the one hand, he elevated Indian
culture, comparing Aztec art to contemporary cubism and calling on
Mexican artists to seek inspiration in pre-Hispanic works. He also advocated

→

---

middling classes, of states that governed by principles of Enlightened
Absolutism, seeing their subjects as populations to be instrumentally
managed, for their own good (1993 [1960]: xiv–xv). For Kedourie
nationalist ideology was a reaction to this estrangement – to being the
object, but not the agent of state power.

The crux of his argument unfolds in three acts: the French Revolution,
Immanuel Kant and J. G. Fichte. The doctrines of the French Revolution
in principle overturned the *de facto* world of European politics, where the
right to rule was based on a combination of custom and a realistic acceptance of the demonstrated ability to hold power. By contrast:

The Revolution meant that if the citizens of a state no longer approved
of the political arrangements of their society, they had the right and the

→

a return to forms of collective Indian land tenure undone by liberal land reforms. On the other hand he was eager for Indians to learn Spanish so that they could join the larger Mexican nation. As Brading puts it: 'he revived the emphasis on the pre-Hispanic civilisations which had formed an essential part of creole patriotism, but substantiated it by excavation and reconstruction of imposing monuments' (2001: 529).

The Aztec civilization and the Mexican Revolution have provided key symbols of Mexican national identity, the first representing a heritage from before Spanish colonization, the second a reassertion of indigenous identity against European hegemony. In the Revolution Emiliano Zapata's insurgent troops were led into battle by another key national symbol, the emblem of the Virgin of Guadalupe. The Virgin derives from the syncretism of Catholicism and indigenous religious beliefs in the colonial period (2001: 530). According to legend, the Virgin appeared to a Christianized Indian commoner in 1531, ten years after the Spanish conquest, speaking to him through his native Nahuatl language, and through a miracle helped him to convince the Archbishop to build a shrine in her honour. The site of the vision and the shrine had been the location of a pre-Hispanic temple to the fertility goddess Tonatzin, and the Virgin is normally portrayed as brown-skinned, thus she represents a certain indigenization of Catholic symbolism. Eric Wolf (1958) argued that the symbol of the Virgin resonated with different sets of meanings for the Indian and Mestizo populations, for the former representing their right to recognition within the new social and ideological order and for the latter validating their 'racially mixed' status as an entitlement to national membership, rather than exclusion from it. Thus, the symbol of the Virgin of Guadalupe has historically condensed divergent social experiences of the Mexican nation.

power to replace them by others more satisfactory. As the Declaration of the Rights of Man and the Citizen had it: 'The principle of sovereignty lies essentially in the Nation; no body of men, no individual, can exercise authority that does not emanate expressly from it.' Here, then, is one prerequisite without which a doctrine such as nationalism is not conceivable. (1993 [1960]: 4–5)

Contemporaneously Kant (1724–1804) was working out his ethical philosophy and its political implications. Without going into much philosophical detail, Kant's mission was to argue that 'the good will, which is the free will, is also the autonomous will. For it to be good, it has to choose good freely, and what that good shall be, the will itself legislates for itself' (Kedourie) 1993 [1960]: 16). In short, there can be no moral responsibility without such freedom. Thus, in opposition to the principles of Enlightened Absolutism, Kant advocated in his essay on *Perpetual Peace* (1794) that every state should be a republic of some form, in which the laws could be made to express the autonomous will of the citizens (1993 [1960]: 22). In subsequent generations, figures such as Herder (1744–1803), Fichte (1762–1814) and Schelling (1775–1854) elaborated and transformed this notion of self-determination, in increasingly romantic tones. In their hands, the very meaning of the individual is dependent on its social relations, and thus the Kantian idea of autonomy becomes submerged in the idea of an organic, self-governing cultural group with its own state. Kedourie pays particular attention to Fichte, who says in *The Foundations of Natural Law* (1796):

> In a product of nature, no part is what it is but through its relation with the whole, and would absolutely not be what it is apart from this relation . . . similarly, man attains a determinate position in the scheme of things and fixity in nature only by means of civil association; he attains a particular position with regard to others and to nature only because he is in a particular association . . . Between the isolated man and the citizen, there is the same relation as between raw and organized matter . . . In an organized body, each part continuously maintains the whole, and in maintaining it, maintains itself also. Similarly, the citizen with regard to the state. (Fichte, quoted in Kedourie 1993 [1960]: 31–2)

For Fichte as for Herder, a key element in this organic social unity was language, and individuality and will are most fully realized within the language community. Thus the tight bonds demanded by romantic nationalism between language, culture and the state. For Kedourie this is the dangerous model for all subsequent nationalisms. He was well aware that Kant cannot be regarded as a nationalist in these terms, in fact the romantics fundamentally reversed Kant's emphasis on the autonomy of the individual conscience, but his emphasis on self-determination was a key ingredient in the idea of nationalism that would develop. Indeed, one of the most interesting things about Kedourie is his grasp of the deep and paradoxical interconnection between individualism and collectivism in the modern era. To those other modernists such as Gellner, who tended to view such ideology as a functional reflection of material conditions, his rejoinder is that the idea originated and often spread well ahead of industrialism and capitalism. While he does not regard an account of the ideological process as a sufficient explanation of actual historical events, which always involve other factors, he regards the ideology of nationalism as a distinctive causal process in history, which needs to be understood as such (1993 [1960]: 137–40).

Two Tricky Cases

The sequence of thinkers we have traced so far is, of course, a contrivance. While it helps flesh out the idea of a continuum from cultural to ideological conceptions of nationalism, the complexity of the ideas involved means that some placements in the sequence are a bit arbitrary. I want to consider two more theorists who are worth discussing here but that I find particularly difficult to fit into this schema. Doing this may help counterbalance the artificial suggestion of a typological series above.

My first case is Benedict Anderson's highly influential characterization of nations as 'imagined communities' (1991). Early on in the book he signals his intention to treat nationalism as a 'cultural artefact' (1991: 4) and to sidestep the idea of nationalism as an ideology:

> What I am proposing is that nationalism has to be understood by aligning it, not with self-consciously held political ideologies, but with the large cultural systems that preceded it, out of which – as well as against which – it came into being. (1991: 12)

The phrase 'large cultural systems' is telling here, because culture is frequently conceived more on the model of a relatively contained system of symbols, ideas and associated identities, whereas Anderson clearly has in mind something bigger, closer to what is sometimes meant by terms such as *Weltenschaung* (worldview) and civilization. Also significant is the use of the term 'consciousness' (1991: ch. 3) to describe the phenomenon he is concerned with. The early chapters of the book (1–3) and the two chapters appended to the revised edition (10 and 11) tell us the most about the relationship between culture, consciousness and what Anderson means by 'imagined communities'. His celebrated notion of 'print-capitalism' and its effects on languages (see Chapter 4) provides the key mechanism of change, but it is specifically fundamental understandings of time and space that define the new style in which national communities are imagined.

Anderson tries to capture the historical shift that led to nationalism by defining two very different kinds of 'simultaneity' (1991: 24). In medieval Europe community beyond the strictly local was imagined in a very different manner than today. All space and time were bound together by a 'simultaneous' relationship to a transcendent heavenly order. The political community of the dynastic realm was organized around a 'high centre' deriving its legitimacy from the divine, not the people:

> In the modern conception, state sovereignty is fully, flatly, and evenly operative over each square centimetre of a legally demarcated territory. But in the older imagining, where states were defined by centres, borders were porous and indistinct, and sovereignties faded imperceptibly into one another. (1991: 19)

The imagined community of medieval Christendom, which aided in the legitimation of the worldly dynastic realms, was constituted as a relationship between the mundane and sacred worlds, a relationship mediated by the sacred language of Latin, commanded by the clergy, which was essentially, not arbitrarily, the linguistic channel to the divine. The image of this world that Anderson presents is of an open-ended array of peoples oriented through dynasties and churches towards kings and popes in this world, and through them to a heavenly order standing outside of time. He exemplifies this 'timeless' perspective by considering:

> the visual representations of the sacred communities, such as the reliefs and stained-glass windows of mediaeval churches, or the paintings of early Italian and Flemish masters. A characteristic feature of such representations is something misleadingly analogous to 'modern dress'. The shepherds who have followed the star to the manger where Christ is born bear the features of Burgundian peasants. The Virgin Mary is figured as a Tuscan merchant's daughter. In many paintings the commissioning patron, in full burgher or noble costume, appears kneeling in adoration alongside the shepherds. What seems incongruous today obviously appeared wholly natural to the eyes of mediaeval worshippers. (1991: 22)

This history-less simultaneity is counter-posed by Anderson to the new, modern, secular conception of 'homogeneous empty time' (1991: 24). Now time becomes like an endless expanse of blank space laid under a grid, measurable into discrete and equivalent units. This new simultaneity appears in many guises. Intimately linked to the phenomenon of print-capitalism is the rise and spread of the newspaper, which invites its readers, wherever they are, to jointly survey events across the world that have occurred in the last day or week. The experience neatly slices up and evenly distributes the experience of the 'present' (1991: 33). Similarly the naming of new colonial towns and cities in the Americas after their partners in the old world – New York, Nueva Leon, Nouvelle Orléans – implied not replacement, but a hiving off of exactly the same thing. The people in these urban locales understood themselves as living lives somehow both separate from and parallel with their namesakes in Europe (1991: 187). This mindset also directed the colonial state in its efforts to classify and regulate colonial populations. Through censuses ethnicities were classified and to various degrees created, through cartography territories were mapped and administered, and through archaeology the remains of past ways of life were museum-ized, catalogued and narrated into a single tradition:

> The 'warp' of this thinking was a totalizing classificatory grid, which could be applied with endless flexibility to anything under the state's real or contemplated control: peoples, regions, religions, languages, products, monuments, and so forth . . . The 'weft' was what one could call serialization: the assumption that the world was made up of replicable plurals. The particular always stood as a provisional representative of a series, and was to be handled in this light. (1991: 184; see also 1998: ch. 1)

Finally, and perhaps most profoundly, the orientation to a timeless sacred beyond gives way to a secular narrative in which nations become like persons with biographies, explained and justified by their ability to anchor their present selves in a coherent past. Novel republican revolutions in the US (1776) and France (1789) initially had little need for historical justification, but as time wore on and other nationalisms followed suit, all nations, each an example from the series 'nations', had to moor themselves in the grid of world history, remembering and forgetting pieces of the past as needed (1991: 187–206).

More recently Anderson has contemplated ongoing shifts in the mapping of nations onto space and time, stimulated by the continuing evolution of all forms of communication. Contemplating what he calls 'long-distance nationalism' he observes:

> the communications revolution of our times has profoundly affected the subjective experiences of migration. The Tamil bus-driver in Melbourne is a mere dozen sky-hours away from his *land van*

herkomst. The Moroccan construction worker in Amsterdam can every night listen to Rabat's broadcasting services and has no difficulty in buying pirated cassettes of his country's favourite singers . . . The Filipina maid in Hong Kong phones her sister in Manila, and sends money in the twinkling of an electronic eye to her mother in Cebu. (1998: 68)

And so on. At the other end of the social scale, affluent citizens of wealthy core post-industrial states who ethnically identify with their co-nationals in external homelands are much more able to engage in homeland politics through funds and other resources, yet without bearing the burdens of social strife in those homelands. Anderson worries that the disarticulation of networks of national communication from territorial location and political domain is laying the groundwork for highly unaccountable forms of nationalist politics (1998: 74). While the modern grid of simultaneity that enabled the new imagining of national community remains basically the same, the restless march of capitalism and technology is making it possible not just to imagine parallel elsewheres (cf. Fuglerud 2001), but to move and act much more rapidly across the entire grid.

Having broached the question of narration, let me briefly consider a recent contribution by the political scientist Rogers M. Smith, *Stories of Peoplehood* (2003). Smith's premise is that political scientists have not paid adequate attention to how political memberships and identities are generated. To help correct this he articulates a variable and encompassing concept of 'political peoples', which includes all kinds of organized and mobilized social groups. Having said this, he is primarily concerned with ethnic and national groups. For Smith such groups are constituted through 'stories of peoplehood', which cultivate feelings of collective worth and trust among members. He argues that such stories are necessary for political life, not diversionary fabrications. Thus, while such stories are in some sense inherently political, he conceives of them as part of a cultural, rather than narrowly ideological fabric of ideas (2003: 48–9). To be effective such stories must do three things: (1) cultivate trust and worth among co-members; (2) do the same between leaders and followers; and (3) maintain a sufficient correspondence with reality. He stresses that the meanings of these stories will diverge between leaders and followers.

Smith defines three main types of 'stories', focusing on the third. 'Economic stories' promise material security and prosperity, attesting to leaders' abilities to deliver the goods. 'Political power stories' argue that the power and self-determination of the people will be enhanced by a particular mode of political constitution and/or allegiance to those who rule. 'Ethically constitutive stories' define a people as carriers of certain ultimate values, transmitted across generations. Here, senses of worth and trust arise not out of hopes for economic or political success, but out of commitment to intrinsic goods, more immune to the vagaries of political life. Such stories 'are more likely to be religious or quasi-religious, kinship-like, and gendered than economic or political power stories' (2003: 69), providing particularly enduring bases to collective identities. However, all three types of story are basic, and normally found woven together. The special importance of ethically constitutive stories is that they express the uniqueness of a people in specifically moral terms. Economic and political stories are more generic and ethically ambiguous (e.g. liberalism, communism), thus less compelling. Moreover, ethical stories get foregrounded when economic and political powers are faltering or manifestly morally questionable, needing compensatory legitimation, or when the ideas, institutions and practices that sustain them are threatened.

Over the course of the book, Smith moves from formulating his 'stories of peoplehood' as a tool of description and analysis, to trying to render it as a normative justification for the idea of political community. In effect, there are good ways and bad ways of making and advancing stories (2003: 158). The final chapter examines the concrete example of American peoplehood, advocating a secular and historical approach to constructing American identity. Smith criticizes ideologically conservative attempts to use history to essentialize an unchanging American people by idealizing the 'founding fathers'. In their stead he advocates an admittedly prescriptive story of Americans as a 'pioneering people' disposed towards political experimentation and adaptation, thus inclined towards progressive reformism in politics. Leaving aside his normative claims, Smith's approach is interesting in this context for the way it treats the cultural fabric of national identity as woven out of competing and conflicting stories. There are similarities here to Hutchinson's notion of nations as 'zones of conflict', and in a manner similar to Hutchinson's concern with moral regeneration, Smith sees ethically constitutive stories as not just serving interests, but constituting values. But Smith's argument is ultimately for a dialogical understanding of what politics is, a process that inevitably makes peoples, whereas Hutchinson begins with peoples, elaborating the different and conflicting ways they pursue national goals.

Box 8.4   Contesting the Official Narrative of Eritrean Nationalism

An Italian colony since the late 1880s, Eritrea became a British protectorate after the Second World War, until it was federated into Ethiopia in 1952 as an autonomous region. Forceful integration by the Ethiopian state led to resistance, first in the 1960s by the largely Muslim Eritrean Liberation Front (ELF), and then from the 1970s by the broader and more secular Eritrean People's Liberation Front (EPLF). (Regarding religion the majority of Eritreans are fairly evenly split between Sunni Islam and the Eritrean branch of the Oriental Orthodox Church.) In 1991 after 30 years of insurgency the EPLF established *de facto* independence, formalized by a UN-supervised referendum in 1993. Since then Eritrea has had tense relation with its neighbours on all sides, seeing further wars with Yemen (1996), Ethiopia (1998–2000) and hostile relations with Sudan.

Sara Dorman (2005) has examined the interplay of official and unofficial narratives of the nation in Eritrea, highlighting the way supposedly neutral researchers and journalists become a part of the nation-building process, both wittingly and unwittingly. Born of a liberation struggle that has left a deep impression on society and culture, the official narrative emphasizes the solidarity, self-reliance and incorruptibility of the Eritrean people. One of its key sub-themes is the gender equality generated by women's full participation in the military struggle. The government-generated discourse is one of a multi-ethnic and multilinguistic society, secular and recognizing the roles of both Islam and Christianity, fostering economic growth in the private sector and avoiding dependency on

→

Conclusion

Benedict Anderson's global shift in worldview is perhaps too encompassing to fit under the headings of culture or ideology, and Rogers Smith's stories of peoplehood are perhaps too sociologically embedded to be regarded as ideology, but too limited to the realm of political discourse to be viewed as culture. Obviously, this all depends on how one defines ideology and culture, and the difficulty in classifying is perhaps a testament to the originality of their ideas. The main point, however, is not to fixate on definitions, but to appreciate the diversity of concepts that have been formulated to try to grasp the cultural-ideological dimension of nationalism – *mythomoteurs*, banal deixis, invented traditions, aesthetics of beauty, misguided philosophy, spatiotemporal worldview, stories of peoplehood. We should also ask two things. First, to what degree are these concepts shaped by the concrete cases they were devised to engage with?

→
foreign aid. Many outside commentators have looked on in admiration, seeing this case as an exceptionally progressive movement that has avoided the pitfalls of earlier, more Marxian liberation movements (e.g. Angola, Mozambique, Zimbabwe).

Dorman points out, however, that this discourse arises out of a hegemonic state born of years of widespread military mobilization. This intensely solidaristic national identity is actively cultivated by granting citizenship to expatriates of the Eritrean diaspora, by national youth service programmes and continuing military service, by tight controls on local government, by restricting the autonomy of NGOs and regulating development funding through government ministries, and by the dominant party of government's (PFDJ) monopolization of extensive parts of the private sector. Moreover, counter-discourses are suppressed. Teachers and researchers writing about the failings of government have been dismissed from university posts; Jehovah's Witnesses who have refused military conscription on religious grounds have been jailed for long periods; in 2001 a group (senior movement leaders, journalists) calling for party reforms of the PFDJ were imprisoned indefinitely without charge. Other critics have noted that the celebrated gender equality of wartime has not translated into changes in women's status within the household and society in general. And yet outside observers have been slow to pick up on these critical counter-discourses, although they are starting to catch up. This contemporary example from one of the newest states on the globe reminds us how easily a multiplicity of competing national narratives can become obscured by the dominant state-led story, even when events are not buried in the mists of time.

The oscillation between cultural and political forms seems particularly suited to the Irish case; the blatant inventing of traditions seems particularly pronounced in industrializing Europe; nationalism as an aesthetic seems to have a special relationship to German romanticism; contending stories of peoplehood seems a particularly apt way to describe multicultural debates over national identity in an American liberal democracy. Second, to what degree does the historical proximity and accessibility of the subject matter determine its conceptualization? The archaeology and history of the ethnic polities of the ancient Near East leave us fragments of the legitimating myths inscribed on stones and preserved in politicized lore, the *mythomoteurs*; it is much more difficult from the records we have to determine if something like 'banal deixis', or the 'invention of tradition' was going on then, though one suspects they were. The concepts we employ may be calibrated to the degree of descriptive resolution we can achieve. Some are more broad-brushed, others more finely detailed.

Finally, my point in this chapter has been to look at analyses of nationalism along the plane of ideation, taken as the most inclusive term, of both culture and ideology. This is not to say that any of these writers would deny the importance of more material factors. Hobsbawm and Anderson, with stronger intellectual debts to Marx than most, would probably give capitalism, class and technology a larger role in causal explanation than most. The ethno-symbolists, in the manner of Weber, would tend to see ideational processes as having considerable consequences within broader perimeters set by material circumstances. But all would acknowledge some sort of interplay between the material and the ideational. Here we have simply been isolating the latter and comparing various conceptual tools for its analysis. In the next chapter I will explore some other senses of the concept of culture deriving from the anthropological tradition, which tend to cut across the material/ideal dichotomy.

Further Reading

Smith (1986) is still the seminal statement of what would become his ethnosymbolic approach. Armstrong (1982: ch. 5) and Hutchinson (2001) are also key sources for understanding this approach. Smith's (2001b) entry on 'Durkheim and Nationalism' in Leoussi (2001) provides insight into his general perspective. The special issue of *Nations and Nationalism* on ethno-symbolism (2004, volume 10, parts 1/2) provides one of the better statements by Smith of his position along with many engagements with his work by other scholars in the field. Along these lines see also Özkirimli's (2003) postmodernist critique of Smith and Smith's rebuttal (2003b). Regarding conceptions of nationalism that treat it more as ideology, Billig (1995), Hobsbawm and Ranger (1983) and Kedourie (1993 [1960]) are essential readings. Mosse's (1991, 1985b, 1990) nuanced historical analyses deserve to be more widely read. For more postmodern treatments of culture and nationalism from the perspective of literary studies see Bhabha (1990) and Berlant (1996). For a general survey of the concept of culture see Jenks (2005); for the concept of ideology see McLellan (1995).

9
Rethinking Culture

In the previous chapter we surveyed some approaches to nationalism that emphasized culture, but in ways that often merged with notions of ideology. I am inclined to follow Eric Wolf (1999: 4) in using 'ideas' and 'ideation' as the covering terms for cognitive phenomena and processes, restricting 'ideology' to that subset more clearly caught up in the deliberate making and unmaking of social power. I am not, however, inclined to treat 'culture' as 'the other half', the non-power-laden subset of ideation, for two reasons. First, I view culture as much more than ideas – as a complex set of relations among ideas, sentiments, identities, organizations and practices, which are constituted both mentally and physically. The analytic dimension of ideation is much too narrow to capture this complexity. Second, far from culture being evacuated of power, I argue that it is precisely power which pulls together 'this complex set of relations'. The aim of the rest of this chapter is to elaborate and defend this concept of culture, and highlight the problems it raises for nationalism studies.

There is critical intent in what follows. Much of the literature that invokes culture in its conception of nations and nationalism, while not entirely neglecting power, seriously underplays the role of power in culture. This is especially true of the ethno-symbolic approach as Anthony Smith conceives of it. However, much of the literature we have explored in this book is particularly rich in suggesting the interplay of power and culture. So another part of my purpose is not so much to critique an absence, as to move into the foreground what I consider to be a key aspect of understanding nationalism – the power/culture relationship. After examining this relationship in the next two sections, I return one last time to two classic 'cultural' themes in nationalism studies – language and religion. While my purpose is to review key issues under these headings, my approach to them is broadly informed by the perspective on culture essayed below.

The Hazards of Culture

This and the next section take a detour through some of the anthropological literature, not just because I am trained as an anthropologist and tend

201

to see the world that way but because in recent decades anthropologists have wrestled with problems besetting the concept of culture in ways that nationalism studies has not yet. Anthropological debates about the viability of the culture concept are acutely relevant.

The concept of culture used in the discipline of anthropology, especially in its North American variety, has developed along certain lines. From its early days, particularly under the seminal influence of Franz Boas (1858–1942) there has been a strong tendency to conceptualize culture through an analogy to language, and to continue to turn to linguistics for guidance in understanding culture (Briggs 2002). Moreover, this analogy is to language conceived in a particular way: to language as a system of implicit, unconscious rules that structure speech and generate meanings. Thus, culture has often been conceived as a relatively bounded and integrated system of enduring norms and values, transmitted collectively and habitually from generation to generation, the comprehensive awareness of which is generally unavailable to cultural members, just as we acquire language without explicitly learning its grammar. This linguistic analogy tended to be reinforced by trends in the institutionalization of academic disciplines in the US after the Second World War. An influential programmatic statement by the sociologist Talcott Parsons and the anthropologist Alfred Kroeber argued that there should be a clear division of intellectual labour between sociology and anthropology (1958; see Friedman 1994: 68). They held that the concepts of 'sociology' and 'culture' had largely overlapped in the formative period of the two disciplines, but that the time had come for an 'analytical discrimination':

> We suggest that it is useful to define the concept *culture* for most usages more narrowly than has generally been the case in the American anthropological tradition, restricting its reference to transmitted and created content and patterns of values, ideas, and other symbolic-meaningful systems as factors in the shaping of human behavior. On the other hand, we suggest that the term *society* – or more generally, *social system* – be used to designate the specifically relational system of interaction among individuals and collectivities. (Kroeber and Parsons 1958: 583, emphasis in original)

In short, bees and ants have a kind of society, but no culture to speak of. Thus, the Geertzian concept of culture cited in the last chapter, with its emphasis on meaning and symbolization, conforms to this prescription and exemplifies the dominant tendency in anthropology (see Foster

2002), one widely influential beyond anthropology. This conception carries with it certain assumptions and attendant difficulties. In recent decades anthropological critiques of the culture concept have called either for its fundamental reformulation, or its abandonment. A series of criticisms have been put forward, as have rebuttals (see Brightman 1995; Kuper 1999; Yengoyan 1986). I boil these down to three lines of criticism particularly salient for more culturalist approaches to nationalism: (1) dangers of interpretation; (2) illusions of boundedness and continuity; and (3) obscuring power.

Dangers of Interpretation

Charles Briggs (2002) argues that the linguistic analogy for culture, with its assumption that the deeper patterns of culture are inaccessible to those subject to it, privileges the anthropologist as the external interpreter and translator of culture. Cultural distance can facilitate a degree of objectivity and insight, but as Roger Keesing (1987) has noted the role of the interpreter is also hazardous. The interpreter's search for deeper meaning and inner connections can concoct as well as discover these. For instance, as I argued in Chapter 3, from the presence of a language of kinship in nationalist discourses we cannot easily infer cultural understandings of the national group as a kin group. References to 'brotherhood' and 'bonds of blood' may reflect such understandings, but they may also be conventional metaphors for other kinds of social ties, or believed as such only in temporary, heightened contexts, not to be confused with the common sense that guides everyday life. Because language is polysemic, reading nomenclature with such literalism is risky. For this reason, Walker Connor's (1994: 196–209) attempts to demonstrate such beliefs on the basis of the declarations of political leaders is much too thin to make the case. What is needed is something more like George Mosse's extensive explorations of the idea of race and its relation to practices of science and aesthetic ideas of beauty during a particular period of Germany's history (1985a, 1991).

To Keesing's observation about the hazards of reading too deeply I would add another: having one's attention drawn to the loudest, most blatant symbols, while less obvious symbolic processes may be more consequential. As a specialist on nationalism and Scotland I have become used to encountering people whose knowledge on the subject rests almost exclusively on Hugh Trevor-Roper's celebrated essay in Hobsbawm and Ranger's (1983) *The Invention of Tradition*, demolishing the 'authenticity' of the Scottish kilt. Trevor-Roper accurately showed that the modern

'short' kilt, now used primarily for formal dress occasions, and the associated panoply of clan tartan patterns, were largely creations of the eighteenth and nineteenth centuries, although adapted in the first instance
from the much older *breacan* or 'belted plaid'. The crux of his argument,
however, is that the modern kilt is a key symbol of Scottish identity and
national spirit, and that it is a fabrication (literally!) invented by non-
Scots. The implication is that Scottish national identity and nationalism
are similarly inauthentic, and not to be taken seriously. The weakness of
this argument for understanding contemporary Scottish nationalism is
that the symbolism of the kilt, while obvious and routine, is not terribly
important. While it does some work of, in Billig's terms, banally sustaining the category of Scottishness, like his unwaved flags, it is not a focus
of identity or political contention. One does not have to wear the kilt to be
recognized as Scottish, speaking Scots or Scots-Gaelic are much more
important identity markers. As I indicated toward the end of Chapter 5,
recent Scottish nationalism has been fuelled more by a notion of Scots as
more social democratic in values than the English, and Margaret
Thatcher as a symbolic hate figure has played a much more important
role in mobilizing nationalist sentiments. A much more diverse and
sometimes subtle complex of symbols has leant expression to Scottish
nationalism, the importance of tartanry is exaggerated (see Hearn 2000).

Illusions of Boundedness and Continuity

Eric Wolf once posed the question: 'Culture: Panacea or Problem?'
(1984), arguing against viewing cultures as 'integral wholes carried by
social isolates' (1984: 393). Wolf had a gift for locating cultures in their
historical and political economic contexts, and demonstrating the way
cultural patterns arise out of complex interactions with exogenous forces.
For instance, he tracks the transformation of the 'six nations' of the
Iroquois Confederacy, an alliance of linguistically distinct clusters of
matrilineages located around the upper drainage of the Hudson river, over
the seventeenth century. These people had lived by horticulture and hunting,
with some raiding of neighbouring groups, and had reciprocal spheres of
social power for men and women. But with the rise of the European fur
trade in beaver skins the confederacy became an organization competing
for the dominance of the local fur trade, with Dutch and then English backing and guns, attempting to marginalize French-backed native groups. In
this context hunting, warfare and male power became much more central,
until fragmenting alliances weakened the confederacy and finally the
American War of Independence ended English patronage (Wolf 1982:

165–70). Wolf's point is that this culture, or '*ethnie*', was radically trans-formed over these centuries, and cannot be understood apart from its external connections.

Robert Brightman (1995) argues, and I agree, that the charge that anthropology has long laboured under a rigidly bounded and unchanging concept of culture, while not unfounded, is exaggerated. Awareness of these conceptual pitfalls can be found throughout the history of the disci-pline. Nonetheless, the problems raised are ones students of nationalism should take care to consider as well. In what sense was the culture of France in 1539, 1789 and 1968 'the same'? Does Castro's ailing commu-nist Cuba today have the same culture it did in the 1960s, or under the preceding Batista dictatorship? Wherein, exactly, does the continuity lie? What symbols and values do we focus on to convey that continuity? If this becomes problematic over a few decades, how much more so over several centuries? This is not to argue that there are no salient historical continuities, nor to deny that there is such a thing as culture and that it is relevant. But it is to question the idea that culture is peculiarly stable and persistent, or primarily a matter of symbols and boundaries.

Obscuring Power

The mutually defining conceptions of language and culture that have long shaped anthropology carry an assumption that easily misleads. The idea of an integrating force generated by a system of rules and values that carries on below the level of everyday awareness suggests that culture is a matter of unarticulated consensus, something fundamentally 'shared' through symbols. Employed uncritically the concept tends to by-pass the question of power and its role in making 'consensus', in apportioning what is 'shared'. Drawing on the ideas of Michel Foucault and Pierre Bourdieu, Lila Abu-Lughod (1991) has argued that this problem with the concept of culture is insuperable, and that we should instead think in terms of fields of contradictory discourses and heterogeneous practices, in order to avoid a false holism. Keesing (1987), while not prepared to throw culture overboard, has called for a more qualified view of cultural knowledge as: '*distributed* and *controlled* . . . Cultures are webs of mysti-fication as well as signification. We need to ask who *creates* and *defines* cultural meanings, and to what ends' (1987: 161–2, emphasis in original). Similarly, Wolf maintained that:

> The construction and maintenance of a body of ideological commun-ications is . . . a social process and cannot be explained merely as the

formal working out of an internal cultural logic. The development of an overall hegemonic pattern or 'design for living' is not so much the victory of a collective cognitive logic or aesthetic impulse as the development of redundancy – the continuous repetition, in diverse instrumental domains, of the same basic propositions regarding the nature of constructed reality. (1982: 388)

Wolf's point about 'redundancy' resembles Billig's notion of banal representations permeating the social environment, and again reminds us of the conceptual fluidity between culture and ideology. What I am trying to highlight here is that the culture concept easily invites us to brush over power relations that are constitutive of culture. If we return to Anthony Smith's conception of ethno-symbolism quoted in the last chapter, we find that it is strikingly silent about the difficulties outlined above:

Given the many economic and political ruptures between pre-modern and modern collective cultural identities in the same area, any conti-nuity between *ethnie* and nation had to be located in the cultural and symbolic spheres. This in turn led to the adoption of the term 'ethno-symbolism' for an approach that sought to establish relations between the different kinds of collective cultural identity by focussing on elements of myth, memory, value, symbol, and tradition that tended to change more slowly, and were more flexible in meaning, than the processes in other domains. (2004: 196)

Along with many of the commentators we have been discussing, I would argue that this search for cultural and symbolic continuity between *ethnie* and nation purchases historical depth at the price of a rather super-ficial notion of culture. The slow rate of change and semantic flexibility of the cultural stuff that Smith makes central might be viewed as more of a problem than a virtue for explanation. For surely it is the historically specific and shifting concatenations of meanings and values, how they are forged by power relations, and altered by circumstances, that we want to understand. The remarkable persistence of myths and symbols is due in part to the fact that they are polysemic, changing their meanings over time, and thus obscuring as much as illuminating the processes in ques-tion. Again, I am not making a case against culture as a conceptual tool, but against culture conceived with the accent on stasis, boundedness and continuity.

Another Sense of Culture

Before the 1950s the anthropological concept of culture was frequently no more than a container for whatever collection of mental and physical artefacts the ethnographer might need to describe and organize. Thus, Clark Wissler's 1929 *Introduction to Social Anthropology* defined culture as 'the mode of life followed by the community' (quoted in Bidney 1944: 30), and Boas's definition, while bearing the stamp of the linguistic analogy we have noted, was similarly broad: 'Culture embraces all the manifestations of social habits of a community, the reactions of the individual as affected by the habits of the group in which he lives, and the products of human activity as determined by these habits' (1944: 30). Although there were lively debates about the processes that shape culture, what generally comes across in the writings of this earlier period is a notion of culture as a loosely cohering set of beliefs, behaviours and artefacts. The main reason for this rather nonchalant concept was probably that the object of study was largely predefined by the method of ethnography – the direct study of relatively small social groups over long period of time, with a view to the thorough description of their 'way of life'. Moreover, these groups had usually been further predefined by the practices of colonial administrations in their management of populations. This ethnographic practice tended to lead to a kind of 'descriptive integration' (Wolf 1982: 14), cataloguing cultural components and their functional relations, and at their best bringing these into a vivid, holistic account of a circumscribed sphere of social life.

While often neglecting questions of historical process and wider fields of social relations, as we have seen, these earlier researches had the limited but important merit of seeking interconnections across the full range of social life, weaving together the ideational and the material, the mental and the physical. It is also notable that this process of descriptive integration was frequently aided by another complementary concept, 'social organization', that put more specific emphasis on social groups, relations and dynamics (see Boas 1940: 356–78; Firth 1956, 1964; Lowie 1947). The criticisms of the culture concept reviewed above are salutary, but I want to suggest that there may also be value in returning to the past to make a new departure. In his critique Wolf maintains that

> the culture concept is no panacea – it is, if anything, but a starting point of inquiry. Its value is methodological: 'look for connections!' But it still takes work and thought to discover what those connections might be and, indeed, if any connections exist. (1984: 394)

In the first instance, I would recommend that those interested in a cultural understanding of nationalism worry a bit less about the power of myths and symbols, and a bit more about seeking connections, not just in the dimension of ideation but across the full range of social life in the particular case in question. In the second instance, I would argue that we can make some headway in understanding what makes the components of culture 'somehow hang together' (Deutsch 1953: 88) if we relate this minimal notion of culture back to our discussion of power and organization.

Let me state it bluntly at first: the universal human need for power adequate to daily life leads to diverse forms of social organization, and such organization operates across a range of social phenomena, to adumbrate – ideas, symbols, values, sentiments, identities, institutions, formal and informal organisations, technologies, practices and procedures and so on. Culture is the interconnections among such phenomena, causally determined by the social organization of power. It is not culture that binds, but power. Power, in binding, creates culture. While this may render culture as an epiphenomenon of power, it also regards culture as an essential conceptual tool for tracing the workings of power. In keeping with the previous discussion, specific concentrations of power, organization and culture do not exist in tidy, bounded packages. These are better imagined as centres of gravity, whose fields of 'pull' overlap and interact with other such centres, in relations that can either reinforce or conflict. There is no need to privilege the social form of the ethnic group or nation as the carriers of culture. The global Catholic Church has power and organization, and thus a culture peculiar to it, as do economic firms, well-organized professions, landholding elites, academic departments, urban street gangs, even families, and so on *ad infinitum*. Some kinds of culture are generated precisely by imposed organization and the limited possibilities for power, such as among prison populations. In this conception, because we all participate in multiple, cross-cutting organizational contexts, participating in various subcultures, we are all in some sense 'multicultural'. We pay special attention to ethnicities and nations to the degree that they have power and are effectively organized, whether through movement organizations, Hechter's 'governance units' (2000: 9), or states.

Because culture in these terms is understood as a kind of *relation*, rather than an *object* (cf. Ollman 1976), it becomes particularly difficult to illustrate by examples. The idea of culture put forth here is a ramifying network of relations that bleed into other such networks, not a set of circumscribed, meaningful symbols. Even the 'laundry list' at the beginning of the last paragraph is misleading, because it directs attention to a set of basic categories, rather than the relations between them. Nonetheless, let me try at least to suggest by illustration what I am getting at. Consider the myths surrounding the iconic episode of Serbian history, the Battle of Kosovo in 1389, in which Prince Lazar died on the battlefield defending the Christian faith and the Serbian nation. In the nationalist hagiography that grew up around this event in the following centuries, Lazar became a sacrificial Christ figure, betrayed by a fellow nobleman in the role of Judas, heroically accepting his own death but, like Christ, prepared for resurrection along with the Serbian nation (Hastings 1997: 130–2). This myth has been put in service of various political projects in modern times, most recently in the Serbian claims on Kosovo and the conflict there in 1998. Clearly the set of symbolic equations in this myth: Prince Lazar = Christ = Serbia are very meaningful for many Serbians, and this symbolic package provides a way for imagining a shared identity and destiny. This kind of symbolic analysis, which is only sketched here, is valuable and illuminating, and I am not arguing against doing it. But by my reckoning this myth is best viewed as a component in a field of ideology, not as in and of itself an 'example' of culture. A better grasp of how this myth is caught up in culture is gained by considering the rapprochement between Slobodan Milosevic's government and the Serbian Orthodox Church after he came to power in December 1987. Reversing communist policies, Milosevic allowed new church construction and expansion, the selling of the Church newspaper at public news-stands, and the celebration of Orthodox Christmas in downtown Belgrade:

> In token of the new atmosphere, the Serbian Orthodox Church cooperated with the Milosevic government in marking the six hundredth anniversary of the battle of Kosovo on 28 June 1989. In Orthodox services connected with the commemoration, pictures of Milosevic could be seen among the religious icons. (Ramet 1996: 180)

Culture lies not so much in the symbol of the battle of Kosovo and Prince Lazar (although its not a bad place to start), as in how they 'hang together' in this 'new atmosphere', in this evolving set of relations among church, state, citizens and believers, relations that could be traced out much further. These relations were shaped, but not comprehended, by the machinations of Milosevic and Church leaders. Those machinations operate within wider fields of power and culture that are not of their making. Thus, I am not simply advocating an instrumentalist approach to the analysis of national symbols (Brass 1991). I am suggesting that such symbols need to be located in the shifting gravitational fields of organizations and their powers, and that the relations we become aware of when we do this are culture.

Language

We have encountered two main types of arguments about the relationship between language and nationalism. The one, more associated with primordial approaches, emphasizes language as an object of affect and sign of social identity and authenticity (Fishman 1972). The other, more associated with modernist approaches, emphasizes the technical effects of language, and especially printing and literacy, in expanding and accelerating communication within national groups (Deutsch 1953). These arguments are quite compatible, the difference is a matter of emphasis. Indeed, Benedict Anderson's (1991) argument about the relationship between 'imagined communities' and 'print-capitalism' can be viewed as an attempt to bring them together (see Chapters 4 and 8). For this reason Anderson's approach comes closer to exemplifying what I mean by a cultural analysis, as opposed to an approach that focuses more strictly on the ideational and symbolic role of language. Let me fill in this rather polarized view a bit by examining the relationship between language and nationalism under four headings: (1) as functional communication; (2) as a symbol of community; (3) as a medium of status marking; and (4) as a medium of cognition and ideology.

As Functional Communication

Gellner's thesis, that a basic requirement of society in modern industrialized nation-states is a standardized written language supported by widespread literacy (1983: 35–8), seems overstated when one considers viable multilingual states such as Switzerland, where four languages are officially recognized: German, French, Italian and Romansh. Nonetheless, it hard to deny the force of Gellner's argument, that common language facilitates the need of modern society for 'modularity' among its members, in the face of constant economic change and restructuring. Even in the case of Switzerland, although all four languages have been officially recognized since 1998, almost three quarters of the population live in the German-speaking region and almost one quarter lives in the French-speaking region, where German and French are respectively the languages of official business and education. So there is a much greater degree of linguistic uniformity than might at first appear. Similarly, the rising role of Spanish as a second language in the United States, while creating social tensions, is not likely to upset the role of English as the dominant language. For Gellner's thesis, it is not linguistic homogeneity, but the presence of a dominant variety that is key. Modern societies are highly stratified, and the demands for mobility, and thus literacy and command of the linguistic standard, fall much less on those at the bottom of the hierarchy. In fact, linguistic marginality for such populations may be seen as reinforcing the stratification system and thus functional for the national economy as a whole.

As we have seen, it has frequently been argued that the rise of widespread printing in vernaculars, combined with expanding literacy among middle classes, were prerequisites for the development of nationalism. While not gainsaying the importance of these changes, if applied too mechanically this thesis may obscure other ways in which the written and spoken word, in combination with organizational structures, can achieve the widespread dissemination of ideas and foment popular movements. Reading is only one way of taking in ideas, and the spread of new ideologies such as Protestantism or nationalism, while no doubt facilitated by expanding literacy, probably also relied on the verbal dissemination of these ideas by the literate to the illiterate, especially in settings where the speaker's authority is sanctioned. The Scottish Reformation (1560–7), which I would regard as proto-national, led to the development of an extensive system of basic schooling in Lowland Scotland in the seventeenth century, boosting popular literacy. But the earlier phases of the Reformation probably relied more on the effects of literacy within the reforming clergy and their supporters in the nobility and urban middling ranks, which in turn disseminated these ideas orally through social networks and the crucial role of ministers in the pulpit. Adrian Hastings has made a similar point about the impact of missionizing and literacy in Africa:

The effect of a relatively small number of books in a community which has, hitherto, had none or very few is far greater than people in a world used to a surfeit of books can easily realise, and it extends far beyond the literate. Thus the impact of a vernacular literature in shaping the consciousness of communities hitherto untouched by printing in, say, late nineteenth- and early twentieth-century Africa could be enormous. It is not that everyone, or most people, could read. The social impact of written literature may even be greater when that is not the case. What can be so decisive in such circumstances is the mediation of the authority of the written text across certain privileged forms of orality. (1997: 23)

As a Symbol of Community

Many nationalists, in the style of Herder, have sought to define national identity in terms of a distinct linguistic patrimony, despite the profound problems of delimiting languages. Consider this example:

> The language-dialect situation along the border between the Netherlands and Germany is an interesting one. Historically there was a continuum of dialects of one language, but the two that eventually became standardized as the languages of the Netherlands and Germany, Standard Dutch and Standard German, are not mutually intelligible, that is a speaker of one cannot understand a speaker of the other. In the border area speakers of the local varieties of Dutch and German do still remain largely intelligible to one another, yet the people on one side of the border say they speak a variety of Dutch and those on the other side, a variety of German. On the Dutch side, the residents of the Netherlands look to Standard Dutch for their model; they read and write Dutch, are educated in Dutch, and watch television in Dutch. They say they use a local variety, or dialect, of Dutch in their daily lives. On the other side of the border, German replaces Dutch in all equivalent situations. The interesting linguistic fact, though, is that there are more similarities between the local varieties spoken on each side of the border than between the one dialect (of Dutch?) and Standard Dutch, and the other dialect (of German?) and Standard German, and more certainly between that dialect of German and certain south German and Austrian dialects of German. (Wardhaugh 1992: 27–8)

Such examples are often used to argue the difficulties of defining nations in terms of distinct, bounded languages, and they serve this purpose very effectively. Other prime examples include the distinctions between Hindi and Urdu, and between Serbian and Croatian, both pairs having substantial structural similarities, but being defined as different languages by their users, because of different modes of writing, and associations with distinct religious and national traditions (Wardhaugh 1992: 26–7). But demonstrating the weak correspondence between the distribution of 'objective' linguistic features and communities defining themselves as nations should not make us think that language is irrelevant but rather make us ask how, then, it is relevant. Sociolinguists have struggled to articulate an analytic concept of 'speech communities' defined by shared patterns of speech. Because of examples like the ones we have just seen, many have found definitions based on objective features of the spoken language too narrow, turning instead to subjective aspects of language:

> We must also acknowledge that using linguistic characteristics alone to determine what is or is not a speech community has proved so far to be quite impossible because people do not necessarily feel any direct relationship between linguistic characteristics A, B, C, and so on, and speech community X. What we can be sure of is that speakers do use linguistic characteristics to achieve group identity with, and group differentiation from, other speakers. (Wardhaugh 1992: 118)

Thus, when language serves as a symbol of community, the actual distribution of linguistic structures (grammar, vocabulary, etc.) is not really the issue. What matters is that the speakers themselves perceive their speech variety as belonging under a certain heading, either Dutch or German in the case above. The symbolization of community is partly a matter of policing boundaries, as with the stringent opposition to loan-words from English in France (e.g. *le weekend*), but it is also a matter of orienting identity to a valued core – to the standard variety taught in schools, to the idea of a literary canon, to folk traditions of verbal arts, as in humour, to notions of characteristic national speech styles, such as laconic, argumentative, flamboyant and so on. Though such character-izations may be impossible to substantiate as generalizations about national populations, and may be cross-cut by contrasting characteriza-tions of regional or ethnic speech communities, it matters little. What matters is that aspects of language that are positively valued and identi-fied with are construed in national terms.

As a Medium of Status-marking

Language frequently reveals aspects of our social standing, both gener-ally and in specific situations. Dialects can mark us out as working or upper class; the use of a more formal speech style or ritualized markers of 'politeness' may be required when there is distance between the social statuses of those conversing; the use of terms of address (e.g. title, last name, first name) can indicate whether two speakers view each other as equals or ranked by an authority relationship. Of particular relevance to nationalism is the role of diglossia, a situation in which there is a relatively stable coexistence of high status (H) and low status (L) varieties of language, associated with other ethnic or class boundaries in the society. These are frequently differences along a language continuum, such as French (H) and Haitian Creole (L) in Haiti, or Standard German (H) and Swiss German (L) in Switzerland, but can also involve separate languages, such as Norman French (H) and English (L) in England for about three centuries after 1066. C. A. Ferguson suggests that classic diglossic situations tend to have roots in pre-democratic/colonial societies in which there is sharp stratification between a literate elite and a much larger, non-literate population (1972: 247). Many of the paradigmatic nationalisms of the fragmenting Habsburg Empire involved acute examples of diglossia, as between German (H) and Czech (L) in Bohemia. As Ferguson observes:

> Diglossia seems to be accepted and not regarded as 'a problem' by the community in which it is in force, until certain trends appear in the community. These include trends toward (1) more widespread literacy (whether for economic, ideological or other reasons), (2) broader communication among different regional and social segments of the community (e.g. for economic, administrative, military, or ideological reasons), (3) desire for a full-fledged standard 'national' language as an attribute of autonomy or of sovereignty. (1972: 247)

Thus, modern democratic societies with advanced capitalist economies are incompatible with classic diglossia, and instead there tends to be an ambiguous balance between a somewhat privileged 'standard' and a counterbalancing positive evaluation of regional and class dialects, arising partly from the influence of popular mass culture celebrating these dialects. Swiss German is often highly valued in Switzerland as sign of a national identity distinctive from Germany, thus weakening the historical high/low relationship between this pair. Standard German increasingly serves as a functional asset and less as a status marker. Nonetheless, tensions over the prestige and opportunites afforded by different languages remain salient in modern states. It is an interesting question whether the relationship between English and Spanish in the United States is a high/low one, a new quasi-diglossia, just a growing bilingualism among part of the population, or a complex combination of both. Russian is currently experiencing the decline of its former 'high' status vis-à-vis titular languages in many of the former republics of the Soviet Union (Laitin 1998). The Soviet Union was modern in many respects, and Russian existed alongside titular languages in the republics that were written and officially recognized. However, the incorporation of the communist economy into the political bureaucracy meant that the language of the bureaucratic hierarchy, Russian, was in some sense the ultimate H variety.

As a Medium of Cognition/Ideology

There is another line of argument tracing back to Herder, which emphasizes the way language shapes perception and understanding (Wardhaugh 1992: 218–25; see also Box 2.3, p. 34). A classic statement comes from Edward Sapir in 1929:

> Human beings . . . are very much at the mercy of the particular language which has become the medium of expressions for their society. It is quite an illusion to imagine that one adjusts to reality essentially without the use of language and that language is merely an incidental means of solving specific problems of communication or reflection. The fact of the matter is that the 'real world' is to a large extent built up on the language habits of the group . . . We see and hear and otherwise experience very largely as we do because the language habits of our community predispose certain choices of communication. (1985: 162)

In its more extreme forms that emphasize the determining effects of deep grammatical structures on consciousness (Whorf 1956), this argument is highly contentious. Multilingual people seem to live in one reality mediated in different ways by their different languages, not in multiple realities divided by those languages. But the more general point, that language helps render our thoughts and feelings in implicit and habitual forms, is more sustainable. Speakers of a language often share conventions, not just at the level of grammar, but in the patterns of association and metaphor that pervade language. We noted above how aspects of language can become explicit symbols of community and objects of positive evaluation. Here we are concerned with the implicit workings of language, recalling Billig's (1995) stress on the banal ways discourse reinforces national identity.

Consider the way words and ideas become strongly associated through repeated use. For instance, for many Americans (but not all), 'America' is automatically situated in a web of close associations with 'freedom', 'democracy', 'individualism', 'God' and so on. In Britain one finds chains of association between 'immigrant' and 'non-white', 'non-Christian', 'poor', 'criminality' and so on. Activating this series of associations is what we mean when we accuse politicians, purportedly using a neutral discourse about immigration policy, of 'playing the race card'. These are not logically necessary connections, but rather a selection established out of a huge range of possibilities, routinized through popular discourse. Such webs of ideational *cum* ideological associations ramify throughout a language, interconnecting and reinforcing one another. They are neither hard-wired into the grammatical structures of the language, nor consciously and deliberately chosen by their users (apart from the odd ideologue). This process of association is a fundamental and unavoidable aspect of language, ever susceptible to ideological currents and manipulation.

Language is also unavoidably suffused by metaphors. George Lakoff and Mark Johnson offer a minimal definition: '*The essence of metaphor is understanding and experiencing one kind of thing in terms of another*' (1980: 5, italics in original). They suggest that certain basic metaphors pervade English, such that arguments are routinely likened to war ('He *shot down* all of my arguments') and time is likened to money ('He's living on *borrowed* time') (1980: 4–9). Metaphorical thinking can be found throughout nationalist discourses. Even where racial conceptions of the nation are eschewed, the metaphor of the nation as an organism, as a single being persisting and growing through time ('This nation can look back on its history with pride'), is so obvious we often forget it is there. As we saw in Chapter 4, the proto-nationalism of the Protestant reformers in Britain drew heavily on a metaphor likening the nation (both England and Scotland) and its struggles to those of ancient Israel (Hastings 1997: 195–6). The terrorist attacks on the US on 11 September 2001 were quickly construed on the model of the Japanese attack on Pearl Harbor precipitating the American entry into the Second World War, and soon Saddam Hussein was being likened to Hitler. Thus, the moral associations Americans have with the Second World War were transferred to the new 'War on Terror'. Again, specific languages do not prescribe specific metaphors, but the use of metaphor, as a basic aspect of how language and the mind work, is inevitable.

Language evolves to serve practical human needs for communication and coordination of behaviour. It does this at various levels, providing a basic means for communication at the level of phonology and syntax, while also encoding, albeit more fluidly than is often assumed, all sorts of descriptive and normative assumptions about the world at the level of semantics. In this way, apart from any issues of how people identify as members of a linguistic community, language has fundamental organizing effects, facilitating the coordination of behaviour by sustaining both explicit and implicit understandings about reality among users of the same language. The sense of incompetence and disempowerment one experiences when trying to accomplish simple verbal tasks in a context where one does not command the language in use is raw evidence of this fundamental organizing capacity of language. On the other hand, as a marker of communal identity and icon of communal heritage, language organizes people in another way, less pragmatically and more ideologically. In this regard language becomes a criteria for social inclusion or exclusion, a core value to be praised and protected, a social good the national population and their leaders can lay claim to and defend. Here the language itself becomes a symbol suffused with sentiments, not a medium for coordinating behaviour, but a value for orienting and motivating behaviour. In short, language organizes behaviour (1) in the functional-pragmatic way emphasized by Gellner, (2) by naturalizing and rendering habitual assumptions about reality that are often ideologically charged, as emphasized in different ways by Sapir and Billig, and (3) by symbolizing ideas and feelings about shared community, as stressed by Fishman. Language is a diffuse and spontaneous mode of social organization, which gets seized upon and utilized by more formal and authoritative forms of organization, such as campaigning groups, political parties and ultimately states. The latter kind of social organization in effect harnesses the former. All quests for power, national or not, need to control language to some degree, but in the case of nationalism this relationship becomes particularly convoluted, because language becomes both the medium and the object of power.

Religion

Discussions of the relationship between religion and nationalism tend to run along three lines (cf. Smith 2003a: 13–14): (1) questions of the historical roots of modern nationalism in the Judeo-Christian tradition; (2) the role of religions in providing crucial organizational and ideological resources for nationalisms; and (3) questions about whether religion and nationalism both ultimately address the same human need for meaning and moral authority. I will take these in turn.

*Questions of the Historical Roots of Modern Nationalism in the
Judeo-Christian Tradition*

This argument has been put forth most forcefully by Adrian Hastings
who maintains that:

> The nation and nationalism are both . . . characteristically Christian
> things which, in so far as they have appeared elsewhere, have done so
> within a process of westernisation and of imitation of the Christian
> world, even if it was imitated as western rather than Christian. (1997:
> 186)

He stresses the way the Bible, and more specifically the Old
Testament, provided a template for imagining the nation and its moral
and political causes. This is augmented by: (1) the institutional role of the
medieval European Church in fostering the legitimacy of rulers among
the ruled; and, most distinctively, (2) the role of Christianity 'as a religion
of translation' (1997: 194) lacking a true 'sacred language' (*contra*
Benedict Anderson's claim that Latin functioned in medieval Europe as a
sacred language) and therefore amenable to dissemination through local
vernaculars, a process which Hastings argues began well before the
Reformation. These points suggest why Christianity was well suited to
enabling the formation of nationalism, but not why it trumps other religions in this purpose (cf. Grosby 2001b: 109–13). Hastings notes that the
Jews 'may well be called the true proto-nation' (1997: 186), having a core
identity structured around a religious tradition, language and literature,
but that identity became distributed over a variety of ethnicities. And
crucially, their religious institutions were not articulated with political
ones in the same way that Christian ones were, being more confined to a
private sphere. Thus, Jewish nationalism, in the form of Zionism, only
developed in the late nineteenth century under the general pressures of
European nationalism.

Even more starkly, despite sometimes articulating with nationalism in
the twentieth century (see Suleiman 2003), Hastings views Islam as
'profoundly anti-national' (1997: 187). A lengthy quote provides the
crux of Hastings argument of why Islam, unlike Chrisitianity, is antipa-
thetic to nationalism:

> Here there was from the start a political model – the world empire
> based on the *umma*, a community of faith, but based also on the
> possession of a single, and genuinely sacred language. Not only was

the explicit model of Islam together with its early history opposed to anything like a multitude of nation-states, unlike Christianity, it was also opposed to linguistic diversity. Its culture was not one of translation but of assimilation. This is a point which . . . was made already by an observant Arab in the sixteenth century who became a Christian and a monk of Dabra Libanos in Ethiopia. Enbaqom wrote his *Anqasa Amin*, 'The Door of the Faith', in 1540 during the Jihad of Gran. It was an apologetic work comparing Islam and Christianity to prove the superiority of the latter and one of his most interesting arguments was that the Qur'an is the book of a single language, Arabic, while the Bible exists in twenty languages and he cites many of them to prove that Christianity can be at home anywhere. Enbaqom put his finger on quite a crucial divergence between the two religions. The Muslim attitude to the Qur'an made translation almost impossible. For the religious person it has to be read, recited out loud five times a day, or listened to in Arabic. In consequence the whole cultural impact of Islam is necessarily to Arabise, to draw peoples into a single world community of language and government. And this is what it did. Even the language of Egypt disappeared before it, except as a Christian liturgical language. Nations are not constructed by Islam but deconstructed. That is a fact of history, but it is a fact dependent upon theology. Recognition of it should make it all the clearer that the construction of nations within the Christian world was not something independent of Christianity, but, rather, something stimulated by the Christian attitude both to language and the state. (1997: 201)

Hastings also argued that within Christianity it was specifically the reformed varieties strongly linked to particular states via national churches that were most conducive to nationalism, paradigmatically in England. This state–church linkage has been echoed to a degree in the post-Byzantium autocephalous Eastern Orthodox Churches of Russia, Serbia, and Greece. Christianity's countervailing universalist and anti-statist tendencies, evidenced in the Catholic Church and smaller Protestant sects such as the Mennonites and Quakers, have been more impervious: 'small non-state churches and very large, highly international, churches are those least affected by nationalism' (1997: 205). (For a set of interrogations of Hastings' argument, see Grosby [2003], Llobera [2003], Magaš [2003] and Smith [2003c].)

The Role of Religions in Providing Crucial Organizational and Ideological Resources for Nationalisms

Regardless of whether Christianity was the unique historical seedbed of nationalism, there is little doubt that it and other religions have at times provided key institutional and ideological resources for nationalism. Despite considerable variations within and across religions, churches, monasteries, synagogues, mosques and so on are all formal organizations, with material resources in the form of property, land, wealth and social resources in the form of personnel with skills, influence, networks and hierarchical command structures (Bax 1991). A few examples involving the Catholic Church will help illustrate. On the one hand, expansive church bureaucracies can 'frame' the daily life of a people, replacing the agency of the state in areas such as education, and fostering a relatively unpoliticized collective identity. In the nineteenth century the Catholic Church in Ireland fulfilled many of the socializing functions of the modern state, consolidating while also controlling an Irish Catholic identity in opposition to the British state (Inglis 1991; Ruane and Todd 1996). In a similar way the Church both 'caged' and cultivated a religious *cum* national identity among Catholics in Quebec, which later became more politicized and secularized during the 'quiet revolution' of the 1960s. Alternatively, when national identities have become politicized, religious organizations can help harbour and focus opposition, providing key resources for the nationalist project. During the later years of the Franco dictatorship in Spain (1939–75) the Catholic Church, particularly centred on the Benedictine abbey of Montserrat, became a focus for the preservation of Catalan language and identity in embattled opposition to Franco's Castilianizing government in Madrid (Conversi 1997: 125–9). Similarly, the role of the Catholic Church in Poland in sustaining an underground opposition to communist rule (1945–89), stimulated by the popularity of the late Pope John Paul II, is well known. Similar examples can be found for other religions. This is not to suggest that religious institutions naturally align themselves with nationalism, on the contrary they often accommodate themselves to the state structures they find themselves in, and resist the politicizing and secularizing impulses of nationalism. But under the right circumstances there are convergences. The general point here is that we should not let our attention be drawn so quickly to the ideational resources of religion for nationalism, which I address next, that we neglect this more pragmatic role of religious organization.

Paul Brass (1991) has scrutinized the way religiously derived symbols have fed into communal conflicts between Hindus and Muslims in South

Asia, often manipulated by elites in those communities. In the case of the episodic cow protection movements that have arisen among Hindus in India since the 1880s, in objection to Muslim practices of killing and eating cows, the issue

> was not central to the political elites who dominated the leading political organizations of Indian nationalism and Muslim separatism. It was central to the Hindu religious leaders, revivalist and orthodox, and it later became a useful symbol for Hindu communal organizations committed to a Hindu definition of Indian nationalism. (1991: 79)

Just as the protection of the revered cow has been a matter of respecting Hindu sensibilities, the protection of religiously based *shari'a* law for the Muslim community has been important, thus requiring a certain zone of jurisdictional concessions to *ulema* authority within the standardized civil code of India. According to Brass:

> In effect a tacit bargain has been struck in modern India whose terms are that Muslims will not be allowed to violate Hindu feelings by slaughtering cows, while the Muslims retain the right to have a separate system of civil laws. This bargain could have been struck at any time before independence had it not served the interests of Hindu religious elites and Muslim political elites to keep the issues alive. It was not struck because Hindu revivalists found the symbol of the cow invaluable in uniting Hindus, because the Muslim political elites found the cow protection issue useful to demonstrate the dangers of Hindu majority rule, and because both Hindu and Muslim political elites found the issue of the Sharia valuable in recruiting the support of the *ulema* in their conflicts with each other for political influence. (1991: 82)

Thus, in Brass's analysis, while religious customs obviously inform the identities of the two communities, their political significance is highly situational, depending on the balance of forces between multiple elite factions in both communities. Brass's 'instrumentalist' approach here exemplifies the treatment of religious ideas as malleable symbolic resources for nationalism.

We have already encountered the basic idea that the concept of the Hebrew nation in the Old Testament was a key ideological metaphor for the conceptualization of Christian nations. While drawing his illustrations primarily from the Judeo-Christian tradition, which seems to have provided ideas particularly suited to imagining the nation, unlike Hastings, Anthony Smith (2003a) sees a more fundamental derivation of nationalism from religion in general and, unlike Brass, he sees symbolic processes as determined at a much deeper level. Smith is clear that nationalisms are opposed in many ways to religions, particularly in their this-worldly as opposed to other-worldly attitude to the resolution of human alienation. But there are continuities that go deeper than simply the borrowing and adapting of symbolic motifs, to an underlying similarity of social form:

> We must go beneath the official positions, and even the popular practices, of modern nationalisms to discover the deeper cultural resources and sacred foundations of national identities; and that in turn means grasping the significance of the nation as a form of communion that binds its members through ritual and symbolic practices. (2003a: 18)

For Smith the symbolic themes of religion and nationalism share four 'basic dimensions': community, territory, history and destiny (2003a: 31). Thus, he observes how the Hebrew idea of a community formed through a unique covenant with God has carried over to numerous 'Christian' nations, sometimes combined with notions of a providential world-historical mission for the nation, either by protecting the faith, or by defending and advancing other secularized but still ultimate values (see Hastings 1999; Templin 1999). He argues that the idea of a sacred relationship to a particular territory, again the prototype being God's giving a specific homeland to the Jews, is echoed in the reverence for national territories and their distinctive aesthetic beauties in the eyes of many nationalists, and in their claims to those territories. Regarding history, as we have seen the idea of 'golden ages' in the nation's past figure prominently in Smith's symbolic analysis. Here the connections to religious traditions are somewhat looser, but he hears echoes of religious ideas of Eden and paradise in the idealization of the past. However, myths of national heroes and their great cultural achievements also serve to consolidate the essence of a positive national identity, providing a touchstone that can be referred to in times of crisis. They stand midway between an Eden in a 'time before time', and the present reality. Finally, Smith emphasizes an ethos of sacrifice for the nation by its people, reworking some of the themes of George Mosse's writings seen in the last chapter. Here it is not so much private grief, as public memory and commemoration of individual and collective sacrifices that matter, especially in regard to war and genocide. As with the notion of covenants, the idea of sanctification through sacrifice, and the acceptance of a difficult but divinely appointed destiny, has deep roots in the Judeo-Christian religious tradition. Again, this sense of sacrifice and destiny can take a more secularized form but is often deeply imbued with religious sentiments.

The idea of ethnic election, of a people chosen by God, or in a more secular perspective, by history itself, binds together these religious themes in Smith's account of nationalism. Peter van der Veer (1999) has found striking parallels in the construction of Hindu identity in the nineteenth and twentieth centuries. On the one hand, early philological studies that identified the underlying connections between the Indo-European languages attributed these similarities to a language-bearing Aryan race, which genetically linked upper caste Hindus with their British colonizers. Religious reformers used this idea to imagine a superior Hindu/Aryan race, degenerated by external influences (Dravidian, Muslim, Dalit) but still a font of all modern civilization and capable of being restored to its original virtue and glory. On the other hand, this racial concept of the nation was complemented by a spiritual one. Reformers developed notions of 'Hindu spirituality' in opposition to 'Western materialism', reinterpreting the Vedanta (the Upanishads and their tradition of interpretation) and codifying diverse ascetic practices into 'the ancient system of Yoga'. These processes fed into an agenda of revitalizing the Hindu nation, while also making Hindu religious practices more accessible to Westerners. The combined idea of the Hindus as a spiritually superior race, first developed in the second half of the nineteenth century, continues to shape Hindu nationalism to the present day.

At first this would seem to confirm Smith's notion of a universal formal affinity between religion and nationalism based on ideas of ethnic election. However, van der Veer also stresses that these developments were very much a response to the impact of Orientalism, that is, 'the various Western accounts of the thought, religion and history of colonised peoples in Asia' (1999: 422). The notion of a unified Hindu people following a distinct religion in a given territory (and defined against the Muslim population) is heavily shaped by Western scholarship and colonial administration. As van der Veer observes:

Hindus do not have a Semitic concept of a 'chosen people'. What they do have is the opposite: a concept of 'chosen gods'. Hindus may choose personal gods from their pantheon much in the same way as Catholics in the Christian tradition may choose their patron saints. One chooses the god to whom one feels most attracted. Some of these gods are saviour gods in the theological sense that they can grant liberation from the cycle of rebirths. There is no Hindu notion, however, of a 'covenant' between god and his 'chosen people' as in the Semitic tradition. It is important to make this conceptual difference clear, because it highlights the fact that many of our theories about the relation between religion, ethnicity and nationalism, as well as about secularisation and secularism, are based upon Christianity and/or the Judeo-Christian tradition. Hinduism, Buddhism, Shintoism and even Islam (despite its Semitic origins) do not easily fit these theories. At the same time, however, despite this difference the impact of Western concepts (which are partly rooted in Christianity) on these other religions in the modern period has been so fundamental that it allows us to explore the theme of 'chosen people' further. In India the impact on Hinduism is sometimes called the 'semiticisation of Hinduism'. (1999: 419)

This observation points us back to Hastings' argument about the peculiar influence of Christianity on nationalism, an influence then broadcast throughout the world via colonialism, orientalism and missionization, under the rubric of 'modernization'.

Questions about Whether Religion and Nationalism both Ultimately Address the Same Human Need for Meaning and Moral Authority

Fundamentally, Smith's argument about 'chosen peoples' hinges on the transmutation of religious sacredness into national authenticity. For him the communion of the nation revolves around the core idea of 'authenticity' – that which is true, unique, necessary and the ultimate source of value:

One could argue, then, that religious sanctity, the category of the sacred in traditional religions, has become transmuted in the nationalist belief-system into a secular authenticity. But, not only does the latter function within nationalism in much the same way as the former does in traditional religions – that is, to separate and 'forbid' certain objects; it is also located at the heart of a new religion, the 'religion of the people', a religion that is equally binding, ritually repetitive, and collectively enthusing – the defining qualities of all religions, in Durkheim's view – as any earlier religion had been. Equally, the cultivation of authenticity, which stands at the heart of nationalist belief-systems, provides the essential means to an inner-worldly salvation. Rediscovering one's roots and cultivating one's true self are central to the salvation drama of nationalism. (2003a: 40)

Thus, Smith's approach can be viewed as a variation on Durkheim's (1965 [1915]) classic argument that the sacred objects of religious worship are, in fact, symbolic representations of the community doing the worshipping, to wit, the nation (see Smith 2001b). In a complex argument Steven Grosby (2001b) has questioned the Durkheimian tendency to equate religion and nationalism, arguing that despite their similar social functions in generating social solidarity through symbol and ritual, the key objects of 'transcendence' for religions and nations are, in fact, quite different. According to him, religions achieve transcendence through an orientation to an 'other-worldly' source of ultimate meaning, whereas nations do so through an orientation in this world to 'vitality', by which he means a notion of life-force flowing through, and cognitively embodied in, relations of kinship, lineage and territorial attachment. These two orientations to transcendence permeate, but also exist in tension with one another. He suggests that we can assess

> the extent to which religion is a factor in the constitution and continued existence of nationality based on the degree to which the this-worldly objects of reference to vitality, lineage (ethnicity) and territory, are incorporated into a particular religion. Put abstractly, where the this-worldly loci of vitality are elements within the religion, then there exists a convergence between religion and nationality. Where they are absent, then there exists a considerable degree of tension between religion and nationality. (2001b: 109)

Thus, localized, 'pre-axial' religious traditions where worship is focused on ancestors and gods of lineages, households and sacred places, constitute the ideal conditions for convergence, whereas the 'axial' (i.e. world) religions of Islam, Buddhism, Judaism and Christianity tend towards a separation of these orientations to the transcendent. There is a world historical trend of divergence between these two principles. However, once again, he suggests that Judaism and Christianity are more compatible with the vitalism of nations, the former because of its merging of lineal identity and territorial attachment with its monotheism, the latter because of its inheritance of this same ideational complex, but also because its doctrine of acceptance of worldly power ('Render to Caesar the things that are Caesar's', Mark 12:17) has made it more open to affiliation with ethnic and territorial power. For Grosby there is an elaborate historical *pas de deux* between religions as the transcendent source of meaning, and nations as the transcendent source of vitality.

In a short speculative essay entitled 'The Goodness of Nations' at the end of his book *The Spectre of Comparisons* (1998), Benedict Anderson has pondered the ability of nations to become the vessels of goodness in a secularized world. In very different terms, he echoes Grosby's concern with the lineal continuity of the nation as an object of transcendence. The dilemma is that nations, unlike religions, are so clearly grounded in the mundane and profane world, caught in the compromises of history and worldly venality. Where religions claim to judge the affairs of this world from the standpoint of God or revealed wisdom (albeit problematically mediated by mortals), nationalism can offer no such empyrean standpoint. So it must use a trick of the imagination, whereby the nation in the present is judged from the perspective of distant ancestors in the past, or by descendents in a far-away future. In each case, the distance of times past and the hypothetical nature of the future render our judges as anonymized co-nationals, 'impartial spectators' with the necessary sympathy for our condition, but cleansed of compromising moral entanglements. Have we honoured and been true to those in the past? Will those in the future happily recognize themselves in us? As we have seen, some people see their nations as divinely sanctioned and have no need of this moral device. But Anderson seems to think that in a world where God is for many, if not dead, in semi-retirement, the nation is called upon to provide an alternative source of moral grounding, not just in the sense of being something blessed, but in providing the ultimate judges of our actions in the present.

Talal Asad has argued that the idea that religion is essentially about the human need for ultimate values and meaning is a specifically modern and Christian view of the matter (1983: 245). This view was engendered by the development of the modern state and its need to largely restrict religion to a sphere of private moral and psychological concerns, a process that was enabled by new ideological notions of 'the secular' and 'secularization' (Asad 1999). He sees a danger in projecting our own peculiarly modern concerns with alienation and meaning in a de-authorized world onto the whole of human history. Asad's approach is to suggest, first, that our ideas of religion and secularism are interdependent ideological constructs arising in the modern period and, second, that we should avoid universalizing ahistorical conceptions of 'religion' and 'secularization' and attend more closely to the particular ways that power creates religion (and secularism).

While I suspect that a certain amount of alienation and need for meaning is perennial and not peculiarly modern, I agree with Asad that the fixation on these terms in defining religion neglects the important role of power. Religions are not just cosmological sources of meaning, solace and immortality – they are traditions of profound meditations on the nature of power (as God said to Job: 'Where were you when I laid the foundations of the Earth?' Job 38:4) and at the same time attempts to gain power and come to terms with power in the real world. Likewise, nationalisms are not simply about the need for authenticity or the belief in vitality, but practical attempts to create power in this world by advancing combined claims to identity, territory and jurisdiction. Given this it is no surprise that the two should intertwine in myriad ways, because power is the linchpin that connects sacred and secular universes (cf. Poggi 2001: chs 4 and 5). I suspect that it is in tracing out common concerns with power that the most revealing connections between religion and nationalism in actual cases are to be found. Anderson's accent on the search for an authoritative standpoint from which the nation can judge itself comes closer to the mark for me, because the notion of authority, however imaginary, implies a concern with the power that underwrites that authority. Anderson's nationals don't just want to be deemed 'good', they want the power to judge themselves so. From our modern perspective we tend to think that the nation needs to have 'God on its side' so that it can be assured of its righteousness, but there is an older, more fundamental and more enduring reason – so that it will prevail.

Conclusion

We know that language and religion are frequently very significant for nationalism because they supply symbolic resources for articulating nationalist claims, for defining national communities and anchoring identities. But I have been trying to suggest that their significance goes deeper than this. Language is important for nationalism because it is a fundamental medium for the very constitution of power, one which, through its overall patterning, can organize behaviour in explicit and implicit ways, orienting it towards centres of national power. Religion, for its part, can provide nationalism with crucial formal organizational structures and resources, which can seize upon and channel more nebulous religious ideas and sentiments, orienting them to nationalist causes. But perhaps more fundamentally, religions are about the ultimate nature of power, and our relationship to it. When nationalism aligns itself with religion, it partakes in its vital orientation to ultimate power. It is conventional to regard language and religion as quintessentially cultural processes because of their roles in provisioning humans with meaning. They do this, and in so doing they make our lives 'hang together' not just by providing meaning, but by orienting us to power.

Further Reading

For an extensive treatment of the anthropological debates about the culture concept see Brightman (1995). The articles by Keesing (1987) and Wolf (1984) are worth reading in full. On language and nationalism Deutsch (1953), Fishman (1972). Weber (1976) and Anderson (1991) remain essential readings. From a broadly rational choice perspective the work of David Laitin has been highly influential (1992; 1998). All of Billig (1995) is about nationalism and language in the broadest sense, but especially the second chapter. Fairclough (1989) advocates the critical study of language and power, with implications for the study of nationalism. On religion and nationalism Hayes (1960) is a seminal statement. Major recent works on this topic include: Grosby (2002), Hastings (1997), Smith (2003a) and van der Veer (2001). Van der Veer and Lehmann (1999) provide a good collection of case studies, plus the more theoretical essays by Asad and Anderson discussed above. The special issue of *Nations and Nationalism* (1999, volume 5, part 3) on 'chosen peoples' is also a good resource. Eickelman (1998) and Zubaida (2004) are good initial sources on the relationship between nationalism and Islam.

10
Conclusion: Power, Culture and Nationalism

This book has sought to critically survey some of the core literature on nationalism, scrutinizing the conceptual tools with which we make sense of it. The underlying argument has been that there are problems with both primordialist and modernist approaches, and that the fruitfulness of framing debates in terms of this antinomy may be exhausted. Instead, I have suggested that we need to clarify our concepts of power and culture, developing these in dialogue with the substantive empirical study of nationalism. I have tried to formulate and present general concepts of power and culture in this way. Because power and culture are fundamental constants in social relations, they bear on anything we might study, not just on nationalism. But this is not to suggest that nationalism itself is a fundamental constant – rather, it is a historically emergent permutation on the dynamics of power and culture. Moreover, arguing for the basic relevance of these concepts for understanding nationalism does not constitute a 'theory' of nationalism, it merely directs our attention in certain ways. Genuine theories need to define sets of variables and offer hypotheses about how they co-vary, supporting these with empirical material. That is a different kind of project, and not what is attempted here. I have offered not a theory, but a 'point of view', that generates criticisms, observations, speculations and arguments.

I begin this conclusion by summarizing the major points that have been made *en route* in the preceding chapters. I then go on explore three important areas of research and debate that have been left largely aside: (1) multiculturalism, pluralism, the accommodation of ethnic differences and the regulation of ethnic conflict; (2) normative critiques and defences of nationalism; and (3) postmodern approaches to nationalism. This should give those interested in these topics an initial sense of what they involve. At the same time I have tried to indicate why these have fallen mostly outside the purview of this book, as a way of further clarifying the position I have taken. I conclude with some speculative reflections on where the future of nationalism might take us.

Ten Summary Theses

The following list of core theses is presented not in order of importance, but roughly in the order that they were made in the book, although some points were made in different ways in various places. As I have said, they do not add up to a single argument, but rather emerge out of a point of view. They are also meant to suggest areas that we should explore and develop in future research.

1

As a school of theory 'primordialism' barely exists – it is more a broad tendency than a unified perspective. On the one hand, supposed major proponents of the perspective such as Anthony Smith abjure the label, on the other hand, rather diverse concerns are bundled under this heading: (1) with defining nationalism primarily in terms of ideologies of kinship and descent; (2) with tracing the roots of nationalism into premodern forms of ethnicity; and (3) with the fundamental role of sentiment and affect in constituting nationalism.

2

Understanding the role of the emotions in the constitution of nationalism is important, but so far under-theorized. There is a tendency to simply draw attention to the use of symbols, and then assume their emotional efficacy. A more sophisticated understanding of both how symbols do (and do not) work, and how human beings are emotionally constituted, needs to be developed and then brought to bear on nationalism.

3

Debates about the historical depth of nations are somewhat artificial, in that they hinge as much on how one defines nations and ethnic groups (*ethnies*), and what questions one is asking about them, as on matters of substantive historical fact. Regarding any particular case, looking for historical depth and continuity in terms of symbolic forms may yield a very different interpretation from tracing continuities in the organization of power.

4

Modernity tends to be misconceived as a relatively 'steady state', as a stage of historical development, creating a deceptively static notion of a context in which nationalism reaches full development. In the last 500 years or so there has been an intensification and acceleration of technological, demographical and political economic processes, changes that are continuing apace. Nationalism appears to be a rather malleable artefact of this unstable environment. We lack the historical perspective to confidently define 'modernity' as a stage of social evolution, as opposed to a transition period between stages.

5

A concomitant of the previous point is that the idea of 'uneven development', broadly defined as social inequalities between populations generated by economic and political interactions, remains relevant for the study of nationalism. Uneven development does not always cause nationalism, but it is frequently implicated in nationalism.

6

Modernity, whatever it is, can be usefully understood through the lens of urbanization. Our attention to the territorial state tends to obscure the ways that cities in particular, and the dynamics of competition between urban centres, are the crucible in which national identities and movements are forged. Nationalism is ultimately an urban phenomenon that often dresses in the garb of the countryside.

7

Liberal democratic regimes, far from transcending nationalism, routinize it, incorporating it into the very structures of politics. Competition to advance combined claims about what unites a national population and how they should be governed, keeps nationalism on a 'slow boil' in liberal democracies, even where there are no strong conflicts over territorial jurisdiction. Appreciating this point helps us to recognize the ongoing importance of nationalism in countries such as the United States.

8

Nationalism is a particular variant on the general human propensity to pursue power through forms of social organization. To understand nationalism, we need to pay close attention to the organizational means and opportunities, the dynamics of power-making, that recur across various instances. Key processes include: (a) the way more centralized, authoritative and formal organizations capitalize on more diffuse and extensive modes of social organization such as language and popular faith; (b) the way core organizations of nationalist mobilization are embedded within larger organizations (including the state itself) and articulate across fields of organizations; (c) the way modern states are composed out of social organizations that are both historically 'found' and 'created' by the state; and (d) the way political and social leadership arises out of 'interstitial positions' in the social hierarchy, especially when the relatively 'elite' strata of a social group embedded within a larger society finds itself either threatened in its position, or blocked from advancement within that larger society.

9

Nationalism studies, like social science in general, is vexed by blurry conceptual distinctions between ideology and culture. I advocate the following distinction: *ideology* is the more or less deliberate use of ideas in the making and unmaking of social power (*ideation* covers social cognition in its entirety); *culture* is the way all kinds of social phenomena (ideational, emotional, institutional) appear to 'hang together' due to the influence of organizational centres of power. Thus, the ways I conceptualize culture, power and social organization are highly interdependent.

10

This perspective suggests that attempts to define culture, nations and nationalism primarily in terms of systems of symbols and meaning are inadequate. Such symbolic processes are better viewed as examples of ideology that blend into broader fields of ideation, and that also need to be understood in relation to the relevant centres of socially organized power. As I have said: 'power, in binding, creates culture'.

Multiculturalism, Pluralism, Accommodation and Conflict

The questions of how much ethnic heterogeneity a nation-state can tolerate, and how best to accommodate such diversity, are long-standing ones (Glazer and Moynihan 1963; Aron 1974; Lijphart 1977; Hall, J. A. 1996; Smooha 2002a). In the last couple of decades the term 'multiculturalism' has increasingly been used to label both: a) societies with considerable ethnic diversity; and b) a social philosophy that advocates the defence and celebration of such diversity. However, it should also be noted that this term is most commonly applied to liberal democracies whose ethnic diversity is a combined result of European colonization and settlement, successive waves of labour immigration, in some cases histories of slavery, and the social embedding of indigenous peoples, prime examples being Canada, Australia and the US. The colonial and post-colonial societies of Africa, the Middle East and South-East Asia have more often been referred to as 'plural societies', sometimes implying weaker levels of overarching political, economic and cultural integration. Thus both terms tend to identify ideal types within a wide variety of situations around the globe. In other words, it is less clear how countries such as Switzerland or Brazil fit within this rubric (on the multicultural/plural distinction, see Rex 1997 and Kuper 1997). Moreover, even within these headings one must pay attention to variations. As John Rex (1995) points out, multicultural situations confronted by the social democratic welfare states of Western Europe, Canada and the US have very different origins: the first having more to do with immigration from former colonies, the second being heavily shaped by Québécois claims to autonomy and the third being formed by the legacy of slavery and the black civil rights movement.

Rex (1997) has tried to square the circle of ethnic diversity and national community by focusing on the distinction between public and private domains. He suggests that a healthy multicultural society requires a common public culture, underpinned by legal, political, economic and educational institutions, in which the notion of equality of individuals prevails, but that there should also be space for a private domain of family, kinship, religion and some aspects of education, in which more circumscribed ethnic identities, values and bonds are appropriate and deserve protection. Thus, he hopes that the public/private distinction can reduce conflicts between minority 'ethnic' cultures and majority 'civic' cultures by assigning each to its own domain. Some accommodation of ethnic differences like this is probably the common-sense view of many people living in multicultural societies. However, a society's 'public culture' usually privileges what is also the private culture (language, religion, etc.) of the dominant ethnic group. Moreover, the line between the public and the private is often not as clear as we might like it to be. When should a minority's beliefs and practices allow them to opt out of public laws and obligations (e.g. military service)? When should the state grant special rights and privileges to minority groups (e.g. to education in their mother tongue, to occupy traditional lands)?

Thus, much of the discussion about multiculturalism has been framed within discussion of 'the rights of minority cultures' (Kymlicka 1995). Will Kymlicka (2001) has long argued that national and ethnic cultures are an important part of human flourishing, and that recognizing group-specific rights for ethno-cultural minorities has a proper place within liberal political regimes (cf. Van Dyke 1977; Walzer 1980; Margalit and Raz 1990). He observes that defenders of multiculturalism tend to oper-ate with one of two models (cf. van den Berghe 2002). The first, much like Rex's division of domains, argues that the state and its laws should be neutral and not discriminate between individuals and groups, respect-ing culture, but treating it as a private matter. The second, closer to his own position, recognizes that granting collective rights specific to partic-ular cultural groups may be justified and even necessary if their way of life is to be respected and protected. This does pose the problem, however, of how to define membership in the entitled group (by descent and marriage?), and who defines it – the group or the state? And ethnic groups are evolving social entities, legal codification of aspects of their existence can direct their development as well as protect group interests. Similarly, Kymlicka also notes that minority collective rights can be construed as serving two distinct purposes. On the one hand, they can protect minority groups against the domination of other larger and/or more empowered ethnic groups. On the other hand, they can sanction the right of the minority group to regulate the behaviour of its members with-out outside interference (1995: 9–14). There are very complex issues here of balancing group rights against individual rights, while also recogniz-ing that individuality, with its inherent value, for many people necessar-ily takes shape within naturally occurring collectivities that they are born into.

Given such puzzles, and there are many others we haven't touched on here, the question arises: does multiculturalism pose a fundamental threat to the idea of the nation-state – is it the unhinging of the nation? I am inclined to say no, at least not necessarily. In fact, the growth of multi-cultural discourses and their institutionalization in law, in states such as the US, Canada and Australia, might better be construed as a new phase of nation-building, in which notions of the overarching national identity are reconfigured and rearticulated in order to keep pace with social change and shifting distributions of social power. Multiculturalism is not just a set of dilemmas, it is also a collective identity discourse in its own right.

Several of the authors we have discussed in this book have been concerned with the problem of regulating ethnic and nationalist conflict, especially when prone to tip over into violence (e.g. Hechter 2000, Horowitz 1985; Mann 2001; Snyder 2000). Such discussions tend to work more with the concepts of 'plural' or 'deeply divided' societies (Smooha and Hanf 1992) rather than 'multiculturalism', and to define problematic contexts as 'multinational' rather than simply 'multi-ethnic', to underscore the depth of social cleavages. The exact 'problem' being addressed in this literature varies, creating some ambiguity. Sometimes it is the actual outbreak of inter-ethnic violence, sometimes a more general condition of political instability and sometimes it is the domination of one ethnic/national group over others. But the last of these problems can sometimes help prevent the first (Lustick 1979), and political instability may not be a 'problem' for those seeking political change.

John McGarry and Brendan O'Leary have noted some general conditions that tend to ameliorate these problems:

- internal territorial segregation which permits self-government ('good fences make good neighbours');
- demographic dominance (where a large group is sufficiently secure not to fear the minority (or minorities) and behaves in a generous way);
- demographic stability (where one or more groups are not outgrowing or 'outfalling' one another); and
- a history of pre-democratic co-operation amongst ethnic political elites which gives the post-authoritarian state a reasonable chance of promoting accommodation. (1993: 16)

To this one might add that where powerful forces of assimilation are at work the need to regulate ethnic relations diminishes, but this literature is largely concerned with situations where this 'natural' remedy has not happened and is not likely. These discussions have two closely related concerns: a) to identify political-institutional features that appear to contribute to political stability in deeply divided societies; and b) to recommend the application of such principles to cases of instability and conflict. Arend Lijphart's early and influential argument identifying models of successful 'consociationalism' (1977) and 'power sharing' (1991) in pluralistic countries such as the Netherlands, Belgium, Austria, Switzerland and Malaysia, recommends a political system in which ethnic/national groups: share in the executive power of the state; have substantial governmental autonomy; have veto power over important issues (especially for minorities); and observe proportionality in the allocation of parliamentary representation and other social goods. This is viewed as assuring a balance of power between ethnic groups, entrenching the rights of minority groups. However, others argue that by 'building in' an ethnic dynamic to politics, such arrangements may ultimately be prone to abuse by ethnic elites and reinforce factionalism in worsening conditions. Lijphart once held up Lebanon as a model of consociationalism, but had to amend his position after the outbreak of bloody civil war there in the 1970s (Hechter 2000: 136–7; Snyder 2000: 328–31).

Ian Lustick (1979) argues that consociational explanations of political stability have been overemphasized, and need to be balanced by a realistic appreciation of the role of hegemonic control by a dominant ethnic group in creating stability. Like it or not, domination rather than cooperation may be the most common explanation for political stability in plural societies, and he goes so far as to suggest that such domination may be preferable to outright anarchy and violence. McGarry and O'Leary (1993) have expressed reservations about this last claim, suggesting that if taken too far it can justify all manner of political repression in the interests of 'stability'. Their concern is to argue alternatively that in some cases partition and/or secession provide justifiable solutions to ethnic conflict, and that these strategies do not conflict in principle with liberal democracy. While accepting that reality never offers neat one-to-one correspondences between ethnic groups and territories, that demarcating 'a people' is always difficult and that secession/partition is likely to be attended by conflict and violence, they nonetheless maintain that the democratic principle of self-determination, given new impetus with the end of the Cold War and collapse of the USSR, requires that this option remains on the table, regardless of the difficulties. For them, achieving sovereignty may be the only way some peoples have of safeguarding their interests and well being. Particularly relevant here are the problems of minority groups embedded within what Sammy Smooha has called 'ethnic democracies': political regimes that combine the basic principles and institutions of democracy with the ascendancy of one core majority nation that dominates society through the political regime. For Smooha, Israel is a key example of this problematic and 'deficient' type of democracy (2002a, 2002b).

Donald Horowitz (1991) has offered another alternative to Lijphart's consociationalism, which rather than entrenching the political interests of ethnic groups seeks to use political institutions to create alliances across ethnic boundaries, to moderate ethnic conflict. Thus, he advocates de-aligning the distributions of ethnic populations and territorial sub-units in federal systems, and the use of voting systems that require majorities larger than the largest ethnic group, thus obliging politicians to court support beyond their own ethnicity. However, there is a paucity of empirical cases with which to test these recommendations. Jack Snyder argues that Horowitz is 'on the right track', but that his largely institutional mechanisms need to be complemented by breaking down media barriers to public discourse across ethnic boundaries and the de-ethnicization of key government agencies of courts, police and armed forces (2000: 332). For him the long-term though difficult goal is the cultivation of a civic democracy that can erode democracy's ethnic forms.

In keeping with his general historical argument that nationalism first arose when the indirect rule of old empires was increasingly being replaced by the direct rule of centralizing dynastic states, Michael Hechter (2000: 139–59) argues that the main solution to nationalist conflict lies in the creation of federal systems that afford a balance of centralization and decentralization, and a degree of autonomy within territories for national groups. Snyder is more sceptical about 'ethnofederal' systems, such as Yugoslavia, arguing that they heighten and politicize ethnicity (2000: 327–8). Hechter recognizes the potential fragility of federal solutions, and that their empirical track record is mixed, but maintains that with the proper observance of procedural justice by the central state over and above ethnic interests, and the institutionalizing of protections for minority cultures, federalism can potentially provide the best balance between centripetal and centrifugal ethno-political forces. What all this suggests is that within the very general categories of ethnic conflict and political instability actual cases are very particular and may call for particular solutions that are not easily captured in a single set of general prescriptions.

As I think the preceding demonstrates, this entire area of discussions tends to slide back and forth between descriptive and normative arguments, which is a problem, though perhaps unavoidable given the subject matter. My purpose in this book has been to concentrate on how we describe, conceptualize and understand nationalism, leaving the moral and practical problems largely to one aside. This is not because I deny their importance or urgency, but because I believe that to engage in normative and prescriptive arguments well one must spend some of the time developing a more descriptive and analytical understanding of the subject in question separately, in its own right. Doing this helps reduce the degree to which our grasp of reality is distorted by our normative assumptions. It is also the case that this literature straddles the division between 'ethnic politics' (the pursuit of ethnic group interests that does not challenge the basic political framework) and 'nationalism' (combined claims to identity, jurisdiction and territory) as defined in the

Introduction (Chapter 1), and thus falls partially outside the purview of this book. The literature above usefully draws our attention to the blurriness of this conceptual boundary.

Normative Critiques and Defences

Debates about how to manage multiculturalism and ethnic conflict shade into a more purely normative political theory literature, which addresses whether nationalism as a whole is, in principle, defensible. What I have just said about how the literatures surveyed above relate to the purposes of this book obviously applies here as well. And again, I can only adumbrate the range of positions taken. Nonetheless, let me try to give a general sense of what is at stake in these more philosophical discussions. They could be roughly distributed under the headings of 'those opposed', 'those in favour' and 'those abstaining'.

Michael Ignatieff (1999a) has provided one of the more strident voices for the opposed. For him nationalism is not just a collective identity – not a controversial position in itself – but a kind of collective identity that necessarily must overvalue itself by opposing and devaluing other such identities. Nationalism is a form of narcissism, which can only see in other national groups negative and inverted versions of itself, to be demonized. While he sometimes writes positively about 'civic nationalism' (1999b), it is clear that this is primarily a euphemism for liberalism, and that true nationalism is for him 'ethnic nationalism' (Beiner 1999b: 24, footnote 56). The only cure in his view is a thoroughgoing liberal individualism:

> The essential task in teaching 'toleration' is to help people see themselves as individuals, and then to see others as such – that is, to make problematic that unthought, unconsidered fusion of personal and group identity on which racism depends. For racism and intolerance are, at a conceptual level, procedures of abstraction in which actual, real individuals in all their specificity are depersonalized and turned into ciphers or carriers of hated group characteristics. (1999a: 101)

Ignatieff's easy slide from 'nationalism' to 'racism' in this passage signals the associations nationalism has for him. Maurizio Viroli (1995) similarly casts nationalism as a dark force, but for him the remedy is not liberal individualism, but republican patriotism:

The language of patriotism has been used over the centuries to strengthen or invoke love of the political institutions and the way of life that sustain the common liberty of a people, that is love of the republic; the language of nationalism was forged in late eighteenth-century Europe to defend or reinforce the cultural, linguistic, and ethnic oneness and homogeneity of a people. Whereas the enemies of republican patriotism are tyranny, despotism, oppression, and corruption, the enemies of nationalism are cultural contamination, heterogeneity, racial impurity, and social, political, and intellectual disunion. (1995: 1–2)

Thus, while many almost equate patriotism and nationalism, Viroli makes a strong distinction, seeing a tradition of patriotic republican thought, traced back to classical Rome through such figures as Rousseau and Machiavelli to Livy, as the best antidote to a malign nationalism. He champions the value of strong commitments to a social and political collectivity, it is how that collectivity is conceived that is the problem. Arguing from a more cosmopolitan perspective, Judith Lichtenberg (1997) acknowledges the need for intermediate forms of association between the individual/family and the state, and that cultures and nations will sometimes provide these, satisfying important human needs for community and support. But she also raises doubts about the partiality, towards fellow nationals and a shared way of life, which national membership seems to entail. Even if this is couched not as a denigration of other national groups (*pace* Ignatieff), but simply a positive preference for one's own national group that nonetheless respects others, there may be clashes of incompatible values and interests that cannot be resolved within a common political framework. She expresses the hope that in working through such clashes cultures and nations can change, and overarching public cultures can accommodate and synthesize their component nations, gradually forging a more universal (and in some sense less national) framework of interests and values.

Bhikhu Parekh accepts that the defenders of nationalism, which we will discuss next, are ultimately trying to find 'how best to ensure the unity and stability of the modern state' (1999: 320), but he again objects that nationalism is in its nature homogenizing and reifying, and thus a dangerous foundation for this purpose. He argues that the underpinnings of the modern state do not require such allegiances and are, in fact, more abstract, structural and procedural. To the degree that it achieves legitimacy, it does so by observing the impartial rule of law among citizens, by pursuing the common good of all citizens and by satisfying socially diverse needs and demands – that is, by accommodating rather than over-coming heterogeneity. While these ideals may be realized imperfectly, or the success of their realization contested among citizens, nonetheless it is they, not some shared vision of the nation, that can and should ultimately garner support for the modern state.

Of 'those in favour' Roger Scruton (1999) mounts a defence from the position of classic British political conservatism. There is a strong sense in Scruton's writings that the sheer weight of cultural inheritance – language, religion, history – cannot be disregarded, and sets very real limits to human sociability. But beyond this there is a more philosophical argument about the nature of identity and personhood in modern states. While the characteristic bases for collective identity have changed over history, from kinship, to religious creeds, to territorial jurisdiction, the basic need for political community to be based on some exclusive conception of a 'we' opposed to a 'they' is universal and constant. Echoing a point made by Durkheim (1964 [1933]: 212–16), the crux of the matter for Scruton is that the 'social contract' that binds the citizens of modern states, if it is to be stable, must ultimately rest on something more fundamental and enduring:

> The nation is not . . . conceived as an accidental and defeasible contract between strangers; it is a hereditary entitlement, a burden of duty, a call to sacrifice. Unlike a contract, the bond of membership is disinterested: I am *given* to it, and it to me, by the very fact of my exis-tence. My debt to the nation is a debt of gratitude and piety . . . however transient this or that form of nationhood might be, the need to which it ministers is a human universal. Benedict Anderson puts the point well: 'If historians, diplomats, politicians and social scientists are quite at ease with the idea of "national interest", for most ordinary people of whatever class the whole point of the nation is that it is inter-estless. Just for that reason it can ask for sacrifices.' (Scruton 1999: 289)

Other defenders have tried to make the case for nationalism on liberal rather than conservative foundations. David Miller (1995) argues that while embracing the principle of nationality will affect one's liberalism and may come into conflict with some versions of liberalism (e.g. those that strongly prioritize individual autonomy), there are conceptions of liberalism and nationalism that are compatible. Much of his argument rests on a distinction between 'ethical universalism' and 'ethical particu-larism'. The former assumes that we have obligations to our fellow human beings simply by merit of our shared humanity, the latter maintains that our obligations arise out of the particular nature of our relations, we are always already encumbered by concrete social ties that must be taken into account in our ethical reasoning. For Miller there is truth in both positions, but taking ethical particularism seriously is what leads him to argue that nationality is a legitimate form of identity, that comes with certain moral bonds and implications. Thus for him it is reasonable to maintain that we owe special obligations to our fellow nationals that we do not owe to non-members of our nation. While the ethical particularism of the nation risks forms of chauvinism that may need to be checked by forms of ethical universalism, it also can provide the basis for stronger arguments towards fairness and equitable distributions of social goods among co-nationals.

Charles Taylor (1999) builds on the modernist arguments of Gellner, Anderson and Greenfeld to argue that nationalism is for some an unavoidable path for attaining a modern identity that enjoys recognition and respect. In outline, he argues that modernity requires us not just to be modular and adaptable to the modern economy in Gellner's terms, but to realize our self-worth and dignity as equal citizens able to participate fully in the public deliberations of democracy. To the extent that certain ethnic/national identities are systematically marginalized in the public discourse about the polity they are a part of, they will be excluded from one of the basic moral entitlements of modernity, which is to have one's nationality invested in one's citizenship. He observes that this frustration sometimes takes the form of defensive and illiberal ethnic nationalisms, as in disintegrating Yugoslavia, that are indeed retrogressive. But he maintains that when nationalists pursue 'a liberal regime of rights and equal citizenship' (1999: 242), as in Quebec, this should be understood as part of a legitimate struggle to achieve a fully modern identity with adequate dignity.

The case for 'liberal nationalism' has also been strongly put by Yael Tamir (1993). Her argument, however, is for the transcendence of the traditional nation-state idea, which in a way returns us to the discussion of multiculturalism. Much like the ethno-symbolists, she sees nations as cultural communities bound together by values, myths and symbols, and she sees intrinsic value in their ability to confer meaning and identity on their members. She recognizes the impossibility of a world where each nation has its own state, and that no state, no matter how liberal, can be entirely value neutral. Thus she proposes a judicious balance between recognition and a degree of self-determination for cultural groups, and an overarching liberal political framework:

We can now summarize the characteristics of a liberal national entity. This entity will endorse liberal principles of distribution inwards and outwards; its political system will reflect a particular national culture, but its citizens will be free to practice different cultures and follow a variety of life-plans and conceptions of the good. The political entity described here differs from the traditional liberal entity in that it introduces culture as a crucial dimension of political life. Its unity rests not only on an overlapping consensus about certain values essential to its functioning, but also on a distinct cultural foundation. Membership in this entity will be more accessible to certain individuals, capable of identifying the political entity as their own, than to others. Consequently, even if governing institutions respect a wide range of rights and liberties and distribute goods and positions fairly, members of minority groups will unavoidably feel alienated to some extent. Alienation rather than a deprivation of rights is to be acknowledged as the main problem affecting members of national minorities. (1993: 163)

Thus, Tamir recognizes irresolvable tensions between culture and politics, but argues that a type of liberal state that more loosely binds together its embedded cultures is what we should aspire to.

I am myself something of an abstainer (although I agree with Miller that our ethical lives have an unavoidable particularist dimension that must be taken into account, if not always in national terms). This ambivalent position is perhaps best articulated by Margaret Canovan (1996). Her most basic argument is that twentieth-century political theory has largely disregarded the question of nationalism, preferring to explore such ideas as democracy, justice, rights, freedom, equality and so on, while at the same time implicitly relying on some notion of national community to supply the requisite social power and consensus needed to motivate the pursuit of these more explicit ideals. For Canovan, any attempt to build a normative political theory on the principle of nationhood will founder on the fact that, as social constructions arising in the real world, the ideological content of nationality cannot be philosophically prescribed, and will always be susceptible to taking dark and pathological forms. On the other hand, more cosmopolitan theories espousing universal political norms have little hope of existing beyond the realm of theory, lacking the practical political foundation of concrete human interests and commitments in the real world. When it comes to political theory we are caught between the devil of particularism and the deep blue sea of universalism (see also Canovan 2001). In the end Canovan concludes that we are stuck with 'muddling through', trying to find an 'earthly home' for our 'humane ideals of universal rights, justice and democracy' in the messy world of nations and states (1996: 139–40).

My acceptance of the need to 'muddle through' does not, however, imply that there is no point in making strong normative arguments for and against nationalism. While I believe we are stuck for the time being with having to find a middle path that neither transcends nor uncritically commits to nationalism, instead moderating, compromising and dealing with troubled situations on a case by case basis, nonetheless our ability to muddle though as wisely as possible depends on having a clear sense of the normative conceptual landscape, illuminated by arguments articulated at the extremes (which is not to say extremist arguments). These arguments are not so much positions one must either subscribe to or reject, as tools for refining critical judgement in actual circumstances.

Postmodern Approaches

Finally, I have not drawn much on what might be called postmodern approaches to the subject. As Rachel Walker has observed, the term has an overabundance of referents, which makes it difficult to define (2001: 611–16). She identifies three interpenetrating strains. First, 'historical' or 'epistemic' postmodernism, claims that we are living through the demise of the modern era and the formation of a new, postmodern era. The second, 'methodological' postmodernism, which draws particularly on the analytic techniques of linguistics and literary studies and has been influenced by such figures as Ferdinand de Saussure, Roland Barthes and Jacques Derrida, aims primarily at 'deconstructing' its objects of study by treating them as texts that can be shown to be inherently contingent, incomplete and indeterminate in regard to meaning. The third strain of postmodernism, which she identifies as 'positive', draws more on the work of Michel Foucault, using some of the deconstructive techniques of methodological postmodernism to generate critiques of modernist phenomena while also posing emancipatory responses to the power relations that characterize modernity.

We cannot explore these strains in any detail here. Instead, I will simply identify some key themes in work where postmodern approaches have been brought to bear on questions of nations and nationalism, and then consider a few representative examples of such work, which variously draw on the strains Walker identifies. In brief:

- Postmodernism often argues that nations and nationalism, especially in the guise of the mythicalized nation-state, both epitomized modernity and are currently coming to an end, no longer tenable in a globalizing world.
- Postmodernism often maintains that nations and nationalism are primarily narrative and discursive formations (patterned ways of thinking and talking about, and acting in, the world), and are best understood as such, whatever their correspondence with a more 'material' reality.
- Postmodernism has paid special attention to processes of social identity formation, stressing that identities are always formed in a dialectic with other identities, such that identities are mutually constituting and internally incomplete and unstable.

Stuart Hall's influential writings hover on the margins of postmodernism. He has argued that modernity was characterized by a series of identities, 'the great stable collectivities of class, race, gender and nation – [that] have been, in our times, deeply undermined by social and political developments' (1996: 342). He sees the nation, for instance, as increasingly stretched by forces (political, economic, ecological) pulling power up from above and down from below. Although he rejects extreme postmodernist theses about the absolute impossibility and indeterminacy of identity, he accepts that the terms of identification are undergoing a significant historical change, and advocates a new, more reflexive relationship to ethnic identity that situates itself consciously in changing relations to other identities (cf. Bauman 1992).

Craig Calhoun (1993, 1997) places a strong emphasis on the discursive nature of nationalism. Like Hall, he sees modernity as characterized by the rise of large-scale categorical identities, ethnicity and nationalism being paradigmatic cases. These identities make essentializing claims on those they are ascribed to, claims which are evoked in the rhetoric of nationalism:

> Any time a political leader uses the rhetoric of nationalism – rather, for example, than that of communist internationalism – this has significance. When a peasant rebellion claims to represent a repressed nation, this is significantly different from relying on the language of class alone – or of religion. When a novelist (or painter or composer) presents his or her work as embodying the spirit of the nation, this is different from presenting it as the work of a rootless genius or cosmopolitan citizen of the world. It is impossible to define the

commonalities of these diverse forms of nationalism by a single explanatory variable – such as state building, industrialisation, unequal economic development, or *ressentiment*. What is general is the *discourse* of nationalism. It does not completely explain any specific such activity or event, but it helps to constitute each through cultural framing. (1997: 22, emphasis in original)

Thus, Calhoun seeks to tackle the problem of the diversity of nationalism's concrete referents that we raised in the Introduction (Chapter 1) by defining it in terms of its discursive form, regardless of the causal conditions that are variously associated with it (cf. Özkirimli 2005).

The postmodernist approach is perhaps epitomized by the writings of Homi K. Bhabha, (1990) who as a professor of English and Art is particularly committed to a linguistically informed mode of analysis. Bhabha's writing can be allusive and oblique, drawing together influences from Freud, Foucault and Derrida. He offers a particularly emphatic version of our third theme above, which plays upon various semantic tensions the modern nation encounters: between its historical newness and its need to narratively represent itself as ancient; in its need to define itself both with and against threatening 'others' (cf. Kristeva 1993); and in its need to represent itself as homogeneous while being constituted through cultural differences. Fariba Salehi has tried to sum up Bhabha's argument:

The most powerful modern institution that homogenizes and standardizes identity is the nation-state. The nation-state is a gigantic culture industry. A postmodern critique of the nation-state offers a radically different reading of the nation-state, by describing it as an apparatus of power that produces mega-narratives of identity in the name of 'people.' A postmodern theory of the nation-state deconstructs the nationalistic account of the nation-state, and anchors the question of 'national' identity in the locus of the 'other,' and in so doing erases its totalizing boundaries, challenges the political and ideological manoeuvres that assume an essentialist core in the imagined communities, and argues for the hybridity and ambivalence of national identity. (2001: 252)

For Bhabha nationalism and the nation-state are totalizing illusions that can only be seen through by adopting the perspective of those whose identities have been subordinated and marginalized, and rendered problematic by these processes. The inherent indeterminacy of identity is marshalled as counter-tactic to undermine the essentializing force of nationalism. Here again, in the form of critique, there is a strong normative impulse shaping the theory.

Let me draw to a close by returning to the three themes bulleted above. First, it should be clear that the doubts I have expressed about how modernity is conceptualized as a distinct and bounded historical stage have knock-on implications for the 'epistemic' notion of postmodernism. I would regard the immense changes we are living through as a continuation of the rapid and accelerating change that has characterized 'modernity'. Moreover, I would argue that the problems of the grounding of morality and meaning, and tensions between essentialism and relativism, have broadly characterized the entire period in question and, thus, that there is nothing really epistemically novel about recent decades. Second, one might argue that all the works discussed in Chapter 8 under the headings of 'culture' and 'ideology' are in some sense concerned with nationalism as 'discourse', but few if any encountered there would be called postmodernists. This suggests that what distinguishes a postmodernist approach is not just paying attention to discourse, but a stronger thesis about the fundamentally discursive nature of social reality. I have argued against conceptualizing culture in narrowly ideational terms, and in favour of treating it as an effect of the social organization of power. I would make a similar argument regarding the concept of discourse. Discourse is one of the key forms that the social organization of power takes, but it does not comprehend the latter, which needs to be conceptualized in its own right. Third, it seems to me that the model of modernist identity frequently critiqued by postmodernism is chronically overdrawn, and something of a 'straw man'. Processes of identity formation are too subtle to be usefully summed up in an image of a false, essentializing self that is only the negation of its 'others'. Identities and selves have substantive content that develops through relations with others but does not ultimately evaporate into those relations. Moreover, the characteristics of fixity and organization found in identities, nationalist and otherwise, which some postmodernists are inclined to cast as essentializing and totalizing pathologies of Enlightenment and modernity, are, in fact, perennial and necessary aspects of power. The centring of power and identity, their intrinsic organization, is not something that can be theorized away (cf. Brubaker and Cooper 2000).

Postmodernists tend to adopt an attitude of radical scepticism (cf. Douglas 1986) towards nationalism, viewing it as a system of representations with an illusory nature that must be exposed, and then transcended (see Özkirimli 2005). Such a view, by transposing the phenomenon into the plane representations and discourse, can weaken our grasp of nationalism's moorings in social reality, making the task of critiquing it appear easier than it may actually be. I try to regard nationalism with a healthy scepticism, but I see it not as a fragmentary illusion to be transcended, but as a stubborn reality that will, in time, be transformed. To engage with it, as I have tried to do in this book, I think we need to understand and grapple with how the more transitory discourses of nationalism are implicated in enduring human concerns with power that are not so easily transcended. Thus I have treated nationalism as an ascendant type in a long and evolving line of forms of social organization, of concatenations of power and culture. For me this more realist, as opposed to postmodernist, conception of nationalism is a necessary part of taking the subject seriously and recognizing the challenges it poses.

Thinking Ahead

The debates explored above arise because we are thrown into a world of nationalism and must contemplate that situation and its possible futures. Let us conclude with some brief speculations. Modernity has been and continues to be characterized by rapid change. To say that things have changed radically over the latter half of the twentieth century up to the present, in the manner of 'globalization' discourses, is in one sense to say 'more of the same'. Nonetheless, we can briefly summarize some of the main trends that have characterized this period, and bear on the present and the possible developments for nationalism: (1) There has been broadening and deepening of economic interactions across the globe, albeit in highly uneven ways. (2) A new network of non-state power actors with their own distinctive interests, featuring multinational corporations, international banks and international organizations regulating economic and political activities, has developed. (3) Regional political economic blocs of strong interdependencies and shared interests have evolved, centred in North America, Western Europe and Japan/East Asia. (4) The historically less economically developed countries of China and India are seeing accelerated economic growth, still well behind the leading countries but with considerable potential because of their large territories and populations. (5) Despite some post-war economic growth, the less developed countries of the 'south', particularly in Africa and Latin America, have remained relatively powerless in the global political economy. (6) With the collapse of the Soviet Union in 1989, Russia, while still a major regional power, has been weakened as a global power (see Cohn 2005).

In this context, the more powerful modern states have been not so much undermined as increasingly obliged to negotiate power with other states, and with sub-state and non-state centres of power. The decisive economic hegemony of the United States after the Second World War has been relatively reduced, and relations between states are perhaps more hemmed in by growing economic interdependencies. Some weak states have all but collapsed, but weaker states in general have simply continued to struggle with their limited powers and relations of dependency with more powerful states. These trends are more likely to exacerbate than eliminate nationalism as I have defined it – as combined claims to identity, territory and jurisdiction. For the vast majority of people on the planet, their limited social power is grounded in social organizations that in turn are largely housed in territorial states. The shape of the territories in question may change, but de-territorialized social power is a luxury of the few.

There are some things we should watch, however, if we are interested in the future trends of nationalism. If I am correct in regarding cities as the peculiar seedbeds of nationalism, then we should be particularly interested in how urban developments are stimulating nationalism. For instance, it could be argued that the growth of major Chinese cities in southern Export Processing Zones, with the development of a new middle class, is helping to form a new, more typically 'modern' national consciousness in China. In addition to the 'combined claims', I have argued that the modern mode of political legitimation, emphasizing popular sovereignty, is a defining feature of nationalism in the full sense. The true 'end of the nation-state' would entail the decline of this principle of legitimation, and possible replacement by another, in the leading liberal democratic states. There have been debates since the 1970s about a 'crisis of legitimation', but such crises do not seem to have seriously destabilized the leading liberal democratic states (Beetham 1991: 170). I have also argued that the development of mass communication seems to be a key practical condition for nationalism in the modern sense. This directs our attention to changes in modes of communication, such as the die-off rate of minority languages and spread of dominant *lingua franca* such as English, and the possibility for aural and visual electronic communications to reduce the importance of literacy *per se* in the dissemination of ideas. But, as I have argued, language is a diffuse and extensive form of social organization that, while enabling nationalism and its ideologies, does not cause them in and of itself. That requires more focused and authoritative forms of social organization.

Just as modern nation-states evolved out of monarchic polities in Europe, the question of their future is one of how they might be transformed into significantly different power organizations. Can we imagine a world where alternative foci for the social organization of power render states and nations a thing of the past, or at least highly marginalized? Perhaps a global economy, either dystopic or utopian, depending on your point of view, in which multinational corporations are the ultimate centres of power, commanding a certain allegiance from their 'employees' due to their *de facto* power. But the essence of the modern corporate-employee relationship is a weak contract, the ideology of capitalism celebrating the looseness and flexibility of these relations based on personal interest – not deep mutual commitments. Moreover, it is hard to imagine such corporations not needing to rely on the territorial jurisdictions, and sometimes the military strength, of states.

Perhaps some of the present power blocs will continue to grow together, such that entities like the European Union will develop political, ideological and military powers to match its growing economic strength. This is not absolutely impossible, but the existing historically entrenched diversity of Europe suggests that if it does happen, it will take a long time, and probably require considerable stimulation by competition with external centres of power. But if it did, creating a very large 'super-state' with a sufficient degree of communicative integration, a clearer collective European identity and enjoying popular political legitimacy, then I would argue that a kind of macro-nationalism had evolved, clearly quite different in size and scale to its predecessors, but not fundamentally different in type. Moreover, this would not require that the existing nationalities of Europe be obliterated, but simply that they become embedded within and ultimately subordinated to the larger 'macro-nation'.

Finally, perhaps the present patchwork of international agreements and agencies, led by dominant states, and confronted by challenges that could only be addressed by humanity in concert, will eventually coalesce into a true world government, effectively overarching all other allegiances. If it met all the requirements, this would be the same as the case of the European Union, a macro-nation except at the ultimate level. If this were to happen, I would have to take my stand with Liah Greenfeld, who asserts that 'a nation coextensive with humanity is in no way a contradiction in terms' (1992: 7). But 'possible in principle' is very different from 'likely'. As we have seen, organizational complexity entails an integration of sub-organizations, embedded foci of power, which can become the basis of dissent. Even if such macro and even global nationalisms arose, they would be perennially susceptible to this process of fission.

These are just speculations to stimulate our thinking – for now we have plenty of real imagined communities to contend with. The point of view that informs this book regards nationalism as morally ambiguous and historically enduring. I have sought not to praise it, or condemn it, or read it the last rites, but to scrutinize the concepts through which we make sense of nationalism, because we must begin by grasping as best we can the situation we are in.

Further Reading

For overviews of multiculturalism debates see the collections/extracts in: Kymlicka (1995) and Guibernau and Rex (1997). For pluralism and the regulation of national/ethnic conflict see Smooha and Hanf (1992) and O'Leary *et al.* (2001). On normative debates see Beiner (1999a) and McKim and McMahan (1997), both very good edited collections, and Canovan (1996). For introductions to postmodern approaches see Salehi (2001) and especially Walker (2001). Özkirimli (2005) makes a robust case for the normative critique of nationalism and for understanding it in discursive terms.

References

Abu-Lughod, L. (1991) 'Writing Against Culture', in R. Fox (ed.), *Recapturing Anthropology: Working in the Present* (Santa Fe, NM: School of American Research Press).

Anderson, B. (1991) *Imagined Communities: Reflections on the Origin and Spread of Nationalism*, 2nd edn (London: Verso).

Anderson, B. (1998) *The Spectre of Comparisons: Nationalism, Southeast Asia and the World* (London: Verso).

Anthias, F. and N. Yuval-Davis (1989) 'Introduction', in N. Yuval-Davis and F. Anthias (eds), *Women-Nation-State* (Basingstoke and New York: Palgrave Macmillan).

Armstrong, J. (1982) *Nations Before Nationalism* (Chapel Hill, NC: University of North Carolina Press).

Aron, R. (1974) 'Is Multinational Citizenship Possible?', *Social Research*, 41, 4: 638–56.

Asad, T. (1983) 'Anthropological Conceptions of Religions: Reflections on Geertz', *Man*, 18, 2: 237–59.

Asad, T. (1999) 'Religion, Nation-State, Secularism', in P. van der Veer and H. Lehmann (eds), *Nation and Religion: Perspectives on Europe and Asia* (Princeton, NJ: Princeton University Press).

Azaryahu, M. and R. Kook (2002) 'Mapping the Nation: Street Names and Arab-Palestinian Identity: Three Case Studies', *Nations and Nationalism*, 8, 2: 195–214.

Baier, A. (1988) 'Hume's Account of Social Artifice – Its Origins and Originality', *Ethics*, 98: 757–78.

Balakrishnan, G. (ed.) (1996) *Mapping the Nation* (London: Verso).

Barbalet, J. (ed.) (2002a) *Emotions and Sociology* (Oxford: Blackwell).

Barbalet, J. (2002b) 'Introduction: Why Emotions are Crucial', in J. Barbalet (ed.), *Emotions and Sociology* (Oxford: Blackwell).

Barnard, A. (2004) 'Coat of Arms and the Body Politic: Khoisan Imagery and South African National Identity', *Ethnos: Journal of Anthropology*, 69, 1: 1–18.

Barnard, F. M. (ed.) (1969) *J. G. Herder on Social and Political Culture* (Cambridge: Cambridge University Press).

Barth, F. (1969) 'Introduction', in F. Barth (ed.), *Ethnic Groups and Boundaries* (Boston: Little, Brown).

Bauman, Z. (1992) 'Blood, Soil and Identity', *The Sociological Review*, 38: 675–701.

Bax, M. (1991) 'Religious Regimes and State-Formation: Toward a Research Perspective', in E. R. Wolf (ed.), *Religious Regimes and State-Formation: Perspectives from European Ethnology* (Albany, NY: SUNY Press).

Beetham, D. (1991) *The Legitimation of Power* (Basingstoke and New York: Palgrave Macmillan).

Beiner, R. (ed.) (1999a) *Theorizing Nationalism* (Albany, NY: SUNY Press).

Beiner, R. (1999b) 'Introduction', in R. Beiner (ed.), *Theorizing Nationalism* (Albany, NY: SUNY Press).

Bendix, R. (1964) *Nation-Building and Citizenship* (London: John Wiley and Sons).

Bendix, R. (1978) *Kings or People: Power and the Mandate to Rule* (Berkeley, CA: University of California Press).

Benner, E. (2001) 'Is There a Core National Doctrine?', *Nations and Nationalism*, 7, 2: 155–74.

Berezin, M. (2002) 'Secure States: Towards a Political Sociology of Emotion', in J. Barbalet (ed.), *Emotions and Sociology* (Oxford: Blackwell).

Berlant, L. (1996) 'The Theory of Infantile Citizenship', in G. Eley and R. G. Suny (eds), *Becoming National: A Reader* (Oxford: Oxford University Press).

Bessinger, M. R. (2001) 'Violence', in A. J. Motyl (ed.), *Encyclopedia of Nationalism: Fundamental Themes, Vol. 1* (London: Academic Press).

Bhabha, H. K. (ed.) (1990) *The Nation and Narration* (London: Routledge).

Bidney, D. (1944) 'On the Concept of Culture and Some Cultural Fallacies', *American Anthropologist*, 46: 30–44.

Billig, M. (1995) *Banal Nationalism* (London: Sage).

Boas, F. (1940) *Race, Language and Culture* (New York: Free Press).

Bobbio, N. (1989) *Democracy and Dictatorship* (Minneapolis, MN: University of Minnesota Press).

Bottomore, T. (ed.) (1983) *A Dictionary of Marxist Thought* (Cambridge, MA: Harvard University Press).

Bowker, M. (2004) 'Russia and Chechnya: The Issue of Secession', *Nations and Nationalism*, 10, 4: 461–78.

Bracewell, W. (2000) 'Rape in Kosovo: Masculinity and Serbian Nationalism', *Nations and Nationalism*, 6, 4: 563–90.

Brading, D. A. (2001) 'Monuments and Nationalism in Modern Mexico', *Nations and Nationalism*, 7, 4: 521–32.

Brass, P. (1979) 'Elite Groups, Symbol Manipulation and Ethnic Identity among the Muslims of South Asia', in D. Taylor and M. Yapp (eds), *Political Identity in South Asia* (Dublin: Curzon Press).

Brass, P. (1991) *Ethnicity and Nationalism: Theory and Comparison* (London: Sage).

Breuilly, J. (1993) *Nationalism and the State*, 2nd edn (Manchester: Manchester University Press).

Breuilly, J. (1996) 'Approaches to Nationalism', in G. Balakrishnan (ed.), *Mapping the Nation* (London: Verso).

Breuilly, J. (2001) 'The State and Nationalism', in M. Guibernau and J. Hutchinson (eds), *Understanding Nationalism* (Cambridge: Polity Press).

Briggs, C. L. (2002) 'Linguistic Magic Bullets in the Making of a Modernist Anthropology', *American Anthropologist*, 104, 2: 481–98.

Brightman, R. (1995) 'Forget Culture: Replacement, Transcendence, Relexification', *Cultural Anthropology*, 10, 4: 509–46.

Brown, D. (2000) *Contemporary Nationalism: Civic, Ethnocultural and Multicultural Politics* (London: Routledge).

Brubaker, R. (1992) *Citizenship and Nationhood in France and Germany* (Cambridge, MA: Harvard University Press).

Brubaker, R. (1996) *Nationalism Reframed: Nationhood and the National Question in the New Europe* (Cambridge: Cambridge University Press).

Brubaker, R. (1998) 'Myths and Misconceptions in the Study of Nationalism', in J. A. Hall (ed.), *The State of the Nation: Ernest Gellner and the Theory of Nationalism* (Cambridge: Cambridge University Press).

Brubaker, R. and F. Cooper (2000) 'Beyond "Identity" ', *Theory and Society*, 29, 1: 1–47.

Brubaker, R. and D. Laitin (1998) 'Ethnic and Nationalist Violence', *Annual Review of Sociology*, 24: 423–52.

Burkitt, I. (2002) 'Complex Emotions: Relations, Feelings, and Images in Emotional Experience', in J. Barbalet (ed.), *Emotions and Sociology* (Oxford: Blackwell).

Çağaptay, S. (2003) 'Citizenship Policies in Interwar Turkey', *Nations and Nationalism*, 9, 4: 601–20.

Calhoun, C. (1993) 'Nationalism and Ethnicity', *Annual Review of Sociology*, 19: 211–39.

Calhoun, C. (1997) *Nationalism* (Minneapolis, MN: University of Minnesota Press).

Canefe, N. (2002) 'Turkish Nationalism and Ethno-symbolic Analysis: The Rules of Exception', *Nations and Nationalism*, 8, 2: 133–56.

Canovan, M. (1996) *Nationhood and Political Theory* (Cheltenham: Edward Elgar).

Canovan, M. (2001) 'Sleeping Dogs, Prowling Cats and Soaring Doves: Three Paradoxes in the Political Theory of Nationhood', *Political Studies*, 49, 2: 203–15.

Carr, E. H. (1945) *Nationalism and After* (London: Macmillan).

Castells, M. (1997) *The Power of Identity* (Oxford: Blackwell).

Cauthen, B. (2004) 'Covenant and Continuity: Ethno-symbolism and the Myth of Divine Election', *Nations and Nationalism*, 10, 1/2: 19–34.

Chatterjee, P. (1993) *The Nation and Its Fragments* (Princeton, NJ: Princeton University Press).

Chatterjee, P. (1996) 'Whose Imagined Community?', in G. Balakrishnan (ed.), *Mapping the Nation* (London: Verso).

Childe, V. G. (1951) *Man Makes Himself* (New York: New American Library).

Clegg, S. R. (1989) *Frameworks of Power* (London: Sage).

Cohn, T. H. (2005) *Global Political Economy: Theory and Practice*, 3rd edn (New York: Pearson).

Cobban, A. (1994) 'The Rise of the Nation-State System', in J. Hutchinson and A. D. Smith (eds), *Nationalism*, Oxford: Oxford University Press.

Coleman, J. S. (1988) 'Social Capital in the Creation of Human Capital', *American Journal of Sociology* (supplement), 94: S95–S120.

Connor, W. (1978) 'A Nation is a Nation, is a State, is an Ethnic group, is a . . .', *Ethnic and Racial Studies*, 1, 4: 377–400.

Connor, W. (1990) 'When is a Nation?', *Ethnic and Racial Studies*, 13, 1: 92–103.

Connor, W. (1993) 'Beyond Reason: The Nature of the Ethnonational Bond', *Ethnic and Racial Studies*, 16, 3: 373–89.

Connor, W. (1994) *Ethnonationalism: The Quest for Understanding* (Princeton, NJ: Princeton University Press).

Connor, W. (2001) 'Homelands in a World of States', in M. Guibernau and J. Hutchinson (eds), *Understanding Nationalism* (London: Polity Press).

Conversi, D. (1997) *The Basques, the Catalans and Spain: Alternative Routes to Nationalist Mobilisation* (London: Hurst).

Conversi, D. (ed.) (2002) *Ethnonationalism in the Contemporary World: Walker Connor and the Study of Nationalism* (London: Routledge).

Cusack, T. (2000) 'Janus and Gender: Women and the Nation's Backward Look', *Nations and Nationalism*, 6, 4: 541–62.

Dean, M. (2003) 'Michel Foucault: "A Man in Danger"', in G. Ritzer and B. Smart (eds), *Handbook of Social Theory* (London: Sage).

Deutsch, K. W. (1953) *Nationalism and Social Communication*, 2nd edn (Cambridge, MA: MIT Press).

DeVotta, N. (2005) 'From Ethnic Outbidding to Ethnic Conflict: The Institutional Bases for Sri Lanka's Separatist War', *Nations and Nationalism*, 11, 1: 141–60.

Diamond, S. (1995) *Roads to Dominion: Right-Wing Movements and Political Power in the United States* (New York: The Guilford Press).

Díkötter, F. (1990) 'Group definition and the idea of "race" in modern China (1793–1949)', *Ethnic and Racial Studies*, 13, 3: 420–32.

Dorman, S. (2005) 'Narratives of Nationalism in Eritrea: Research and Revisionism', *Nations and Nationalism*, 11, 2: 203–22.

Douglas, M. (1982) *Natural Symbols: Explorations in Cosmology* (New York: Pantheon).

Douglas, M. (1986) 'The Social Preconditions of Radical Skepticism', in J. Law (ed.) *Power, Action and Belief: A New Sociology of Knowledge?* (London: Routledge & Keegan Paul).

Durkheim, E. (1964 [1933]) *The Division of Labour in Society* (New York: Free Press).

Durkheim, E. (1965 [1915] *The Elementary Forms of Religious Life* (New York: Free Press).

Dumont, L. (1986) *Essays on Individualism* (Chicago, IL: Chicago University Press).

Edwards, B., M. W. Foley and M. Diani (eds) (2001) *Beyond Tocqueville: Civil Society and the Social Capital Debate in Comparative Perspective* (Hanover, NH: University Press of New England).

Eickelman, D. F. (1998) 'From Here to Modernity: Ernest Gellner on Nationalism and Islamic Fundamentalism', in J. A. Hall (ed.), *The State of the Nation: Ernest Gellner and the Theory of Nationalism* (Cambridge: Cambridge University Press).

Eley, G. and R. G. Suny (eds) (1996) *Becoming National: A Reader* (Oxford: Oxford University Press).

Eller, J. D. and R. M. Coughlan (1993) 'The Poverty of Primordialism: The Demystification of Ethnic Attachments', *Ethnic and Racial Studies*, 16, 2: 183–202.

Elliston, D. (2000) 'Geographies of Gender and Politics: The Place of Difference in Polynesian Nationalism', *Cultural Anthropology*, 15, 2: 171–216.

Engels, F. (1972 [1884]) *The Origin of the Family, Private Property and the State* (New York: International Publishers).

Eriksen, T. H. (1993) *Ethnicity and Nationalism: Anthropological Perspectives* (London: Pluto Press).

Fabian, J. (1983) *Time and the Other: How Anthropology Makes its Object* (New York: Columbia University Press).

Fairclough, N. (1989) *Language and Power* (London: Longman).

Fekry, A. and S. Nimis (2004) 'Preface', in Montasser al-Zayyat, *The Road to Al-Qaeda: The Story of Bin Laden's Right-Hand Man*, S. Nimis, (ed.), A. Fekry (trans.) (London: Pluto Press).

Ferguson, C. A. (1972) 'Diglossia', in P. Giglioli (ed.), *Language and Social Context* (Middlesex: Penguin).

Firth, R. (1956) *Elements of Social Organisation*, 2nd edn (London: Watts & Co.).

Firth, R. (1964) *Essays on Social Organisation and Values* (London: Athlone Press).

Fishman, J. (1972) *Language and Nationalism: Two Integrative Essays* (Rowley, MA: Newbury House).

Foster, M. (2002) 'Symbolism: The Foundation of Culture', in T. Ingold (ed.), *Companion Encyclopedia of Anthropology* (London: Routledge).

Foucault, M. (1990) *The History of Sexuality, Volume I*, R. Hurley (trans.) (New York: Vintage Books).

Frank, A. G. (1966) 'The Development of Underdevelopment', *Monthly Review*, 18: 17–31.

Frazer, J. G. (1911–15 [1890]) *The Golden Bough: A Study in Magic and Religion* (London: Macmillan).

Freeden, M. (1998) 'Is Nationalism a Distinct Ideology?', *Political Studies* 48, 2: 302–22.

Fried, M. (1967) *The Evolution of Political Society* (New York: Random House).

Friedman, J. (1994) *Cultural Identity and Global Process* (London: Sage).

Frykman, J. and O. Löfgren (1987) *Culture Builders: A Historical Anthropology of Middle-Class Life* (New Brunswick, NJ: Rutgers University Press).

Fuglerud, Ø. (2001) 'Time and Space in the Sri Lanka-Tamil Diaspora', *Nations and Nationalism*, 7, 2: 195–214.

Geertz, C. (1973) *The Interpretation of Cultures* (New York: Basic Books).

Gellner, E. (1959) *Words and Things: A Critical Account of Linguistic Philosophy and a Study of Ideology* (London: Gollancz).

Gellner, E. (1964) *Thought and Change* (London: Weidenfeld and Nicolson).

Gellner, E. (1983) *Nations and Nationalism* (Cornell, NY: Cornell University Press).

Gellner, E. (1994) *Encounters with Nationalism* (Oxford: Blackwell).

Gellner, E. (1995) 'The Importance of Being Modular', in J. A. Hall (ed.), *Civil Society: Theory, History, Comparison* (Cambridge: Polity Press).

Gellner, E. (1996a) 'Do Nations Have Navels?', *Nations and Nationalism*, 2, 3: 366–70.

Gellner, E. (1996b) 'The Coming of Nationalism and its Interpretation: The Myths of Nation and Class', in G. Balakrishnan (ed.), *Mapping the Nation* (London: Verso).

Gellner, E. (1997) *Nationalism* (London: Weidenfeld and Nicolson).

Giddens, A. (1987a) *Sociology: a Brief but Critical Introduction*, 2nd edn (Orlando, FL: Harcourt Brace Jovanovich).

Giddens, A. (1987b) *The Nation-State and Violence* (Berkeley, CA: University of California Press).

Glazer, N. and D. P. Moynihan (1963) *Beyond the Melting Pot* (Cambridge, MA: MIT Press).

Goodwin, J. (1997), 'The Libidinal Constitution of a High-Risk Social Movement: Affectual Ties and Solidarity in the Huk Rebellion, 1946 to 1954', *American Sociological Review*, 62, 1: 53–69.

Gotham, K. F. (2002) *Race, Real Estate, and Uneven Development: The Kansas City Experience, 1900–2000* (New York: SUNY Press).

Grant, S. M. (1998) ' "The Charter of its Birthright": The Civil War and American Nationalism', *Nations and Nationalism*, 4, 2: 163–86.

Greenfeld, L. (1992) *Nationalism: Five Roads to Modernity* (Cambridge, MA: Harvard University Press).

Greenfeld, L. (1993) 'Transcending the Nation's Worth', *Daedalus*, 122, 3: 47–62.

Greenfeld, L. (2001) *The Spirit of Capitalism: Nationalism and Economic Growth* (Cambridge, MA: Harvard University Press).

Grosby, S. (1991) 'Religion and Nationality in Antiquity: The Worship of Yahweh and Ancient Israel', *Archive of European Sociology*, 32: 229–65.

Grosby, S. (1994) 'The Verdict of History: The Inexpungeable Tie of Primordiality – a Response to Eller and Coughlan', *Ethnic and Racial Studies*, 17, 1: 164–71.

Grosby, S. (1995) 'Territoriality: The Transcendental, Primordial Feature of Modern Societies', *Nations and Nationalism*, 1, 2: 143–62.

Grosby, S. (1997) 'Borders, Territory and Nationality in the Ancient Near East and Armenia', *Journal of the Economic and Social History of the Orient*, 40, 1: 1–29.

Grosby, S. (1999) 'The Chosen People of Ancient Israel and the Occident: Why Does Nationality Exist and Survive?', *Nations and Nationalism*, 5, 3: 357–80.

Grosby, S. (2001a) 'Primordiality', in A. S. Leoussi (ed.), *Encyclopaedia of Nationalism* (London: Transaction).

Grosby, S. (2001b) 'Nationality and Religion', in M. Guibernau and J. Hutchinson (eds), *Understanding Nationalism* (Cambridge: Polity Press).

Grosby, S. (2002) *Biblical Ideas of Nationality, Ancient and Modern* (Winona Lake, IN: Eisenbrauns).

Grosby, S. (2003) 'Religion, Ethnicity and Nationalism: The Uncertain Perennialism of Adrian Hastings', *Nations and Nationalism*, 9, 1: 7–14.

Guibernau, M. (2001) 'Globalization and the Nation-State', in M. Guibernau and J. Hutchinson (eds), *Understanding Nationalism* (Cambridge: Polity Press).

Guibernau, M. and J. Hutchinson (eds) (2001) *Understanding Nationalism* (Cambridge: Polity Press).

Guibernau, M. and J. Rex (eds) (1997) *The Ethnicity Reader: Nationalism, Multiculturalism and Migration* (Cambridge: Polity Press).

Hall, J. A. (1986) *Powers and Liberties: The Causes and Consequences of the Rise of the West* (Berkeley, CA: University of California Press).

Hall, J. A. (1993) 'Nationalisms: Classified and Explained', in *Daedalus*, 122, 3: 1–28.

Hall, J. A. (1996) 'How Homogeneous Need We Be?', *Sociology*, 30, 1: 211–30.

Hall, J. A. (ed.) (1998) *The State of the Nation: Ernest Gellner and the Theory of Nationalism* (Cambridge: Cambridge University Press).

Hall, S. (1996) 'Ethnicity: Identity and Difference', in G. Eley and R. G. Suny (eds), *Becoming National: A Reader* (Oxford: Oxford University Press).

Handler, R. (1988) *Nationalism and the Politics of Culture in Quebec* (Madison, WI: University of Wisconsin Press).

Harvey, D. (2000) *Spaces of Hope* (Edinburgh: Edinburgh University Press).

Hastings, A. (1997) *The Construction of Nationhood: Ethnicity, Religion, and Nationalism* (Cambridge: Cambridge University Press).

Hastings, A. (1999) 'Special Peoples', *Nations and Nationalism*, 5, 3: 381–96.

Hayes, C. (1960) *Nationalism: A Religion* (London: Macmillan).

Hearn, J. (2000) *Claiming Scotland: National Identity and Liberal Culture* (Edinburgh: Polygon at Edinburgh).

Hearn, J. (2001) 'Taking Liberties: Contesting Visions of the Civil Society Project', *Critique of Anthropology*, 21, 4: 339–60.

Hearn, J. (2002) 'Identity, Class and Civil Society in Scotland's Neo-Nationalism', *Nations and Nationalism*, 8, 1: 15–30.

Hearn, J. (2003) 'Big City: Civic Symbolism and Scottish Nationalism', *Scottish Affairs*, 42: 57–82.

Hearn, J. (2005) 'Stories of Peoplehood: The Politics and Morals of Political Membership, Rogers M. Smith', *Contemporary Political Theory*, 4, 2: 195–6.

Hechter, M. (2000) *Containing Nationalism* (Oxford: Oxford University Press).

Held, D. (1996) 'The Decline of the Nation State', in G. Eley and R. G. Suny (eds), *Becoming National: A Reader* (Oxford: Oxford University Press).

Herrnstein, R. J. and C. A. Murray (1994) *The Bell Curve: Intelligence and Class Structure in American Life* (New York: Free Press).

Heywood, A. (1994) *Political Ideas and Concepts: An Introduction* (Basingstoke and New York: Palgrave Macmillan).

Hobsbawm, E. (1983a) 'Introduction: Inventing Traditions', in E. Hobsbawm and T. Ranger (eds), *The Invention of Tradition* (Cambridge: Cambridge University Press).

Hobsbawm, E. (1983b) 'Mass-Producing Traditions: Europe, 1870–1914', in E. Hobsbawm and T. Ranger (eds), *The Invention of Tradition* (Cambridge: Cambridge University Press).

Hobsbawm, E. (1992) *Nations and Nationalism since 1780: Programme, Myth and Reality*, 2nd edn (Cambridge: Cambridge University Press).

Hobsbawm, E. (1996) 'Ethnicity and Nationalism in Europe Today', in G. Balakrishnan (ed.), *Mapping the Nation* (London: Verso).

Hobsbawm, E. and T. Ranger (eds) (1983) *The Invention of Tradition* (Cambridge: Cambridge University Press).

Hohenberg, P. M. and L. H. Lees (1985) *The Making of Urban Europe, 1000–1950* (London: Harvard University Press).

Horowitz, D. L. (1985) *Ethnic Groups in Conflict* (Berkeley, CA: University of California Press).

Horowitz, D. L. (1991) 'Making Moderation Pay', in J. Montville (ed.), *Conflict and Peacemaking in Multiethnic Societies* (New York: Lexington).

Howard, M. (1994) 'War and Nations', in J. Hutchinson and A. D. Smith (eds), *Nationalism* (Oxford: Oxford University Press).

Hroch, M. (1996) 'From National Movement to the Fully-formed Nation: The Nation-building Process in Europe', in G. Balakrishnan (ed.), *Mapping the Nation* (London: Verso).

Hroch, M. (1998) 'Real and Constructed: The Nature of the Nation', in J. A. Hall (ed.), *The State of the Nation: Ernest Gellner and the Theory of Nationalism* (Cambridge: Cambridge University Press).

Hroch. M. (2000) *The Social Preconditions of National Revival in Europe* (New York: Columbia University Press).

Hroch, M. (2004) 'From Ethnic Group Toward the Modern Nation: The Czech Case', *Nations and Nationalism*, 10, 1/2: 95–108.

Hume, D. (1978 [1740]) *A Treatise of Human Nature*, 2nd edn, L. A. Selby-Bigge and P. H. Nidditch (eds), (Oxford: Oxford University Press).

Huntington, S. P. (1998) *The Clash of Civilizations and the Remaking of the World Order* (London: Touchstone).

Hutchinson, J. (1987a) *The Dynamics of Cultural Nationalism, The Gaelic Revival and the Creation of the Irish State* (London: Allen and Unwin).

Hutchinson, J. (1987b) 'Cultural Nationalism, Elite Mobility and Nation-Building: Communitarian Politics in Modern Ireland', *British Journal of Sociology*, 38, 4: 482–501.

Hutchinson, J. (1994) *Modern Nationalism* (London: Fontana).

Hutchinson, J. (2000) 'Ethnicity and Modern Nations', *Ethnic and Racial Studies*, 23, 4: 651–69.

Hutchinson, J. (2001) 'Nations and Culture', in M. Guibernau and J. Hutchinson (eds), *Understanding Nationalism* (Cambridge: Polity Press).

Hutchinson, J. (2004) 'Myth Against Myth: The Nation as Ethnic Overlay', *Nations and Nationalism*, 10, 1/2: 109–24.

Hutchinson, J. and A. D. Smith (1994) *Nationalism* (Oxford: Oxford University Press).

Huysseune, M. (2000) 'Masculinity and Secessionism in Italy: An Assessment', *Nations and Nationalism*, 6, 4: 591–610.

Ignatieff, M. (1993) *Blood and Belonging: Journeys into the New Nationalism* (London: BBC Books).

Ignatieff, M. (1999a) 'Nationalism and the Narcissism of Minor Differences', in R. Beiner (ed.), *Theorizing Nationalism* (Albany, NY: SUNY Press).

Ignatieff, M. (1999b) 'Benign Nationalism? The Possibilities of the Civic Ideal', in E. Mortimer (ed.), *People, Nation and State: The Meaning of Ethnicity and Nationalism* (London: I. B. Tauris).

Ingilis, T. (1991) 'The Struggle for Control of the Irish Body: State, Church, and Society in Nineteenth Century Ireland', in E. R. Wolf (ed.), *Religious Regimes and State-Formation: Perspectives from European Ethnology* (Albany, NY: SUNY Press).

Jacobs, J. (1985) *Cities and the Wealth of Nations: Principles of Economic Life* (New York: Viking).

Jayawardena, K. (1986) *Feminism and Nationalism in the Third World* (London: Zed).

Jenks, C. (2005) *Culture*, 2nd edn (London: Routledge).

Kamenka, E. (1976) 'Political Nationalism – The Evolution of the Idea', in E. Kamenka (ed.), *Nationalism: The Nature and Evolution of an Idea* (London: Edward Arnold).

Keating, M. (2001) *Nations Against the State: The New Politics of Nationalism in Quebec, Catalonia and Scotland*, 2nd edn (Basingstoke and New York: Palgrave Macmillan).

Kedourie, E. (1993 [1960]) *Nationalism*, 4th edn (London: Blackwell).

Keesing, R. M. (1987) 'Anthropology as Interpretive Quest', *Current Anthropology*, 28, 2: 161–9.

Kemper, T. D. (1978) *A Social Interactional Theory of Emotions* (New York: Wiley).

Kertzer, D. (1988) *Ritual, Politics and Power* (New Haven, CT: Yale University Press).

Kirchhoff, P. (1968) 'The Principles of Clanship in Human Society', in M. Fried (ed.), *Readings in Anthropology, Vol. II*, 2nd edn (New York: Thomas Y. Crowell Co.).

Kjeilen, T. (2004) 'Islamism', in T. Kjeilen (ed.), *Encyclopaedia of the Orient*, Oslo, Norway, last modified 11 September 2004. URL: http://lexicorient. com/cgi-bin/eo-direct.pl?islamism.htm

Klima, A. (1993) 'The Czechs', in M. Teich and R. Porter (eds), *The National Question in Europe in Historical Context* (Cambridge: Cambridge University Press).

Kohn, H. (1967) *The Idea of Nationalism* (New York: Collier).

Kövecses, Z. (2000) *Metaphor and Emotion: Language, Culture and Body in Human Feeling* (Cambridge: Cambridge University Press).

Kristeva, J. (1993) *Nations Without Nationalism* (New York: Columbia University Press).

Kroeber, A. L. and T. Parsons (1958) 'The Concepts of Culture and of Social System', *American Sociological Review*, 23: 582–3.

Kuper, A. (1999) *Culture: The Anthropologists' Account* (London: Harvard University Press).

Kuper, L. (1997) 'Plural Societies', in M. Guibernau and J. Rex (eds), *The Ethnicity Reader: Nationalism, Multiculturalism and Migration* (Cambridge: Polity Press).

Kymlicka, W. (ed.) (1995) *The Rights of Minority Cultures* (Oxford: Oxford University Press).

Kymlicka, W. (1999) 'Misunderstanding Nationalism', in R. Beiner (ed.), *Theorizing Nationalism* (Albany, NY: SUNY Press).

Kymlicka, W. (2001) *Politics in the Vernacular: Nationalism, Multiculturalism and Citizenship* (Oxford: Oxford University Press).

Laitin, D. (1992) *Language Repertoires and State Construction in Africa* (Cambridge: Cambridge University Press).

Laitin, D. (1995) 'National Revivals and Violence', *Archives of European Sociology*, 36: 3–43.

Laitin, D. (1998) 'Nationalism and Language: A Post-Soviet Perspective', in J. A. Hall (ed.), *The State of the Nation: Ernest Gellner and the Theory of Nationalism* (Cambridge: Cambridge University Press).

Lakoff, M. and G. Johnson (1980) *Metaphors We Live By* (Chicago, IL: Chicago Univerity Press).

Lan, D. (1985) *Guns and Rain: Guerrillas and Spirit Mediums in Zimbabwe* (Berkeley, CA: University of California Press).

Layder, D. (2004) *Emotion in Social Life: the Lost Heart of Society* (London: Sage).

Lazar, M. M. (2001) 'For the Good of the Nation: "Strategic Egalitarianism" in the Singapore Context', *Nations and Nationalism*, 7, 1: 59–74.

Leoussi, A. S. (ed.) (2001) *Encyclopaedia of Nationalism* (London: Transaction).

Leoussi, A. S. and S. Grosby (eds) (2003) *Nationality and Nationalism*, 4 vols (London: I. B. Tauris).

Lichtenberg, J. (1997) 'Nationalism, For and (Mainly) Against', in R. McKim and J. McMahan (eds), *The Morality of Nationalism* (Oxford: Oxford University Press).

Lijphart, A. (1977) *Democracy in Plural Societies: A Comparative Exploration* (New Haven, CT: Yale University Press).

Lijphart, A. (1991) 'The Power-Sharing Approach', in J. Montville (ed.), *Conflict and Peacemaking in Multiethnic Societies* (New York: Lexington).

Llobera, J. (1994) *The God of Modernity: The Development of Nationalism in Western Europe* (Oxford: Berg).

Llobera, J. (2003) 'A Comment on Hasting's *The Construction of Nationhood*', *Nations and Nationalism*, 9, 1: 15–18.

Lowie, R. (1947) *Primitive Society* (New York: Liveright).

Lustick, I. (1979) 'Stability in Deeply Divided Societies: Consociationalism versus Control', *World Politics*, 31, 3: 325–44.

Lynch, M. (2002) 'In Search of the Scottish Reformation', in E. J. Cowan and R. J. Finlay (eds), *Scottish History: The Power of the Past* (Edinburgh: Edinburgh University Press).

Magaš, B. (2003) 'On Bosnianness', *Nations and Nationalism*, 9, 1: 19–24.

Malinowski, B. (1948) *Magic, Science and Religion, and Other Essays* (New York: Free Press).

Mann, M. (1986a) *The Sources of Social Power, Vol. I* (Cambridge: Cambridge University Press).

Mann, M. (1986b) 'A Crisis in Stratification Theory? Persons, Households/ Families/Lineages, Genders, Classes and Nations', in R. Crompton and M. Mann (eds), *Gender and Stratification* (Cambridge: Polity Press).

Mann, M. (1988) *States, War and Capitalism* (Oxford: Blackwell).

Mann, M., (1992) 'The Emergence of Modern European Nationalism', in J. A. Hall and I. C. Jarvie (eds), *Transition to Modernity: Essays on Power, Wealth and Belief* (Cambridge: Cambridge University Press).

Mann, M. (1993) *The Sources of Social Power, Vol. II* (Cambridge: Cambridge University Press).

Mann, M. (1996) 'Nation-states in Europe and Other Continents: Diversifying, Developing, not Dying', in G. Balakrishnan (ed.), *Mapping the Nation* (London: Verso).

Mann, M. (2001) 'Explaining Murderous Ethnic Cleansing: The Macro-Level', in M. Guibernau and J. Hutchinson (eds), *Understanding Nationalism* (Cambridge: Polity Press).

Mann, M. (2002) 'The Crisis of the Latin American Nation-State', accessed at the author's website: http://www.sscnet.ucla.edu/soc/faculty/mann/articles_site.htm

Mann, M. (2003) *Incoherent Empire* (London: Verso).

Margalit, A. and J. Raz (1990) 'National Self-Determination', *Journal of Philosophy*, 87, 9: 439–61.

Mavratsas, C. V. (1999) 'National Identity and Consciousness in Everyday Life: Towards a Sociology of Knowledge of Greek-Cypriot Nationalism', *Nations and Nationalism*, 5, 1: 91–104.

Mayall, J. (1990) *Nationalism and International Society* (Cambridge: Cambridge University Press).

McClintock, A. (1996) ' "No Longer in a Future Heaven": Nationalism, Gender and Race', in G. Eley and R. G. Suny (eds), *Becoming National: A Reader* (Oxford: Oxford University Press).

McCrone, D. (1998) *The Sociology of Nationalism* (London: Routledge).

McCrone, D. (2001) *Understanding Scotland: The Sociology of a Stateless Nation*, 2nd edn (London: Routledge).

McGarry, J. and B. O'Leary (1993) *The Politics of Ethnic Antagonism* (London: Routledge).

McKim R. and J. McMahan (eds) (1997) *The Morality of Nationalism* (Oxford: Oxford University Press).

McLellan, D. (1995) *Ideology*, 2nd edn (Minneapolis, MN: University of Minnesota Press).

McNeill, W. (1974) *The Shape of European History* (New York: Oxford University Press).

Mill, J. S. (1996 [1861]) 'Nationality', in S. Woolf (ed.), *Nationalism in Europe, 1815 to the Present* (London: Routledge).

Miller, D. (1995) *On Nationality* (Oxford: Oxford University Press).

Morgan, L. H. (1985 [1877]) *Ancient Society* (New York: Holt).

Morriss, P. (2002) *Power: A Philosophical Analysis*, 2nd edn (Manchester: Manchester University Press).

Mortimer, E. (ed.) (1999) *People, Nation and State: The Meaning of Ethnicity and Nationalism* (London: I. B. Tauris).

Morton, G. (1996) 'Scottish Rights and "Centralisation" in the Mid-Nineteenth Century', *Nations and Nationalism*, 2, 2: 257–80.

Mosse, G. (1976) 'Mass Politics and the Political Liturgy of Nationalism' in E. Kamenka (ed.), *Nationalism: The Nature and Evolution of an Idea* (London: Edward Arnold).

Mosse, G. (1985a) *Toward the Final Solution: A History of European Racism* (Madison, WI: University of Wisconsin Press).

Mosse, G. (1985b) *Nationalism and Sexuality: Middle-Class Morality and Sexual Norms in Modern Europe* (Madison, WI: University of Wisconsin Press).

Mosse, G. (1990) *Fallen Soldiers* (Oxford: Oxford University Press).

Mosse, G. (1991) *The Nationalization of the Masses* (Ithaca, NY: Cornell University Press).

Mosse, G. (1995) 'Racism and Nationalism', *Nations and Nationalism*, 1, 2: 163–74.

Motyl, A. J. (ed.) (2001) *Encyclopedia of Nationalism: Fundamental Themes*, 2 vols (London: Academic Press).

Nairn, T. (1981 [1977]) *The Break-Up of Britain*, 2nd edn (London: Verso).

Nairn, T. (1996) 'Internationalism and the Second Coming', in G. Balakrishnan (ed.), *Mapping the Nation* (London: Verso).

Nairn, T. (1997) *Faces of Nationalism*, (London: Verso).

Nairn, T. (1998) 'The Curse of Rurality: Limits of Modernization Theory', in J. A. Hall (ed.), *The State of the Nation: Ernest Gellner and the Theory of Nationalism* (Cambridge: Cambridge University Press).

Nielsen, K. (1999) 'Cultural Nationalism: Neither Ethnic or Civic', in R. Beiner (ed.), *Theorizing Nationalism* (Albany, NY: SUNY Press).

Ohmae, K. (1996) *The End of the Nation State* (New York: HarperCollins).

O'Leary, B. (1998) 'Ernest Gellner's Diagnoses of Nationalism; A Critical Overview, or, What is Living and What is Dead in Ernest Gellner's Philosophy of Nationalism?', in J. A. Hall (ed.), *The State of the Nation: Ernest Gellner and the Theory of Nationalism* (Cambridge: Cambridge University Press).

O'Leary, B., I. Lustick and T. Callaghy (eds) (2001) *Right-sizing the State: The Politics of Moving Borders* (Oxford: Oxford University Press).

Ollman, B. (1976) *Alienation*, 2nd edn (Cambridge: Cambridge University Press).

Özkirimli, U. (2000) *Theories of Nationalism: A Critical Introduction* (Basingstoke and New York: Palgrave Macmillan).

Özkirimli, U. (2003) 'The Nation as an Artichoke? A Critique of Ethnosymbolist Interpretations of Nationalism', *Nations and Nationalism*, 9, 3: 339–56.

Özkirimli, U. (2005) *Contemporary Debates on Nationalism: A Critical Engagement* (Basingstoke and New York: Palgrave Macmillan).

Parekh, B. (1995) 'Ethnocentricity of the Nationalist Discourse', *Nations and Nationalism*, 1, 1: 25–52.

Parekh, B. (1999) 'The Incoherence of Nationalism', in R. Beiner (ed.), *Theorizing Nationalism* (Albany, NY: SUNY Press).

Paterson, L., F. Bechhofer and D. McCrone (2004) *Living in Scotland: Social and Economic Change since 1980* (Edinburgh: Edinburgh University Press).

Penrose, J. (1995) 'Essential Constructions? The Cultural Bases of Nationalist Movements', *Nations and Nationalism*, 1, 3: 391–418.

Penrose, J. and J. May (1991) 'Herder's Concept of Nation and its Relevance to Contemporary Ethnic Nationalism', *Canadian Review of Studies in Nationalism*, 18, 1/2: 165–78.

Pfaff, W. (1993) *The Wrath of Nations: Civilization and the Furies of Nationalism* (New York: Simon and Schuster).

Plamenatz, J. (1976) 'Two Types of Nationalism', in E. Kamenka (ed.), *Nationalism: The Nature and Evolution of an Idea* (London: Edward Arnold).

Poggi, G. (1978) *The Development of the Modern State: A Sociological Introduction* (Stanford, CA: Stanford University Press).

Poggi, G. (2001) *Forms of Power* (Cambridge: Polity Press).

Polanyi, K. (1957) *The Great Transformation: The Political and Economic Origins of our Time* (Boston, MA: Beacon).

Poliakov, L. (1974) *The Aryan Myth* (New York: Basic Books).

Putnam, R. D. (1995) 'Bowling Alone: America's Declining Social Capital', *Journal of Democracy*, 6: 65–78.

Ram, H. (2000) 'The Immemorial Iranian Nation? School Textbooks and Historical Memory in Post-revolutionary Iran', *Nations and Nationalism*, 6, 1: 67–90.

Ramet, S. P. (1996) *Balkan Babel: The Disintegration of Yugoslavia from the Death of Tito to Ethnic War*, 2nd edn (Boulder, CO: Westview Press).

Reicher, S. and N. Hopkins (2001) *Self and Nation: Categorization, Contestation, and Mobilization* (London: Sage).

Renan, E. (1996 [1882]) 'What is a Nation?', in S. Woolf (ed.), *Nationalism in Europe, 1815 to the Present* (London: Routledge).

Reuter, C. (2002) *My Life is a Weapon: A Modern History of Suicide Bombing* (Princeton, NJ: Princeton University Press).

Rex, J. (1995) 'Multiculturalism in Europe and America', *Nations and Nationalism*, 1, 2: 243–60.

Rex, J. (1997) 'The Concept of a Multicultural Society', in M. Guibernau and J. Rex (eds), *The Ethnicity Reader: Nationalism, Multiculturalism and Migration* (Cambridge: Polity Press).

Reynolds, S. (1984) *Kingdoms and Communities in Western Europe, 900–1300* (Oxford: Clarendon Press).

Robinson, F. (1979) 'Islam and Muslim Separation', in D. Taylor and M. Yapp (eds), *Political Identity in South Asia* (Dublin: Curzon Press).

Robinson, F. (1994) 'Islam and Nationalism', in J. Hutchinson and A. D. Smith (eds), *Nationalism* (Oxford: Oxford University Press).

Roseberry, W. (1989) *Anthropologies and Histories* (New Brunswick, NJ: Rutgers University Press).

Routledge, B. (2003) 'The Antiquity of the Nation? Critical Reflections from the Ancient Near East', *Nations and Nationalism*, 9, 2: 213–34.

Ruane, J. and Todd, J. (1996) *The Dynamics of Conflict in Northern Ireland* (Cambridge: Cambridge University Press).

Salehi, F. (2001) 'A Postmodern Conception of the Nation-State', in A. S. Leoussi (ed.), *Encyclopaedia of Nationalism* (London: Transaction).

Sapir, E. (1985) 'The Status of Linguistics as a Science', in D. G. Mandelbaum (ed.), *The Selected Writings of Edward Sapir* (Berkeley, CA: University of California Press).

Sassen, S. (2000) 'A New Geography of Centers and Margins: Summary and Implications', in R. T. LeGates and F. Stout (eds), *The City Reader*, 2nd edn (London: Routledge).

Savage, M. and A. Warde (2000), 'Cities and Uneven Economic Development', in R. T. LeGates and F. Stout (eds), *The City Reader*, 2nd edn (London: Routledge).

Scruton, R. (1999) 'The First Person Plural', in R. Beiner (ed.), *Theorizing Nationalism* (Albany, NY: SUNY Press).

Sekulic, D. (1997) 'The Creation and Dissolution of the Multinational State: The Case of Yugoslavia', *Nations and Nationalism*, 3, 2: 165–80.

Seton-Watson, H. (1977) *Nations and States: An Enquiry Into the Origins and the Politics of Nationalism* (Boulder, CO: Westview Press).

Shilling, C. (2002) 'The Two Traditions in the Sociology of Emotions', in J. Barbalet (ed.), *Emotions and Sociology* (Oxford: Blackwell).

Shils, E. (1957) 'Primordial, Personal, Sacred and Civil Ties', *British Journal of Sociology*, 8: 130–45.

Shils, E. (1995) 'Nation, Nationality, Nationalism and Civil Society', *Nations and Nationalism*, 1, 1: 93–118.

Sider, G. (1986) *Culture and Class in Anthropology and History: A Newfoundland Illustration* (Cambridge: Cambridge University Press).

Slezkine, Y. (1996) 'The USSR as a Communal Apartment, or How a Socialist State Promoted Ethnic Particularism', in G. Eley and R. G. Suny (eds), *Becoming National: A Reader* (Oxford: Oxford University Press).

Sluga, G. (1998) 'Identity, Gender and the History of European Nations and Nationalisms', *Nations and Nationalism*, 4, 1: 87–112.

Sluga, G. (2000),'Female and National Self-determination: A Gender Re-reading of the "Apogee of Nationalism" ', *Nations and Nationalism*, 6, 4: 495–522.

Smith, A. (1984 [1790]) *The Theory of Moral Sentiments*, D. D. Raphael and A. L. Macfie (eds) (Indianapolis, IN: Liberty Fund).

Smith, A. D. (1981) *The Ethnic Revival* (Cambridge: Cambridge University Press).

Smith, A. D. (1986) *The Ethnic Origin of Nations* (Oxford: Blackwell).

Smith, A. D. (1988), 'The Myth of the "Modern Nation" and the Myth of Nations', *Ethnic and Racial Studies*, 11, 1: 1–26.

Smith, A. D. (1989) 'The Origins of Nations', *Ethnic and Racial Studies*, 12, 3: 340–67.

Smith, A. D. (1991) *National Identity* (London: Penguin).

Smith, A. D. (1992) 'Chosen Peoples: Why Ethnic Groups Survive', *Ethnic and Racial Studies*, 15, 3: 436–56.

Smith, A. D. (1994) 'The Problem of National Identity: Ancient, Medieval and Modern', *Ethnic and Racial Studies*, 17, 3: 375–99.

Smith, A. D. (1996a) 'Nations and Their Pasts', *Nations and Nationalism*, 2, 3: 358–65.

Smith, A. D. (1996b) 'Memory and Modernity: Reflections on Ernest Gellner's Theory of Nationalism', *Nations and Nationalism*, 2, 3: 371–88.

Smith, A. D. (1998) *Nationalism and Modernism* (London: Routledge).

Smith, A. D. (1999) *Myths and Memories of the Nation* (Oxford: Oxford University Press).

Smith, A. D. (2001a), 'Nations and History', in M. Guibernau and J. Hutchinson (eds), *Understanding Nationalism* (Cambridge: Polity Press).

Smith, A. D. (2001b) 'Durkheim and Nationalism', in A. S. Leoussi (ed.), *Encyclopaedia of Nationalism* (London: Transaction).

Smith, A. D. (2003a) *Chosen Peoples: Sacred Sources of National Identity* (Oxford: Oxford University Press).

Smith, A. D. (2003b) 'The Poverty of Anti-nationalist Modernism', *Nations and Nationalism*, 9, 3: 357–70.

Smith, A. D. (2003c) 'Adrian Hastings of Nations and Nationalism', *Nations and Nationalism*, 9, 1: 25–8.

Smith, A. D. (2004) 'History and National Destiny: Responses and Clarifications', *Nations and Nationalism*, 10, 1/2: 195–209.

Smith, A. D. and Hutchinson, J. (eds) (2000) *Nationalism: Critical Concepts in Political Science*, 5 vols (London: Routledge).

Smith, R. M. (2003) *Stories of Peoplehood The Politics and Morals of Political Membership* (Cambridge: Cambridge University Press).

Smooha, S. (2002a) 'Types of Democracy and Modes of Conflict Management in Ethnically Divided Societies', *Nations and Nationalism*, 8, 4: 423–32.

Smooha, S. (2002b) 'The Model of Ethnic Democracy: Israel as a Jewish and Democratic State', *Nations and Nationalism*, 8, 4: 475–504.

Smooha, S. and T. Hanf (1992) 'The Diverse Modes of Conflict Regulation in Deeply Divided Societies', *International Journal of Comparative Sociology*, 33, 1/2: 26–47.

Snyder, J. (2000) *From Voting to Violence: Democratization and Nationalist Conflict* (New York: Norton).

Snyder, J. and K. Ballentine (1996) 'Nationalism and the Marketplace of Ideas', *International Security*, 21, 2: 5–40.

Spencer, H. (1860) 'The Social Organism', *Westminster Review*, 17: 90–121.

Spener, D., G. Gereffi and J. Bair (eds) (2002) *Free Trade and Uneven Development: The North American Apparel Industry after NAFTA* (Philadelphia, PA: Temple University Press).

Stanton, W. (1960) *The Leopard's Spots: Scientific Attitudes toward Race in America 1815–59* (Chicago, IL: Chicago University Press).

Stepan, N. (1982) *The Idea of Race in Science: Great Britain, 1800–1960* (Hamden, CT: Archon Books).

Stevenson, D. (1988) *The Covenanters: The National Covenant and Scotland* (Edinburgh: The Saltire Society).

Steward, J. H. (1972) *Theory of Culture Change* (Chicago, IL: University of Illinois Press).

Strange, S. (1996) *The Retreat of the State: The Diffusion of Power in the World Economy* (Cambridge: Cambridge University Press).

Suleiman, Y. (2003) *The Arabic Language and National Identity* (Edinburgh: Edinburgh University Press).

Szporluk, R. (1998) 'Thoughts about Change: Ernest Gellner and the History of Nationalism', in J. A. Hall (ed.), *The State of the Nation: Ernest Gellner and the Theory of Nationalism* (Cambridge: Cambridge University Press).

Tamir, Y. (1993) *Liberal Nationalism* (Princeton, NJ: Princeton University Press).

Tarrow, S. (1994) *Power in Movement: Social Movements, Collective Action and Politics* (Cambridge: Cambridge University Press).

Taubman, G. L. (1997) 'Nationalism. Loss-Gain Framing and the Confederate States of America', *Nations and Nationalism*, 3, 2: 251–72.

Taylor, C. (1999) 'Nationalism and Modernity', in R. Beiner (ed.), *Theorizing Nationalism* (Albany, NY: SUNY Press).

Teichgraeber, R. (1982) 'Rethinking *Das Adam Smith Problem*', in J. Dwyer, R. A. Mason and A. Murdoch (eds), *New Perspectives on the Politics and Culture of Early Modern Scotland* (Edinburgh: John Donald).

Templin, J. A. (1999) 'The Ideology of a Chosen People: Afrikaner Nationalism and the Ossewa Trek, 1938', *Nations and Nationalism*, 5, 3: 397–418.

Thom, M. (1995) *Republics, Nations and Tribes* (London: Verso).

Tilley, V. (1997) 'The Terms of the Debate: Untangling Language about Ethnicity and Ethnic Movements', *Ethnic and Racial Studies*, 20, 3: 497–522.

Tilly, C. (ed.) (1975a) *The Formation of National States in Western Europe* (Princeton, NJ: Princeton University Press).

Tilly, C. (1975b) 'Reflections on the History of European State-Making', in C. Tilly (ed.), *The Formation of National States in Western Europe* (Princeton, NJ: Princeton University Press).

Tilly, C. (1975c) 'Western State-Making and Theories of Political Transformation', in C. Tilly (ed.), *The Formation of National States in Western Europe* (Princeton, NJ: Princeton University Press).

Tilly, C. (1994), 'Entanglements of European Cities and States', in C. Tilly and W. P. Blockmans (eds), *Cities and the Rise of States in Europe, A.D. 1000 to 1800* (Boulder, CO: Westview Press).

Trevor-Roper, H. (1983) 'The Invention of Tradition: The Highland Tradition of Scotland', in E. Hobsbawm and T. Ranger (eds), *The Invention of Tradition* (Cambridge: Cambridge University Press).

van den Berghe, P. (1978) 'Race and Ethnicty: A Sociobiological Perspective', *Ethnic and Racial Studies*, 1, 4: 401–11.

van den Berghe, P. (1995) 'Does Race Matter?', *Nations and Nationalism*, 1, 3: 357–68.

van den Berghe, P. (2002) 'Multicultural Democracy: Can it Work?', *Nations and Nationalism*, 8, 4: 433–50.

van der Veer, P. (1999) 'Hindus: A Superior Race', *Nations and Nationalism*, 5, 3: 419–30.

van der Veer, P. (2001) *Religion and Modernity in India and Britain* (Princeton, NJ: Princeton University Press).

van der Veer, P and H. Lehmann (eds) (1999) *Nation and Religion: Perspectives on Europe and Asia* (Princeton, NJ: Princeton University Press).

Van Dyke, V. (1977) 'The Individual, the State and Ethnic Communities in Political Theory', *World Politics*, 29, 3: 343–69.

Verdery, K. (1996) *What Was Socialism and What Comes Next?* (Princeton, NJ: Princeton University Press).

Viroli, M. (1995) *For Love of Country: an Essay on Patriotism and Nationalism* (Oxford: Oxford University Press).

Walby, S. (1990) *Theorizing Patriarchy* (Oxford: Blackwell).

Walby, S. (2000), 'Gender, Nations and States in a Global Era', *Nations and Nationalism*, 6, 4: 523–40.

Walker, R. (2001) 'Postmodernism', in A. J. Motyl (ed.), *Encyclopedia of Nationalism: Fundamental Themes, Vol. 1* (London: Academic Press).

Wallerstein, I. (1974) *The Modern World System: Capitalist Agriculture and the Origins of the European World-Economy in the Sixteenth Century* (New York: Academic Press).

Walzer, M. (1980) 'Pluralism: A Political Perspective', in S. A. Thernstrom (ed.), *The Harvard Encyclopedia of American Ethnic Groups* (Cambridge, MA: Harvard University Press).

Wardhaugh, R. (1992) *An Introduction to Sociolinguistics*, 2nd edn (Oxford: Blackwell).

Weber, E. (1976) *Peasants into Frenchmen: The Modernization of Rural France, 1870–1914* (Stanford, CA: Stanford University Press).

Weber, M. (1978) *Economy and Society, Vol. 1* (Berkeley, CA: University of California Press).

Wenke, R. J. (1990) *Patterns in Prehistory: Humankind's First Three Million Years*, 3rd edn (New York: Oxford University Press).

West, L. (1997) *Feminist Nationalism* (London: Routledge).

Whorf, B. L. (1956*)* *Language, Thought and Reality: Selected Writings of Benjamin Lee Whorf*, J. B. Carroll (ed.) (Cambridge, MA: MIT Press).

Williams, R. (1973) *The Country and the City* (New York: Oxford University Press).

Wilmsen, E. N. (1989*)* *Land Filled with Flies: A Political Economy of the Kalahari* (Chicago, IL: Chicago University Press).

Wilson, E. O. (1975) *Sociobiology* (Cambridge, MA: Harvard University Press).

Wirth, L. (1995 [1938]) 'Urbanism as a Way of Life', reprinted in P. Kasinitz (ed.), *Metropolis: Center and Symbol of Our Times* (Basingstoke and New York: Palgrave Macmillan).

Wolf, E. R. (1958) 'The Virgin of Guadalupe: A Mexican National Symbol', *Journal of American Folklore*, 71, 279: 34–9.

Wolf, E. R. (1981) 'The Mills of Inequality: A Marxian Approach', in G. D. Berreman (ed.), *Social Inequality: Comparative and Developmental Approaches* (New York: Academic Press).

Wolf, E. R. (1982) *Europe and the People Without History* (Berkeley, CA: University of California Press).

Wolf, E. R. (1984) 'Culture: Panacea or Problem?', *American Antiquity*, 49, 2: 393–400.

Wolf, E. R. (1990) 'Distinguished Lecture: Facing Power – Old Insights, New Questions', *American Anthropologist*, 92, 3: 586–96.

Wolf, E. R. (1999) *Envisioning Power: Ideologies of Dominance and Crisis* (Berkeley, CA: University of California Press).

Wrong, D. (2002) *Power: Its Forms, Bases, and Uses*, 3rd edn (London: Transaction).

Wuthnow, R. (1987) *Meaning and Moral Order: Explorations in Cultural Analysis* (Berkeley, CA: University of California Press).

Yack, B. (1999) 'The Myth of the Civic Nation', in R. Beiner (ed.), *Theorizing Nationalism* (Albany, NY: SUNY Press).

Yengoyan, A. A. (1986) 'Theory in Anthropology: On the Demise of the Concept of Culture', *Comparative Studies in Society and History*, 28, 2: 368–74.

Yuval-Davis, N. (1997) *Gender and Nation* (London: Sage).

Yuval-Davis, N. (2001) 'Nationalism, Feminism and Gender Relations', in M. Guibernau and J. Hutchinson (eds), *Understanding Nationalism* (Cambridge: Polity Press).

Zubaida, S. (1989) 'Nations: Old and New. Comments on Anthony D. Smith's "The Myth of the 'Modern Nation' and the Myth of Nations"', *Ethnic and Racial Studies*, 12, 3: 329–39.

Zubaida, S. (2004) 'Islam and Nationalism: Continuities and Contradictions', *Nations and Nationalism*, 10, 4: 407–20.

Index